THE INVISIBLE JEWISH BUDAPEST

The Invisible
Jewish Budapest

Metropolitan Culture at the Fin de Siècle

M ARY G LUCK

THE UNIVERSITY OF WISCONSIN PRESS

Publication of this volume has been made possible, in part, through support from the George L. Mosse Program at the University of Wisconsin–Madison and the Program in Judaic Studies at Brown University.

The University of Wisconsin Press
1930 Monroe Street, 3rd Floor
Madison, Wisconsin 53711-2059
uwpress.wisc.edu

3 Henrietta Street, Covent Garden
London WC2E 8LU, United Kingdom
eurospanbookstore.com

Printed in the United States of America

Library of Congress Cataloging-in-Publication Data
Names: Gluck, Mary, author.
Title: The invisible Jewish Budapest : metropolitan culture at the fin de siècle / Mary Gluck.
Other titles: George L. Mosse series in modern European cultural and intellectual history.
Description: Madison, Wisconsin : The University of Wisconsin Press, [2016] | ©2016 | Series: George L. Mosse series in modern European cultural and intellectual history | Includes bibliographical references and index.
Identifiers: LCCN 2015036814 | ISBN 9780299307707 (cloth : alk. paper)
Subjects: LCSH: Jews—Hungary—Budapest—History. | Jews—Cultural assimilation—Hungary—Budapest—History. | Popular culture—Hungary—Budapest—History. | Budapest (Hungary)—History—1872–1945. | Budapest (Hungary)—Ethnic relations.
Classification: LCC DS135.H92 B83445 2016 | DDC 305.892/404391209034—dc23
LC record available at http://lccn.loc.gov/2015036814

To the memory of my parents,
Ernő and Irén Gluck

CONTENTS

ILLUSTRATIONS

ACKNOWLEDGMENTS

The idea for this book goes back many years and has its roots in my study of Georg Lukács and his intellectual circle in pre–World War I Budapest. These modernist intellectuals, as I quickly realized, shared much more than common philosophical and aesthetic concerns. Almost without exception, they came from the recently assimilated Hungarian Jewish middle classes. Curiously, this not unimportant fact rarely found its way into their letters, diaries, and autobiographical accounts and left no traces in their literary and philosophical productions. Lukács and his friends did not deny their Jewish origins; they simply considered it an unimportant fact that was redundant to mention. Jewishness was fundamentally irrelevant to their cultural identities and intellectual aspirations. I had no reason to doubt the sincerity of such attitudes, which represented the classic Jewish assimilated outlook of the time. I did wonder, however, whether the cultural experience of assimilation might not be more complex and convoluted than the testimonials of these highly sophisticated Jewish intellectuals suggested. I wondered whether their self-perceptions were not part of a larger, collective story that in its very ordinariness escaped the attention of the historical actors themselves.

This book is an attempt to reveal the silences and omissions that seemed so puzzling to me in my original encounter with the Lukács circle. The search for new ways to tell their story involved many detours and a gradual realization that the conventions of intellectual history were not always adequate for the task. Paradoxically, the major part of the search for new methods involved an extensive and very productive foray into the world of bohemian Paris, which had more similarities with the cultural dilemmas of Central European Jewish intellectuals than I would have thought originally. In fact, my book *Popular Bohemia* proved to be not simply a detour but a necessary stepping stone for conceptualizing the present book on Jewish Budapest.

It gives me great pleasure to acknowledge the extensive intellectual assistance and support that I received in the course of writing this book. David Sorkin was an expert and generous guide in the early stages of formulating this project. Michael Silber has been a long-standing supporter, whose memorable conferences in Jerusalem provided my first introduction to contemporary scholars working in the field of Hungarian Jewish history. Gary Cohen has watched the evolution of this work with warm interest and has helped it along at crucial moments.

On my first of many research trips to Budapest, I received valuable advice from András Kovács and from the late György Bence, who guided me to crucial archival resources I would not have found on my own. Anikó Prepuk has read and commented on several chapters of the manuscript and has provided important orientation in the political history of the period. Miklós Konrád's unusually thorough reading of one of the chapters proved extremely helpful. Tibor Frank generously invited me to his home on several occasions in order to share family lore and professional knowledge about his great-uncle, Mór Wahrmann. Judit Szilágyi facilitated my access to important archival sources at the Petőfi Literary Museum and shared her office with me during a very pleasant summer. Emőke Tomsics expertly advised me on the illustrations for this book and introduced me to the different archives where I could obtain images.

At Brown University, my home institution, Maud Mandel has been generous with her support and encouragement. She read and commented on several chapters of this book and brought to my attention the perspectives of mainstream Jewish historians that I was not always aware of. Saul Olyan brilliantly deciphered a biblical reference in one of my caricatures and helped immeasurably improve the introductory chapter of the book.

I received financial assistance from a number of institutions without which I could not have completed this book. The Memorial Foundation for Jewish Culture, the Stanford Humanities Center, the Posen Foundation, and the Cogut Humanities Center at Brown University provided early support. A timely fellowship from the International Research Center for Cultural Studies (IFK) in Vienna and two sabbatical leaves from Brown University allowed me to complete the writing of the book in Vienna and Budapest. The Humanities Research Fund of Brown University and assistance from the Program in Judaic Studies at Brown University provided generous help with indexing and the purchase of publication rights for the images in the book. György T. Nagy photographed many of the images and illustrations for the book, and James Dorian provided much-needed computer assistance at the final stages of completing the manuscript.

The Mosse Lectures that I delivered at the University of Wisconsin–Madison allowed me to imagine the sequence of chapters that eventually became the final version of this book. I am grateful to John Tortorice for his warm support throughout this project. I particularly appreciate his generous offer to finance the extra illustrations that have been included in this book. During my stay in Madison, David Sorkin and Shifra Sharlin were wonderful hosts who welcomed me with their usual warmth and generosity.

I would also like to thank the editorial staff of the University of Wisconsin Press, in particular Raphael Kadushin, Amber Rose, Carla Marolt, and Sheila McMahon, for their uncommon care and creativity in preparing the final version of the manuscript. I received help from the following archives and libraries in assembling the images for this book: the Budapest Historical Museum/Museum Kiscell, the Collection of Theater History at the Hungarian National Széchényi Library, the Petőfi Literary Museum, the Hungarian Jewish Museum and Archive, the Metropolitan Ervin Szabó Library, Budapest Collection, and the Collection of Historical Photographs of the National Museum. An earlier version of chapter 1 was translated into Hungarian and published in *Múlt és Jövő* in 2012. An abridged version of chapter 3 appeared in *The Hungarian Historical Review* in 2014. I would like to thank the editors of both journals for their permission to use these materials.

My greatest intellectual debt is to Lajos Császi, who has read so many versions of this manuscript that he could present its arguments to friends much more eloquently than I could. Perhaps most important, he has been a constant reminder of the Hungarian liberal perspective in this story that has so tragically disappeared from the everyday politics of the country.

This book is dedicated to the memory of my parents, who, had they lived to read it, might have recognized traces of their city in this account.

THE INVISIBLE JEWISH BUDAPEST

Introduction

Jewish Budapest as a
Symbolic Space

In 1900 Budapest had a Jewish population of roughly 23 percent, making it the second largest Jewish city in Europe. Only Warsaw surpassed it, with a Jewish population of 33 percent. This demographic fact appears startling only because of its virtual absence from official narratives of Budapest. Canonical histories of the city present its story primarily in political terms as the inevitable transition from a German-speaking small town in the mid-nineteenth century into a Hungarian-speaking capital by the fin de siècle.[1] The emergence of Budapest as a major Central European metropolis was undoubtedly a political event reflecting the national and imperial ambitions of the Hungarian state. It was also, however, a cultural phenomenon that gave rise to a complex urban modernity closely associated with the Jewish presence in the city.[2] *The Invisible Jewish Budapest* is an attempt to retrieve the lost contours of this Jewish-inflected cultural world, famous throughout Central Europe for its edgy nightlife, innovative entertainment industry, and bohemian cultural life. I have called this world "invisible" because of its pervasive stigmatization by official culture, which rendered it if not technically invisible then symbolically unacknowledged.

Anti-Semites were the most vociferous and vitriolic critics of modern Budapest, which they directly associated with its Jewish character. In the 1890s, Vienna's anti-Semitic mayor, Karl Lueger, famously coined the term *Judapest* to designate what he took to be overwhelming Jewish influence over the cultural life of the Hungarian capital. The concept of *Judapest* found full-blown ideological iteration during the interwar years under the conservative regime of Miklós Horthy, which labeled Budapest the "sinful city" (*bűnös város*) and vowed to cleanse it of its Jewish elements.[3] The idea of a degenerate and rapacious Jewish modernity that had despoiled Hungarian national culture became the toxic inheritance of right-wing Hungarian politics. Its ambiguous afterlife continues to the present, inhibiting scholarly research or even serious conversation about the subject.

Yet the identification of Budapest as a Jewish cultural space was not exclusively a figment of anti-Semitic imagination or the creation of right-wing ideologues. It existed as a cultural commonplace among contemporaries, who used the figure without feeling the need to define its precise meaning or perimeters. Endre Ady, the great modernist poet who was also a self-declared liberal and philo-Semite, could assume a consensus on this subject when he characterized the modernity of the city in terms of its Jewish character. "It is the Jews," he wrote in an article of 1917, "who created for us [Hungarians] Budapest, along with everything else that from the distance gives the appearance of being European but is nothing but gaudy illusion."[4]

The Jewish Budapest that Ady referred to was not so much a social or political reality as a cultural experience associated with the ambiguities, as well as the challenges, of metropolitan life. Amorphous in the extreme, it lacked stable definition. Its fragmented codes were inscribed in the city's coffee houses, music halls, editorial offices, and boulevards, which embodied the dynamic spirit of the age. Though largely created by Jews, Jewish Budapest was not restricted to Jews and lacked a specifically Jewish face. It is for this reason that the phenomenon has been hard to incorporate into the general history of Hungarian Jewry. As a recent investigator of the Jewish landmarks of Budapest has pointed out, there exists a theoretical and epistemological disconnect between the artifacts of urban culture and their Jewish creators. "How can one describe," the author asks, "that which is *not visible* and write about that which is not Jewish; and yet which . . . still is Jewish, although those who built, shaped and formed it did not do so as Jews?"[5]

These questions form the starting point of my own study, which is concerned not so much with the social and institutional history of the Jews of Budapest as with the development of a uniquely Jewish modernity that became part of the larger Hungarian cultural landscape. Scholars have been deeply divided about the possibility of even talking about the existence of a Jewish modernity.[6] The idea, as the cultural historian Scott Spector argues, has a problematic history in German-speaking Central Europe. Used almost interchangeably by both philo-Semites and anti-Semites, the concept shares "the twin premises that modernism is Jewish, and yet that modernism's Jewishness is somehow hidden and needs to be revealed."[7] Spector notes that the ideological and conceptual instability of the figure makes it difficult to imagine a history of Jewish modernism, but he concedes the possibility of a history of discourses about Jewish modernism. Such a history would focus not so much on essentialist definitions of Jewish modernism as on the cultural work it performs in society.[8] It would circumvent unanswerable questions about the lives and intentions of Jewish modernists and would deal, instead, with issues such as how modernist cultural products functioned and created meanings within particular contexts.

The Invisible Jewish Budapest is informed by this self-reflexive agenda. It argues that the story of Jewish modernity is best studied not through the celebrated achievements of individuals and elite groups but through the everyday narratives, informal practices, and popular rituals of urban life. The shift in focus suggests that the seemingly irresolvable social and political conflicts of society found symbolic expression and partial resolution precisely in the ephemeral, trivial, sometimes vulgar realms of popular culture and commercial entertainment. More generally, it also makes clear that these were the informal spaces where new forms of Jewish sociability and self-identity were invented and made visible in defiance of official liberal ideology committed to rendering Jewish life as invisible as possible within the culture.[9]

In attempting to recuperate the world of Budapest popular culture, I have relied extensively on the work of social historians of the city, who during the past two decades have explored institutions such as the coffee house, prostitution, poverty, and urban developments in Budapest.[10] I am equally indebted to historians of Budapest Jewry, who have studied the physical spaces and the cultural and religious organizations that defined Budapest Jewish life in the later half of the nineteenth century.[11] At the same time, however, the focus of my work and the questions it poses differ from both these genres of urban history. It is situated at the intersection of their concerns and tries to reconstitute the empirical and symbolic spaces where urban history and Jewish history meet and collide. Ultimately, it is interested not just in the city or in the Jews but in the ways a Jewish-identified urban culture constituted itself in the context of the nineteenth-century nation-state.

In his study of twentieth-century New York, the cultural historian Eli Lederhendler articulated some of the theoretical problems involved with such an enterprise.[12] The difficulty of talking about the Jewish-identified city, he suggests, stems in part from the tendency of historians to conflate the city with the Jewish ethnic neighborhood. In fact, these two phenomena represent different conceptual and methodological challenges for the historian. The Jewish ethnic neighborhood, with its "visually and palpably Jewish face," is an empirical space, capable of being identified with its social institutions and physical topography. By contrast, the Jewish-identified city, with its cosmopolitan and modernist culture, is a symbolic concept created by cultural and literary discourses. To illustrate this point, Lederhendler suggests fundamental analogies between the Jewish-identified city and the East European shtetl. Both are metaphorical assertions based on deliberate selectivity that makes no claim to empirical truth.[13] The literary image of the shtetl, it is true, was created by Yiddish writers looking back to a premodern tradition at a moment when East European Jewry faced wrenching social dislocations.[14] By contrast, the Jewish-identified city was the creation of popular journalists who celebrated secular life and individual liberation from tradition. Despite these obvious differences, the juxtaposition of the two images highlights their common discursive dimensions and allows us to treat them as cultural and literary artifacts rather than empirical, social realities.

In seeking to delimit the symbolic boundaries of Jewish Budapest, I have focused on such characteristic institutions as popular journalism, the coffee house, the music hall, the humor magazine, and the mid-cult literary journal, which defined the life and collective experience of the fin-de-siècle city. I have intentionally refrained from imposing the appearance of an artificial unity in my narrative of these institutions, which existed independent of one another and negotiated the encounter between individuals and the city in distinct and characteristic ways. They were, nevertheless, linked with one another not only by their common appeal but also by their implicit or explicit association with Jewish writers, owners, clients, and consumers. Chapter 1 traces the emergence of popular guidebooks and urban narratives in the course of the late nineteenth century, which attempted to define the nature of Budapest urban culture as it assumed the characteristics of an increasingly secular metropolitan center. The inherent political dimensions of this enterprise are explored in chapter 2, which focuses on cultural representations of the so-called Jewish question as it was enacted in the context of two political crises in 1882: the ritual murder trial of Tiszaeszlár and the debate against Russian Jewish immigration. Chapter 3 focuses more fully on the bifurcation of the urban public sphere, which created a sharp distinction between acceptable and unacceptable public discourses about Jewish subjects. Chapters 4 and 5 form the heart of this study, examining the two pivotal expressions of Budapest Jewish public culture. The first was humor or the *Judenwitz*, which found its most important embodiment in the humor magazine *Borsszem Jankó*. The second was the Jewish music hall or Orpheum, which created the forms of a commercial entertainment industry that came to define the very nature of modern Budapest at the fin de siècle. Chapter 6 addresses the anomalies of the Jewish bourgeoisie through the lenses of the mid-cult literary magazine *A Hét*, which gave particularly striking definition to the crisis of Jewish bourgeois identity that characterized the entire period of the fin de siècle.

Perhaps a word also needs to be said about the perspective from which this book is written. I have tried to avoid the aura of nostalgia that commonly surrounds the history of Hungarian Jewry under the Dual Monarchy. In light of the Jewish tragedy of the twentieth century, it is hardly surprising that the monarchy has acquired the status of a golden age in popular imagination. Such positive views, moreover, are more or less consistent with the testimonials of contemporaries. The Hungarian Jewish elite, in particular, was famous for its celebration of Hungarian culture, whose tolerance and enlightenment it considered unmatched among the European nations. My skepticism about such optimistic narratives is an inevitable function of historical hindsight, but it is also conditioned by the nature of my sources, which tend to be drawn from popular culture rather than the bourgeois establishment or the Jewish religious elite. The protagonists of my account are semibohemian journalists, humorists, music hall composers, and cabaret writers who had a distinctly critical and acerbic view of their society. Since it is precisely this critical perspective that has been ignored or suppressed in later histories of the period, I felt it important to give it priority. Of course, the larger truth about Jewish Budapest is that it lacked a unitary voice. Its characteristic feature was the unstable juxtaposition of irreconcilable opposites: optimism with anxiety, conformity with subversion, certainty with ambivalence, rootedness with marginality.

This is possibly the reason why no consensus tale about nineteenth-century Hungarian Jewry has emerged among professional historians. As a recent historian of the period has admitted, the story is fraught with paradox and discontinuity and can only be told in the form of a hypothetical history that would sound something like this: "There existed at one time a happy coexistence between Jews and Hungarians that was unique in Europe, but . . . this relationship simply went sour in the course of time. The alternate version of the story is that these idyllic conditions were precisely the preconditions for the destruction of Hungarian Jewry, which had been rendered politically unsuspecting and defenseless."[15] The story that I recount in the following pages does not contradict the conclusions of this inconclusive historical tale. What it does do is suggest the inadequacies of trying to understand it purely through political or ideological terms. The ultimate goal of this study is not to add complexity to existing interpretations but to open up a new cultural and symbolic space for the history of Central European Jewish experience.

1

Cultural Visions of the Emerging City

The Historical Context

Hungarian Jewry's collective identification with the city of Budapest found ironic depiction in a caricature of 1883 published in the humor magazine *Borsszem Jankó*. The image presented an obviously Jewish figure on his Sabbath walk, surveying with satisfaction the magnificent vistas presented by the recently constructed Andrássy Avenue. The caption under the tableau reads: "How fair are your tents, oh Jacob!"[1] The line was an adaptation from a Jewish liturgical hymn in praise of Israel and intended to convey Hungarian Jewry's unique sense of belonging and symbolic ownership in the city. The surprising juxtaposition of the ancient Biblical text and the modern urban image had complex resonances that conveyed more than mere urban pride. It suggested nothing less than a conceptual, if not historical, overlap between the Biblical homeland and the contemporary city. Budapest appeared as the reincarnation of ancient Jerusalem, the site where the religious past and the secular future found a happy meeting ground. After centuries of wandering among strange lands and hostile people, commented a contemporary, the Jewish Ahasuerus discovered a home in modern Europe.[2]

The remarkable convergence between Jewish hopes and Hungarian realities took place within a specific historical context defined by three interconnected political developments that occurred at almost the same time.[3] The first event was the Compromise Agreement of 1867, which gave rise to an unwieldy but workable constitutional union between Austria and Hungary. The Dual Monarchy, as it came to be known, provided the political frame for an ethnically diverse but politically centralized Hungarian state,

Szombati séta a Sugáruton.

Seiffensteiner Salamon. »Mily szépek a te sátraid, ó Jákób!«

"Saturday stroll along Sugár (Andrássy) Avenue." Published in *Borsszem Jankó* (February 18, 1883). Petőfi Literary Museum.

within which Jews were granted unusual economic opportunities in exchange for Hungarian ethnic assimilation. The second event, closely linked to the first, was the Emancipation Decree of 1867, which granted Jews full political and civic equality in the Habsburg lands. Jewish emancipation unleashed a process of rapid secularization and modernization, which had a particularly dramatic impact on the demographic and cultural life of Budapest. These effects were to find their culmination in the creation of Budapest in 1873, when the three independent municipalities of Pest, Buda, and Óbuda were unified into one capital city. The vast urban renewal project set in motion after unification eventually transformed Budapest into a modern metropolis that increasingly envisioned itself as the rival and potential equal of the imperial city of Vienna.

For Budapest Jewry, the compromise, the emancipation, and the rebuilding of Budapest were symbolically linked and inconceivable in isolation from one another. Even as they learned to balance their Hungarian and Habsburg loyalties in a new sense of citizenship, Jews found satisfying outlets for their civic pride in the emerging city. Jewish capital helped finance the monumental urban renewal projects that transformed the face of Budapest in the

Andrássy Avenue, ca. 1890. Courtesy of Budapest History Museum, Museum Kiscell.

Kigyó (Ferenciek) Square with Klotild Palaces and Elizabeth Bridge in the background, ca. 1902. Courtesy of Budapest History Museum, Museum Kiscell.

Elizabeth Bridge under construction, ca. 1902. Courtesy of Budapest History Museum, Museum Kiscell.

last quarter of the nineteenth century. In turn, urban culture provided large segments of the Jewish population with new social identities that replaced traditional ethnic and religious affiliations. As actors and spectators in the public spaces of the city, Budapest Jews both identified with, and came to be defined by, the urban institutions they had helped create. They celebrated the imposing boulevards, the teeming coffee houses, the lively music halls, and the witty cabarets of the city, in which they saw embodiments of their own, as well as of their city's, modernity.

Observers often remarked on the novel character of fin-de-siècle Budapest, whose precipitous growth and exuberant commercial spirit seemed to resemble an American, rather than a Central European, metropolis. There was an element of instability and symbolic incoherence about the modernity of the city, which defined itself through the fragmented narratives of popular journalism and commercial entertainment rather than the rhetoric of national identity or historical tradition. As late as the 1930s the journalist Béla Bevilaqua reflected on the unfinished, provisional quality of Budapest

Budapest Stock Exchange, ca. 1910. Courtesy of Metropolitan Ervin Szabó Library, Budapest Collection.

urban culture. Unlike Vienna, he mused, the Hungarian capital failed to develop a distinctive urban myth of its own. If there existed a Budapest myth, he speculated, it was that of perpetual self-division and ambivalence that resisted all attempts at stabilization. The typical citizen of Budapest, Bevilaqua claimed, was a restless Hamlet or a wandering Ahasuerus, eternally torn between the empirical and imaginary worlds, "between the earthly and the heavenly Jerusalem."[4]

Hungarian Attitudes toward Budapest

These distinct features of Budapest modernity were not yet visible in 1873, when the city was incorporated as the new Hungarian capital. Conceived by the political leadership that had negotiated the Compromise Agreement of 1867, Budapest was expected to become both a national and imperial city signaling Hungary's political ambitions as a major Central European power.[5] Perhaps no one was more closely affiliated with these ambitions than Gyula Andrássy, the prime minister who laid the political groundwork for the new city. He was, it seems, "constantly preoccupied by the thought of transforming Budapest into the most beautiful city in the world. . . . He envisioned for Hungary a heroic future for which an appropriate capital city was a requisite."[6]

By 1900 Budapest had unquestionably been transformed into an imposing and regal city, with monumental buildings and modern boulevards that rivaled those of Vienna. Yet the city itself failed to live up to the political expectations that had been attached to it. The Hungarian elite that had envisioned and helped bring it into existence never became fully identified with its own creation. Official Hungary increasingly turned to historic symbols and feudal traditions as signs of its legitimacy and collective identity. The Millennial celebrations of 1896, commemorating the founding of the Hungarian state in 896, gave ample opportunity for the ceremonial enactment of a new, explicitly anti-urban national vision. Budapest became the site for the construction of elaborate pseudo-historical monuments, meant to symbolize the premodern roots of the Hungarian state. Processions of office holders in national costumes paraded through the city in reenactments of the indelible continuity between the present and the past. Ironically, the Hungarian elite's anti-urban vision was itself performed as an urban ritual set against the background of modern Budapest.

The new symbolic order found summation in 1896, in a series of lectures delivered at the University of Budapest by the respected literary scholar Zsolt Beöthy. In a dramatic act of mythmaking that actually broke from

Procession celebrating Hungary's Millennium, 1896. Courtesy of Metropolitan Ervin Szabó Library, Budapest Collection.

earlier, liberal national traditions, Beöthy evoked the primitive, Asiatic roots of the Hungarian nation.[7] "Out of the mists of ancient times," he claimed, "the figure of a lone horseman appears before our eyes, as he quietly stands in the flatlands by the Volga looking about him. With his eagle's eyes, he observes the seemingly endless plane, whose every detail is sharply lit by the glaring orb of the sun. He is calm, equally free of fear or fantasy. The only thing that concerns him is what he sees, and his trained eye absorbs everything in the sun-lit flat horizon that a human eye is capable of absorbing from a single angle."[8] There was nothing casual or haphazard about the conception of this enigmatic and solitary horseman. Every detail associated with the figure—the sun-scorched Eurasian planes, his self-possessed manner, his pragmatic gaze—had symbolic resonances that Beöthy's audiences would immediately have recognized. This was not just a distant ancestor of the Hungarian people but also the incarnation of the ideal type of the modern Hungarian individual. Not coincidentally, the type was presented as the direct antithesis of the modern, neurotic, and implicitly Jewish self that populated the coffee houses and boulevards of contemporary Budapest.

Beöthy's artful mythmaking created the symbolic and ideological polarities that would define conceptions of Hungarian nationalism and national character at the fin de siècle. The unspoiled East was juxtaposed to a degenerate West; masculine self-reliance to modern effeminacy; healthy pragmatism to rampant subjectivity. Given the inherent logic of this cultural imaginary, the city could only be conceived of as the antithesis and, in time, the archenemy of national traditions. By the early 1920s the construction of Budapest as a "modern Babylon" was complete. The severing of symbolic ties between modern Budapest and historic Hungary seemed inevitable. "You may well ask," a conservative journalist queried in 1922, "what possible claim this city might have on the nation's stormy, thousand-year-old past?"[9]

Official Jewish Discourses about the City

Significantly, there never developed an explicitly Jewish urban narrative to fill the vacuum left by Hungarian nationalist culture. Individual Jews may have been energized by the possibilities offered by the modern city, but the Jewish religious establishment remained profoundly ambivalent. Not surprisingly, orthodox Jews rejected many aspects of the secular urban world that surrounded them. But the Neolog leadership also viewed with alarm assimilated Jewry's headlong rush to integrate with the modern world.[10] Fearing for the very survival of Judaism under modern conditions, this leadership developed a discourse of crisis about the impact of the city on everyday life that in some respects paralleled the ideological suspicions of Hungarian nationalists.

The leitmotifs of Neolog narratives focused on the erosion of Jewish religious knowledge and cultural practices in the modern world. "Within the span of a generation," lamented a typical article in the official Neolog publication, *Magyar Zsidó Szemle* (Hungarian Jewish review), "we have grown so educated and cultivated that we have discarded everything that our three-thousand-year-old history has consecrated. It has taken the hostility of the outside world for us to turn in on ourselves again and to realize with shame and astonishment the disorganized state of our religious life."[11] "Hungarian Jewry," wrote another observer in a similar vein, "must take firm, unambiguous, and radical action if it wants to ensure that within a decade or two the history of its denomination, the fundamental principles of its religion, and the commandments of its faith will not have sunk into the sea of oblivion."[12]

For many concerned observers, Judaism's encounter with modernity appeared deeply problematic for its long-range survival. In the past, argued one writer, when Judaism found itself face to face with strong, independent cultures in the Greek or Arab worlds, it had been able to respond creatively by producing a new synthesis that actually left Jewish philosophy invigorated and spiritually purified. Recent Jewish responses to European secular culture, however, seemed far more questionable. On the one hand, a small section of Orthodox Jewish scholarship remained closed to the challenges of the new, while on the other, a larger section was uncritically won over to the merely external, material aspects of secular culture. "The prognosis for the future," concluded the author, "appears highly unfavorable in our eyes. In order to survive, a religion needs a collective conscience, and clear, vigorous, and usable concepts. In our case, however, one cannot speak of common views, but rather, of the total absence of such views."[13]

Significantly, none of these critics, who were modernizers in their own way, idealized the Jewish past or wished a return to ghetto culture. They were ready to admit that the average Jew living in a closed Jewish society had been as ignorant of Talmudic scholarship and Jewish philosophy as his secularized descendants. The difference was, however, that the former "practiced the customs of his religion ceaselessly, because this is what his immediate surroundings did. The modern Jew by contrast neither practices Judaism nor sees the practice of Judaism in his environment."[14] Changing patterns of family life, especially among the upwardly mobile bourgeoisie, were frequently blamed for declining religious observance in Jewish families. A common complaint of the time was that Jewish women, who had been traditionally responsible for making of their home "the sacred center of religious life," had abandoned their mission. They had become social butterflies, "at home in society but strangers in their homes," relegating the care of their children to servants and governesses, who understandably had no notion of Jewish traditions. Under these adverse conditions, the religious feelings and memories of the parents, which were often strong and tenacious, became like "shadows with no influence on the consciousness of their children."[15]

The explicit agenda of the Neolog elite was to modernize Judaism by rendering religion philosophically up-to-date and personally meaningful to educated Jews. Religious and ethical instruction, it was hoped, would bring about the rejuvenation of modern Jewish life and character. Such hopes turned out to be quixotic and the crisis of Jewish religious life became a

permanent feature of official Neolog discourse. The theme found its summation in the introduction to the *Zsidó lexikon* (Jewish encyclopedia), published in 1929. "To discover uninhabited lands is a difficult task," proclaimed
the editor, Péter Újvári, "but it is a thousand times more difficult to uncover
the existence of a people who does not know itself. And the Jews who
occupy the Danubian basin do not know themselves; what is worse, they
misunderstand themselves. They live, move, evolve within their history, but
as far as they are concerned, this history is a book sealed with seven seals."[16]

At the heart of the pervasive sense of crisis that haunted Neolog religious
and cultural narratives was an insoluble paradox. The erosion of religious
traditions that they identified as an inevitable result of modernity was also
an integral part of the process of emancipation and assimilation that they
wholeheartedly supported. The task of disentangling the positive aspects of
secularization from its negative consequences proved to be an impossible
undertaking. The Neolog vision of an ethical, rationalized Judaism could not
offer a genuine alternative to modernity. It could only mitigate, not cancel
out, the corrosive impact of the modern world on religious faith and traditional life. Thus, for the vast majority of Budapest Jews, organized religion
became an occasional ritual practice relegated to the peripheries of life
rather than a vital source of collective identity.

The editors of *Magyar Zsidó Szemle* were probably aware of the profound
disjuncture between their high-minded endeavors and ordinary life. They
were even willing to acknowledge it as long as it could be expressed through
a satiric, feminized voice. In one of its early numbers, the review published
a humorous letter from a female reader, reprimanding the editors for the
remoteness of their journal from everyday life and the "female point of
view." Coyly signed as "Georges, but not Sand or Eliot," the letter explicitly
stated its objection in the name of popular culture and the serial novel. "I
definitely want to complain," the elusive reader wrote. "I subscribed to the
Review, which I duly received. But what I found was a huge amount of
scholarly articles, some of which were 'to be continued.' And yet, they are
not even novels or short stories. . . . I feel this journal of ours could use some
liveliness. I have discussed this with my girlfriends and they all agree with
me. But of course, our opinion counts for nothing in your eyes."[17]

The Budapest Flâneur

The challenge of defining how to live under modern conditions was met
not by religious reformers but by the producers of urban popular culture. It

is ordinary journalists, hack novelists, and producers of informal urban texts who shaped people's experiences and expectations of the urban environment. They created images of the modern city, showing its inhabitants what the urban space looked and felt like, how it should be negotiated and consumed, and how its dangers might be managed and guarded against. In performing these tasks, the humble occupation of the commercial journalist was transformed into the heroic role of the flâneur or the privileged observer and interpreter of urban modernity.

The type was invented in early nineteenth-century Paris, where the flâneur came to be associated with a new kind of literary producer who reflected and celebrated the diversity of the urban landscape. Like modern life itself, the external appearance of the flâneur was impersonal and anonymous, defined by the habitual black frockcoat, top hat, and umbrella of the bourgeois man-about-town. He was an indecipherable presence whose distinguishing feature was precisely his lack of personal qualities, his complete anonymity. He strolled through the city, rendering the physical details of the urban world visible and legible, even while he himself remained invisible and illegible.[18] In actual fact, however, the flâneur was a less innocent figure than he appeared. As Priscilla Ferguson has claimed, by asserting the right to guide his readers through the city and explain its capacity for constant flux, the flâneur was actually laying claim to "a new authority over the city as text."[19] He questioned traditional interpretation of the city and asserted a new, more dynamic and democratic vision that strove to express diversity as well as to create unity. The cultural critic John Jervis gave perhaps the most concise depiction of the complexities of the flâneur's vision of urban life. The flâneur saw the city, Jervis noted, in essentially dynamic and contradictory terms. The city was "rational project and the excess of theatricality; . . . pleasure and danger, a site of moral conflict; fragmented, yet interconnected, monolithic, yet heterogeneous; masculine and feminine. It [was] a place of fluidity and diversity, rather than rootedness and community, yet simultaneously reproduced community within itself."[20]

How did this complex perspective find expression in narratives about Jewish Budapest? How did the Jewish flâneur help create symbolic spaces, whose modernity appeared simultaneously Jewish and cosmopolitan? Ultimately, what was the impact of these representations on the related problems of Jewish assimilation and acculturation? The answers to these questions are deeply embedded in the tentative, contradictory, ultimately futile, efforts of contemporary urban chroniclers to render the modern city legible and unified. These early writers of urban texts had no preexistent concept of the city or of modernity. They simply gave voice to the wide-ranging sense of hope, uncertainty, and anxiety that people were likely to experience in the new environment. At the same time, however, they also created stereotypes about urban life and character that helped stabilize and familiarize the city for its inhabitants. Insofar as urban texts were prescriptive as well as descriptive, they fulfilled a positive cultural role in the rapidly modernizing society. They helped create new visions of identity, new patterns of everyday life, which irreversibly linked Jews to the cultural landscape of Budapest.

Guidebooks to the City

The first modern guidebooks appeared in Budapest in the 1860s in the form of cheaply printed pocket-sized booklets offering useful information about the changing city. These were essentially alphabetical listings or inventories of places of business, public life, and amusement that visitors and natives of the city might find equally useful. The goal of the books, as the subtitle of one of the earliest, published in 1864, made clear, was to introduce readers "to the different and most interesting sights of the Hungarian capital, including its public and private buildings, its associations, its commercial, industrial, artisanal, agrarian, and cultural events, and its favorite places of entertainment."[21] The compendium of interesting sights included in these listings was characteristically eclectic, offering no distinction between cultural or commercial pursuits, between highlife and everyday culture, between official and unofficial sights. The content of guidebooks to the city was about museums, theaters, and coffee houses; but also about factories, mills, schools, military barracks, railway stations, government buildings, churches, and graveyards.[22]

In their striving for a panoramic, all-inclusive presentation of the modern city, these urban texts already anticipated the conceptual dilemmas that were to challenge their successors in the 1880s and 1890s. How was it possible to create a comprehensive map of the city? Could one individual grasp and stabilize such a vast subject? Perhaps most elusive of all, what was the meaning of this new phenomenon? These questions were hinted at in a guidebook of 1873, written by Lajos Hevesi, a talented journalist associated with the founding generation of the humor magazine *Borsszem Jankó*. His account of Budapest under construction suggested a city in motion, a place in a constant state of becoming, whose real existence could only be projected into the future, but not understood in the present. "The major streets of Pest," he claimed, "are already transformed or about to be transformed by magnificent boulevards resembling the ones in Paris; the inner city will soon be surrounded by an entire ring of similar boulevards and a brilliantly conceived second ring, which will cut through the most populous neighborhoods, . . . will circulate blood into the veins of the city."[23] Having conjured up a city in motion, without fixed boundaries or character, he raised the inevitable problem of representation. "Ultimately," he complained, "I feel myself approximately like the photographer who attempts to fix in his glass plate the effervescent life of the street; he is compelled to portray every single moving object in the place that it will only occupy in the next moment."[24]

These questions were hardly unique to Hevesi and his contemporaries. The difficulty of representing the city, the allusiveness of city life, has been the inexhaustible theme of popular novelists and historians since the early nineteenth century. It was the emergence of Paris and London that first confronted observers with a new cultural phenomenon that could not be apprehended through conventional categories of representation that were applied to traditional social reality. Struggling to capture the disturbing, disorienting, yet seductive, qualities of metropolitan existence, popular writers of the early nineteenth century developed not just new vocabularies but also new narratives for depicting these unprecedented urban spaces. The city began to appear in their work as a place of hidden passions, exotic personalities, criminal activities, which existed underneath, and apart, from the placid, public façade of the city.[25]

József Kiss and the *Mysteries of Budapest*

The vision of modern Budapest as the site of crime and passion found its most famous incarnation in a seven-volume potboiler of 1874 titled *Mysteries of Budapest* (Budapesti rejtelmek). The author of the text was József Kiss, one of the most celebrated Jewish literary figures of the fin de siècle, who became known for his sentimental ballads of Jewish village life as well as for his pioneering work as editor of the modernist literary weekly *A Hét* (The week). *The Mysteries of Budapest*, however, was not part of his official literary oeuvre. It was published under the fanciful pseudonym of Rudolf Szentessy, a name that self-consciously echoed the hero of Eugene Sue's 1842 bestseller, *Les mystères de Paris*, on which Kiss's own novel was modeled. *The Mysteries of Budapest* presented a scandalous portrait of modern Budapest, in which the seething life of a Jewish ethnic neighborhood, the

Terézváros, was given pride of place as the incarnation of the essence of modernity in the city.

While primarily interested in the life of the Terézváros, Kiss provided by way of contrast a brief detour to the respectable neighborhood of the Lipótváros, where the Jewish commercial elite lived. It was a neighborhood, he informed his readers, of tree-lined streets and handsome apartment palaces, where comfort, good taste, and boredom ruled. The staid and peace-loving inhabitants of the quarter only lost their equanimity when one of their stores failed to open because of bankruptcy. If the male population of the Lipótváros was obsessed with the anxieties of business, its female members were preoccupied with the business of culture. "The ladies of the district," Kiss wrote maliciously, "read French novels in translation. The works of Schiller, Goethe, Heine, and Börne stand in leather-bound volumes on their bookshelves, but only in exceptional circumstances does one encounter the works of Petőfi and Arany."[26] In this pretentious and inauthentic literary fare, Kiss claimed to discern the moral failure of the Jewish financial aristocracy, which "likes to ape the hereditary aristocracy—at least in its faults."[27]

The object of Kiss's narrative was, however, not to criticize the limitations of the wealthy Lipótváros but to celebrate the liveliness of its impoverished neighbor, the Terézváros. This was where the vast majority of the Jewish lower middle classes lived and worked, and it was also where the city's major music halls and places of entertainment were located. On the main thoroughfare of the district, Király Street, Kiss wrote, "one experiences the genuine rhythm of a world city, with its hustle and bustle, its comings and goings, its effervescence and hurried way of life. This is the throbbing heart of the capital, which never sleeps, never rests, and is full of noisy life, even when the city's other districts have already quieted down." The magnetic appeal of Király Street lay in its heterogeneity, in its remarkable ability to blend "eastern confusion, the cacophony of Constantinople, Jewish resourcefulness and Hungarian laziness" into a noisy, chaotic, but seemingly workable unity.[28]

The character of the neighborhood was defined by the intersection of three distinct worlds: commerce, entertainment, and Jewish religious practice. Its pulsating commercial life was reflected in the hundreds of retail stores, food stalls, and itinerant peddlers that jostled one another along the narrow sidewalks and the adjourning streets that opened form Király Street. Every conceivable article was available for sale on this street, which resembled an oriental bazaar rather than a luxury retail district. "There are

"Király Street in rainy weather." Published in *Borsszem Jankó* (March 14, 1869). Petőfi Literary Museum.

no enticing window displays in Király Street," Kiss reminded his readers. "Its stores compete with each other, not in the quality, but in the cheapness of their products. In one place, they offer material for a suit of clothes for two forints [the local currency], its neighbor advertises in large black letters the same product for one forint. A practical people! America in Budapest."[29]

Once the shutters of the stores were lowered at 9:00 p.m., however, the nature of the district changed and the focus of its energies shifted from business to amusement. The bright lights of its musical cafés, beer halls, café chantants, and Orpheums lit up the darkness of the night, and the sound of popular songs and gypsy music streamed out through its open windows and doorways. The quality and reputation of these establishments varied greatly, Kiss admitted, but their close association with disreputable, marginal, and outright criminal elements made them the classic site of bohemia in Budapest. Here were found "unemployed apprentices, shop clerks dismissed for misappropriating funds, and at times, those unfortunates, who had, through no fault of their own, lost their positions. . . . Not a small segment of the regulars were made up of individuals who made their living through the grace of the ladies of the night, in need of gallants to protect them from danger or abuse. The type is referred to as a pimp and represents the most infamous class of mankind."[30]

There was, finally, a third element that contributed to the creative life of the district, and this was the Jewish exotic, enacted through colorful religious celebrations such as the Purim festival, which Kiss presented as "a piece of the Middle Ages resurrected in the midst of modern life."[31] People with white and red makeup, decked out as Harlequins, chimney sweeps, peasant lads and girls, Slovenes, ragged beggars, and other fantastic apparitions, took over the entire street, forcing carriages to proceed at a walker's pace. Groups of revelers congregated in front of the bright entrances of coffee houses to watch improvised performances by Polish Jews in kaftans, "who struck up Yiddish songs and began a frantic dance, until one after another they lost their balance and fell over each other. All this took place amidst applause and enthusiastic cheers from the audience."[32] Kiss concluded his account with the confident assertion that Király Street, with its unmatched vitality and diversity, had no parallels anywhere on the globe:

> Other big cities have narrow dirty streets that swarm with the humble classes of humanity. But no other European capital possesses a Király Street, where one sees intertwined in such close proximity the contrasting elements of life.

Here one finds, trotting along the same road leading to the City Park, the weary nag hauling a hansom cab and the prancing chargers of an aristocratic carriage. Here one sees side-by-side ugliness and beauty, the repulsive and the ravishing sides of life. Király Street is truly unique in the world.[33]

The image of modernity conjured up in these striking streetscapes of the Terézváros was deeply indebted to the tradition of early nineteenth-century melodrama, which first gave voice to the scandalous, disruptive, and conflicted energies of modern life.[34] Kiss seemed aware of the conventions of the genre as well as of the requirements of his role as urban narrator. He undertook the task of guiding his readers through the dangerous underworld of the city by vicariously introducing them to places they would not visit on their own. He was primarily the flâneur who provided impartial information about the teeming, often hidden, life of urban neighborhoods that existed beneath the official surface of the city. On occasion, however, he also assumed the role of Asmodée, the minor devil of eighteenth-century Parisian guidebooks, who removed the rooftops of urban dwellings to reveal their contents.[35]

Collective Editions of Panorama Texts

The simultaneously omniscient and subversive qualities of Kiss's urban writing proved difficult to maintain in the long run. By the 1880s and 1890s the complexity of the city made it increasingly difficult for a single author's work to encompass all its typical sights and features, and the fashion for collaborative volumes became common. Just as importantly, the rise of bourgeois respectability required a more conventional, broadly accepted perspective on the phenomena of modern city life than the one Kiss offered. Both requirements were fulfilled by Henrik Lenkei's edited volume *A mulató Budapest* (Budapest, the city of entertainment), one of the most comprehensive urban texts and guidebooks of the 1890s.

Lenkei brought impeccable literary and social credentials to the task of exploring the cultural landscape of fin-de-siècle Budapest. A poet, playwright, and educator, he was also secretary to the prestigious Izraelita Magyar Irodalmi Társaság (Jewish Hungarian Literary Society), founded in 1894 to promote the translation and publication of Jewish literary and religious texts into Hungarian. In contrast to Kiss's *Mysteries of Budapest*, Lenkai's collection offered no scandalous immersion into the underside of urban life. It was addressed to a primarily respectable bourgeois audience curious about gossip, entertainment, and amusement in the capital city. The articles in the volume focused on such seemingly unobjectionable phenomena as coffee houses, afternoon teas, theaters, museums, libraries, and literary coteries, which all reflected the newly created bourgeois face of the city.

Lenkei's attempt to visualize the topography of urban life in Budapest had shifted considerably since Kiss's efforts to represent it twenty years earlier. By the 1890s the defining features of modernity were associated not with the hidden and disreputable manifestations of popular culture but with the abstract standards of rationality that supposedly reflected an idealized conception of the "West." Budapest was now celebrated precisely for its lack of exotic qualities, which made it indistinguishable from other, "civilized," European cities. As one writer boasted,

> Naturally, Westerners who long for a little exoticism will be most surprised by the Hungarian capital, and perhaps not a little annoyed by its sights. Among our women, the characteristic type of Hungarian beauty is displayed in exactly the same costumes as among Parisian women, while our men . . . wear top hats and long afternoon coats just like the most westernized of the western men. . . . Those tourists, therefore, who seek to discover examples of the exotic East here are requested to kindly move over a little further east and south. There, perhaps, they will discover what they are after.[36]

The "Western" or "European" character of Budapest was invariably associated with the monumental new boulevards on the Pest side of the city, whose modernity was further specified in terms of the symbolism of class. The architectural and aesthetic features of the new boulevards were conceived in terms that enacted the realities of social class. According to this vision, "Andrássy Avenue was the aristocracy of streets, Kerepesi Avenue represented the people, while the Grand Boulevard was the space of the bourgeoisie."[37]

Despite the conscientious efforts of these urban writers, the outlines of the city remained notoriously unstable and incoherent. It is as if the authors themselves were uncertain as to how to view the city, or how they felt about the sights they were depicting. The sense of indeterminacy that defined their enterprise is clearly evident in the following description of the Grand Boulevard. At first sight, the boulevard

> appears to have no character. A mood of everydayness envelops it; it is the bourgeois temper embodied as architecture. It is full of corner houses with

cafes, full of towers and balconies, columned doorways, mansard roofs, plate glass windows, and all this, nevertheless, suggests an endless monotony. . . . In comparison with Andrássy Avenue, people are not impressed [by the Grand Boulevard], but they cannot view it with indifference either. This God knows how many kilometers of apartment palaces is not an ordinary street after all.[38]

The Coffee House as the Site of Urban Modernity

Perhaps no urban institution was surrounded with greater ambivalence than the coffee house, which became the privileged symbol of the city's newfound modernity. "Budapest is the city of coffee houses," proclaimed an urban guidebook of 1891. "Whoever wants to depict the image of the capital city, must paint the portrait of its coffee house."[39] It is questionable whether the actual number of coffee houses in Budapest exceeded those in other cities (according to one estimate, there were roughly five hundred coffee houses in Budapest in 1900), but the intensity of preoccupation with the phenomenon points to its centrality in the collective imagination.

The coffee house was frequently celebrated as a space of sociability and cultural democracy reflecting the new freedom and openness of urban life. In contrast with the aristocratic salon and the noble casino, the modern coffee house was open to all. For the price of a cup of coffee, it was proclaimed, anyone could enter into and participate in a public space that was free of the constraints of the private home and the ceremonials of the public realm. The coffee house was not only a democratic space but also the locus for the production of modern culture. It was the place where novels and poems were written, where literary and artistic doctrines were debated, where magazines and newspapers were edited. A contemporary writer expressed the beneficial aspects of the institution in the following glowing terms: "There is no salon that can compete in elegance with the coffee house of Pest. . . . To be in intimate contact with thousands of people, with every group and class, who discuss their most intimate affairs in front of one's eyes—this constitutes the very definition of heaven for the writer."[40]

Characteristically, however, the modernity of the coffee house could not be fully encompassed in such celebratory depictions. The coffee house had more dubious incarnations as well, which had nothing to do with elegant consumption or intellectual pursuits. It was also frequently seen as a place of corruption and disreputable behavior, where all-night entertainment, gambling, and prostitution were rampant. Equally common were visions of the coffee house as a threat to family life, where women's presence resulted in the neglect of their domestic duties and their roles as wives and mothers. The institution seemed to embody the best and worst aspects of the city, everything people celebrated and feared about the new environment. As metonymy of urban modernity itself, the coffee house was to find its most complex and sustained analyst in the writer-journalist Tamás Kóbor, best known for his naturalistic sketches of urban poverty in fin-de-siècle Budapest.

Kóbor belonged to a generation of Jewish writers who came of age in the 1880s and who were already fully identified with the urban experience. "With his first lines, Kóbor established himself as an urban chronicler," wrote his biographer. "His sensibility lacked any hint of naiveté or nostalgia for idyllic situations."[41] Like so many of his contemporaries, Kóbor found his entry into the life of the metropolis through the coffee house, where he discovered his social circle and his true home. The coffee house offered him an escape from the crushing poverty of his early life in the tenements of the Terézváros.[42] But it also formed an antidote to the threatening anti-Semitic environment of the national political scene. Kóbor's intimate personal relationship with the coffee house was never separate from his larger professional concerns with urban modernity, and the two topics found remarkable synthesis in a sequence of seven articles on the coffee house, which he published on the pages of the literary journal *A Hét* between 1892 and 1893. These essays are worth probing in some detail, since they provide not only a nuanced image of the coffee house but also an exploration of the collective experience of the city's Jewish population that frequented it.

In the first installment of the series, Kóbor made it explicit that the coffee house in his presentation was as much a cultural symbol as a physical place. People went to the coffee house, he pointed out, not simply for the sake of the coffee, the newspapers, or the company but for the "mysterious atmosphere" that fostered a state of incessant emotional excitement and fermentation. "Yes," he elaborated, "the coffee house has become an inescapable part of our lives, the externalization of everything that is inside us, of everything that we long for. Smoke saturates its atmosphere and its characteristic beverage induces sleepless restlessness. It is a place where flirtation imitates love; where haggling pettiness accompanies the search for truth; where the division of labor and the fragmentation of ideas rule triumphant; where the four-penny literature and the sixteen-penny earthly paradise flourish."[43] The coffee house, like modern life itself, was addictive yet disorienting; it

erased the distinctions between truth and falsehood, wholeness and fragmentation, art and kitsch, love and prostitution. The inner duality of the
Budapest coffee house was mapped onto its very physical layout, with its
front doors opening onto the glittering boulevards of the new Budapest
and its back exit leading to the grimy tenements of the Terézváros. A Janus-
faced institution, the coffee house, Kóbor suggested, was the perfect incarnation of a parvenu civilization, characterized by social ostentation and
moral insecurity.

Yet Kóbor went on to destabilize his own critique of the coffee house. The
fake luxury of the institution had a heroic and grandiose side, independent
of its gilt and plush interior. The coffee house was a source of identity and
mobility for the city's uprooted population. It was a mythic place, Kóbor
suggested, comparable to the Garden of Eden, where the Spirit of the Earth
allowed Adam a glimpse into the secret working of nature. In the transfigur-
ing glow of the electric lights, even "the billiard-playing shop assistant, the
beer-drinking apprentice, the Figaro-reading proletarian" assumed heroic
proportions as the new actors on the stage of the modern city.[44]

In his effort to capture the shifting faces of the coffee house, Kóbor had
an uncanny ability to assume multiple identities and perspectives. He presented the coffee house from the point of view of the young worker who on
Saturday evening washes off the grime of the workweek, dons a new suit of
clothes, and takes his girl to the most glittering coffee house on Andrássy
Avenue, where "his money is as good as anyone else's."[45] Immediately after-
ward, however, he assumes the role of the writer and journalist for whom
the cultural democracy of the coffee house was indelibly tied to the com-
mercialization of art and literature. In a world where culture was bought
and sold in the market for pennies, the writer had exactly the same status as
the waiter. Both lived off tips and bowed before the wishes of his clients.
"The tip," Kóbor concluded, "is the foundation of our entire, democratic
way of life. . . . I am not particularly proud, but I find this money grubbing
world humiliating."[46]

The deepest source of Kóbor's ambivalence, however, was reserved for
the sexual and psychological impact of the coffee house on the lives of
urbanites. Like the modern city that it reflected and symbolized, the coffee
house was a place of moral indeterminacy, which threatened the very bedrock of Jewish lower-middle-class existence, the family. The coffee house
was the enemy of domestic life, an ever-present danger to family relations
and to traditional work ethic. In particular, he singled out two aspects of the

institution for extended commentary: its tendency to foster gambling and addiction among men and sexual laxity among women.

Cards, dominoes, and billiards were common pursuits in Budapest coffee houses, but Kóbor focused almost exclusively on the card game, whose addictive quality he compared to the passion for opium and hashish. "The participant knows that he is destroying himself," Kóbor claimed, "but this slow suicide is also the source of his pleasure." The lure of the card table, however, had far greater affinities to modern economic conditions than to exotic escapism. Gambling for Kóbor embodied the dark side of capitalism, with its excess of individualism and its hope for acquiring a quick fortune without effort or hard work. The players sitting around the card table ceased to be just good friends coming together for amusement and relaxation. They were transformed into "deadly enemies, sworn to destroy each other." The disease of gaming had become ubiquitous and practiced in every coffee house of the city, "from the most obscure hole-in-the wall establishment to the most elegant ones. In the former, one finds the professional card sharks, in the latter, the impeccable gentleman, who shoots himself in the head when he loses." The common trait that defines these divergent social worlds was greed, which drew all observers into its dark magic: "Even the kibitzers hold their breath in anticipation: dear God, what will happen? Finally, the suspense is over, the loser retreats into himself and the winner sweeps in the bills with a repulsively eager gesture; and at the end, everyone resumes his mask of blasé indifference."[47]

Even more threatening than the lure of gambling were the sexual temptations of the coffee house, especially the impact it had on women. Significantly, the coffee house posed a threat to the domestic realm in both its afternoon and its nighttime incarnations. Women who spent their days in the coffee house neglected their domestic duties, abandoned their children to the care of strangers, and exposed themselves to potentially undesirable acquaintances whom they would not necessarily have invited into their own homes. The main danger, however, was the coffee house by night, which represented overt sexual danger and a direct competition to the family.

Kóbor devoted an entire article to denizens of the nighttime coffee house such as the female cashier, who sat behind the cash register in all her finery and flashy makeup. A distant cousin of the sexual temptress of the music hall and the Orpheum, the cashier was the modern working girl liberated from the rules of family propriety and patriarchal control. According to Kóbor, she posed a threat to the very institution of marriage, since she captivated the imagination of the male guests and dissipated their interest in respectable women and conventional marriage. Kóbor's concern about the unregulated sexuality of the coffee house was part of a more general perception about the "erotic currents of modern life." These new trends, he concluded, "pollute the man who comes into contact with it and poison the woman as well. The family hearth increasingly loses its poetry . . . [as women] stream into the dazzling atmosphere of the coffee house."[48]

Kóbor's extravagant, at times lurid, evocations of the moral dangers lurking in the depths of the Budapest coffee house undoubtedly gave voice to an undercurrent of anxiety characteristic of the experience of the city's Jewish middle classes. Yet it is important to note that his narrative offered no definitive interpretation about the modern experience in the metropolis. Like the boulevards on which they were found, the meaning of the coffee house, as of modernity itself, remained indeterminate, mobile, and ungraspable.

The Bourgeois Narrative of Urban Culture

By the first decade of the twentieth century, increasing numbers of people began to feel the need to stabilize the proliferating meanings of modernity, to offer a coherent overview of the urban experience. Probably the most important attempt to offer such a narrative was Adolf Ágai's *Utazás Pestről–Budapestre 1843–1907* (Travels from Pest to Budapest 1843–1907), a collection of urban essays, first published in 1908. Ágai, the influential founder and editor of the humor magazine *Borsszem Jankó*, was no stranger to the genre of urban literature. He had spent much of his life as a journalist and humorist, mapping out the cultural terrain and social types of the emerging capital. In many respects, he was the classic incarnation of the Budapest flâneur, whose intimate knowledge and love of the city found expression in a wide range of urban texts, from caricatures, feuilletons, and children's stories to urban essays and satires. In the introduction to his collection, he made explicit his long-standing indebtedness to the tradition of flânerie. He had no intention, he reassured his readers, of writing a "scientific monograph" or of living up to "expectations of perfection" from his readers. His sketches were based on personal experience and observation, and intended to do nothing more serious than to contribute "to a fuller knowledge and a warmer appreciation of the city."[49] Superficially, the general conception of the book was indeed closely modeled on the panorama texts of the 1890s that had attempted to depict the changing landscape of the urban scene.

Ágai's narrative, however, was not simply a recapitulation of the guide-books and urban texts of the past. It was, in fact, a concerted effort to transcend the instabilities and ambiguities of the genre. It attempted to present a definitive synthesis of the life of the capital with the aim of creating a comprehensive vision of Budapest modernity itself. Given the scope of his ambition, Ágai was forced to develop a uniquely personal definition of flânerie that both continued, and yet also repudiated, the tradition. No longer simply the semibohemian journalist associated with the flux of urban life, Ágai's flâneur acquired a number of alter egos, meant to supply intellectual authority, social respectability, and philosophical inevitability to his story. In the course of his account, Ágai alternately assumed the roles of the historian, physician, humanitarian, moralist, and finally artist, in an effort to create a new narrative about the city that had the weight and respectability of the social sciences.

Of these different roles, it was that of historian that Ágai most explicitly acknowledged and identified with. He was following, he claimed, the example of the great French historian Guizot, whose motto, *pour servir à l'histoire de mon temps*, became his own self-proclaimed task.[50] The story he told was that of the remarkable expansion and transformation of Budapest in the course of the later half of the nineteenth century. This transformation, however, was no longer envisioned as random change but rather as historical progress. The unifying theme and organizing principle of the narrative was scientific evolution and the power of technology to change life for the better. The story of Budapest thus became part of a heroic epic that happened to correspond to Ágai's own personal experiences as a young boy in the city. He was, as he vividly illustrated, brought to Budapest on a rickety, horse-drawn carriage in order to begin his formal education in the German-speaking school for Orthodox Jews in the Rumbach Street; he ended as a Hungarian man of letters, traveling in the elegant, red plush-covered compartment of a modern railway carriage.

While celebrating the positive aspects of change, Ágai remained acutely conscious of its human costs. Indeed, an aura of melancholy pervades his account of the destruction of the old city as it transforms itself into its new image. "One views with mixed emotions," he wrote in a typical passage, "the crumbling streets and the emerging squares of the rapidly changing city. It is appropriate to rejoice in the dawn of tomorrow even while looking wistfully back to the days of yesterday. We greet the new and say farewell to the old." For Ágai, the central symbol of the breach between old and new was the relationship between Pest and Buda. Pest represented the dynamism of the modern world, while Buda continued to live in its sleepy and secretive past. Ágai's ultimate sympathies and loyalties in this process were never in question. "I think highly of Buda," he confessed, "but I am not familiar with it, my imagination remains baffled by its monotonous hills and valleys. . . . I confess in all honesty that I have traveled through all the great capitals of Europe, but Buda remains a foreign place to me."[51]

Ágai's function as the historian nostalgically recording the relentless pace of change in the city was only one of his narrative personae. Perhaps more prominent, and certainly more authoritative, was his role as physician giving minute accounts of the hospitals and other institutions of public health that documented the city's modernist credentials. Like many other Jewish intellectuals of his time for whom medicine offered the sole avenue of educational advancement, Ágai, too, earned a medical degree before abandoning the profession for literature and journalism in the 1860s. Unlike the majority of his generation, however, Ágai retained a genuine interest in medicine and brought to his observation of the city the trained eye and scientific expertise of the physician. He spared his readers no details in recounting the inner workings of the city's newly built hospitals and research facilities. His attention was particularly riveted on the institutions set up to house unwed mothers and indigent children, which spoke to both the medical and the humanitarian advances of the time. His evident comfort in the role of the physician was made clear as he forced his readers to accompany him from ward to ward, pointing out for admiration "the sense of cleanliness, order, pragmatism and comfort everywhere." It is hardly surprising that the hero of modern life in Ágai's account turned out to be the physician rather than the artist. As he pointed out, it was the physician who accompanied humanity on its path from birth to death and beyond: "He observes it from its early stages as an ovum and remains on its side even beyond death, seeking in the cold corpse the causes and explanations for why death triumphed over life."[52]

Ágai's medical concerns were closely allied with his humanitarian commitments, which found extensive play in different sections of the book. His advocacy against animal cruelty, especially as manifested in the slaughterhouse of the city, was, perhaps, the most deeply personal of the causes that he espoused. Ágai was ambivalent on the subject of the city's slaughterhouse. He was obviously proud of the ultramodern institution, which, he boasted, was "a virtual model of its kind. There is none, with the possible exception of Chicago, which could compete with it."[53] At the same time, Ágai's compassion for the condemned animals overpowered his scientific detachment. His concern with the suffering of dumb creatures and his ability to empathetically enter into their state of mind makes some of the most compelling and disturbing readings of the volume. He pleaded for humanitarian compassion not only in the case of unwed mothers, destitute children, and animals but of all who suffered, whether on the battlefield or in the slums of the big city. Ágai's concerns extended even to institutions like the Red Cross and the Geneva Convention of 1863, in which he saw the inevitable moral and ethical advance of humanity.

Ágai, the advocate of scientific progress and humanitarian compassion, turned out to be a moralist who viewed with increasing ambivalence such characteristic institutions of urban culture as the coffee house and the music hall. "I have never seen such waste of time as in our coffee houses!" he protested. "It is hard to imagine whether a large part of the clientele of such places even has an honest occupation."[54] Ágai's disapproval of the coffee house found its central focus and justification in the presence of women in these institutions, which in his opinion was a peculiarity of the Budapest scene, totally unknown in Vienna or Berlin. Disapproval of women, especially Jewish women, in Budapest coffee houses was a common theme among cultural critics of the time, and Ágai presented the classic denunciation of the practice. While women gossiped in the coffee house, he pointed out, their children were left at home with servants who poisoned the little ones with words or with bread soaked in alcohol so they can carry on unhindered with their lovers. Ágai's negative views of the coffee house and of women's participation in the public realm were not inconsistent with his otherwise liberal and progressive attitudes on other matters. They were an integral part of a consolidated ideology of progress and stability that increasingly defined the Jewish bourgeoisie of the fin de siècle.

In the final analysis, however, this bourgeois ideology could not provide a stabilizing principle for the experience of the city. Ágai's vision of Budapest, with its proliferating social institutions and growing cultural complexity, ultimately appeared even more fragmented than the earlier accounts of urban writers. On some level, Ágai must have realized this in the final chapter of his book, which gave expression to perhaps his deepest and most deep-rooted identity, that of artist and humorist. The chapter deliberately juxtaposes the heterogeneous, intractably mobile face of the empirical city with the ideal image of a future Budapest created by the fantasy of the humorist.

The contrast between the two versions of the urban phenomenon was suggested through a dream that Ágai supposedly had on New Year's Eve of 1873. The year, of course, was the founding date of modern Budapest and the beginning of the unceasing architectural and historical transformation of the city, which had preoccupied Ágai for much of the earlier part of the book.

Seeking a more reassuring version of Budapest, he fell asleep on his couch to awaken a thousand years later, in the Budapest of 2873. This future city turned out to be a utopian incarnation of the world of *Borsszem Jankó*, perhaps Ágai's most ambitious artistic undertaking. To signal the self-referential intention of his vision, in the humor magazine Ágai actually included a cameo appearance by one of his favorite social types, Daniel Tojás, whose contribution to the imaginary Budapest was honored with an imposing statue in the City Park. In this fantasy city, everything was different from the empirical urban world Ágai had just left behind. In place of the deferential social conventions of nineteenth-century Hungary, Ágai discovered a world of equality where everyone used the informal form of address. The improvement, it seems, was due to the discoveries of a famous bacteriologist of the distant future who had invented the antivirus for "status and title sickness."[55] But the scourge of snobbishness and arrogance was only one of the many social ills that found resolution in Ágai's fantasy Budapest. Through the figure of the charming twenty-year-old guide assigned to show him the sights of the city, Ágai obliquely hinted at the disappearance of the social problem of prostitution as well. As he explained, the young woman was a representative of the institution of certified vestal virgins whose task it was to make visitors welcome in the city and thus to foster the tourist industry. The gypsy problem also found a surprising resolution in this cheerful fantasy of the future city. Ágai was surprised to learn that gypsy musicians had to be imported from Paris because the gypsies remaining in Hungary tended to become building contractors and diplomats and no longer applied their talents to music. Not surprisingly, the Jewish question had also disappeared from the Budapest of the future—not, however, by the elimination of the Jews but by the astronomical growth of their number. In a brilliant parody of the anxieties of anti-Semites, Ágai's guide provided him with the improbable statistics that out of a city of five million inhabitants, twenty million were Jews. The religious sensibilities of the Neolog elite were not spared in this astonishing account of Jewish proliferation, which concluded that the Jews, along with their Christian neighbors, were rapidly converting to Buddhism, which had become the rage of fashionable life.

The Creation of Modern Urban Identity in the City

Ágai's witty repudiation of the urban narrative as a form of social analysis did not imply the ultimate failure of the genre. The modern city could not be contained and stabilized by urban narratives, but urban narratives could contain and stabilize Jewish identities. In the final analysis, Ágai's signal achievement in *Voyage from Pest to Budapest* was not the presentation of a new, synthetic vision of the city but rather the formulation of a new, more authoritative voice for his implicitly Jewish narrator. While retaining many of the characteristics of the flâneur/journalist, Ágai's narrative self also assumed the mantle of respectability of the bourgeois professional. His authority now rested on more substantial grounds than the unmediated personal experience of the flâneur. It was based on the objective laws of progress, science, and morality.

It is impossible not to recognize, in Ágai's complex engagement with the roles of the flâneur and the bourgeois professional, echoes of Hannah Arendt's typologies of the Jew as pariah and parvenu, elaborated in her Jewish essays of the 1940s. Arendt argued that the unfavorable conditions of emancipation forced nineteenth-century Jews to choose between two problematic roles and identities: that of the parvenu and the pariah. The parvenu sought integration in society without ever losing his separateness and accepted at face value the terms of assimilation. He regarded Jews as abstract individuals whose political and legal rights were guaranteed by the liberal state. By contrast, the pariah consciously embraced Jewish difference, confronting mainstream values from the outside. He was never taken in by the political fiction of emancipation and demanded "the admission of Jews as Jews to the ranks of humanity."[56]

Arendt's polarized moral and political categories cannot be separated from her tragic reassessment of the implications of Jewish assimilation. This project, however, looked different from the perspective of the fin de siècle. For enthusiastic advocates of assimilation such as Ágai, the roles of parvenu and pariah did not appear as antithetical or self-limiting choices. On the contrary, they were presumed to be compatible alternatives reflecting the unlimited possibilities and fluid social roles generated by the modern environment. The symbolic boundaries between these identities were as porous as the physical boundaries between the middle-class Lipótváros and the lower-middle-class Terézváros. As is well known, the parvenu Jewish bourgeoisie was a regular visitor to Király Street, sharing with the lower middle classes a taste for scandalous nightlife and popular entertainment. Lower-middle-class pariahs, in turn, were avid supporters of the middle-class ideology of assimilation, even though they often lacked the linguistic skills and cultural capital to realize this ideal. Given the instabilities of Jewish social identities in fin-de-siècle Budapest, it was not surprising that the Jewish parvenu could at times find himself in the role of the pariah, and, by contrast, the pariah could occasionally assume the role of the parvenu.

The caricatures of *Borsszem Jankó* provide numerous illustrations of the inevitably humorous border crossings between parvenus and pariahs. Members of the ennobled Jewish middle classes, for instance, were regularly depicted in ill-fitting Hungarian national costumes with anachronistic swords at their side that posed a public hazard to anyone in their vicinity. These images suggested that the ennobled Jewish parvenu immediately became a pariah once he crossed over into the world of the Hungarian nobility, whose customs he unsuccessfully aped. At the other end of the social scale, people from the lower middle classes were frequently portrayed as comically susceptible to the rhetoric of Hungarian nationalism, which transformed them into ridiculous versions of the parvenu. One such caricature, published in 1869, depicted a Jewish coffee house in the Terézváros, whose regular customers got drunk from the very act of discussing Hungarian politics, even though all they consumed was vast quantities of coffee, hot chocolate, and cake.

These caricatures of Jewish parvenus and pariahs were not the creations of anti-Semitic ideologues but the self-projections of primarily Jewish journalists and humorists. Their ironic images, making fun of Jewish life in all its pretensions and absurdities, addressed a mostly Jewish audience that constituted the enthusiastic readership of *Borsszem Jankó*. The ability of this audience to laugh at itself and to transform the figures of the parvenu and pariah into comic types betrayed a new kind of urban sensibility and cultural competence not easily translatable into the language of politics. Within the world of urban narratives, Jews gained the power to transcend the inevitable contradictions and paradoxes of their social situation. They could, as Ágai ironically suggested in his dream image of Budapest, even abolish the Jewish question as a cultural reality. Urban discourses such as Ágai's challenged the very notion of foundational identities that defined Jews as stigmatized outsiders. By the early twentieth century, Budapest Jews had, in fact, come to see themselves as cultural insiders, if not in Hungary, then certainly in the modern metropolis they inhabited.

In 1908, with the founding of the self-consciously modernist literary journal *Nyugat* (West), Budapest Jews were ready to openly challenge the anti-urban mythology of conservative Hungary. In a provocative essay titled "The City" (A város), Aladár Schöpflin, one of the founding members of the periodical, revisited the archetypal image of the Asiatic Hungarian horseman, conjured up by Beöthy less than a decade earlier. In Schöpflin's version, however, the barbarian horseman was no longer the self-sufficient son of the steppes, reconnoitering for enemies, but an ambivalent marauder, wracked by hate and envy for the cities of Rome and Byzantium. The modern descendants of these invaders, Schöpflin contended, still hated the city, regarding it as "some kind of foreign body within the organism of the nation."[57] But now they were faced with a fait accompli, since Budapest had already become an integral part of the nation. In a deliberate obfuscation of the meaning and content of the word "Hungarian," Schöpflin concluded with the following challenge:

> All resistance is futile: Hungarians have established here, on the banks of the Danube, their own city,—the only truly urban center that the Turanian race has ever succeeded in creating. . . . Yes, we insist that it is we who represent more truly and more faithfully the Hungarian national character than those who want to turn it against us.[58]

The battle for the symbolic ownership of Budapest was openly engaged; it was a battle that neither side could win, nor afford to lose.

The Jewish Question and the Paradox of Hungarian Liberalism

Intimations of Political Violence

Ágai's classic urban text, *Travels from Pest to Budapest 1843–1907*, recounts a disturbing incident of political violence seemingly at odds with the cheerful tenor of the rest of the book. The episode took place at the site of an ancient tree in the hills of Buda called the Normafa, where the city's leisured classes liked to gather for holiday excursions and summer picnics. It was at this spot, Ágai disclosed, that in 1849 the leader of the Hungarian National Guard ordered the hanging of a Jewish peddler on suspicion of spying. The peddler provoked instant suspicion, it seems, even though there was nothing exceptional about his appearance or about the bundle he carried, whose content confirmed his prior claim that it held only needles, thread, and thimbles. What settled the fate of the unfortunate man was the discovery of his tefillin, the small black boxes containing verses from the Torah, which observant Jews wore during morning prayers. The tefillin were assumed to convey military secrets for Hungary's enemies and taken to be a clear sign of the peddler's treachery. It is true that no military plans were actually discovered in the boxes, but the Hungarian soldier reasoned that they either contained such plans in the past, or would contain them in the future.[1]

Ágai failed to attribute special significance to this troubling tale. He presented it as a curious urban legend and a colorful backdrop to the pastoral pleasures of the city. The story, nevertheless, had an ominously contemporary ring and a political charge out of all proportion with its formal role in the narrative. The Normafa lynching took place, after all, not in some distant past but during the revolutionary period of 1849, in the midst of Hungary's brief experiment with liberal democracy and republicanism. Just as importantly, the Jewish peddler was hanged not directly because of his religion but because of his presumed danger to the liberal state. His very presence in the nation was thought to pose a political threat, all the more dangerous for being allusive and conjectural. The physical evidence of his religion became the necessary proof of a prior guilt that was presumed from the beginning.[2]

There is no way of ascertaining the factual accuracy of the Normafa episode, but the emotional and political stakes involved in the story were real enough. The nightmare vision of civic exclusion and political violence evoked by the incident pointed to a potentially lethal ideological realm beyond the literary conventions and collective experiences of Ágai's urban text. It was the barely acknowledged projection of collective political anxieties evoked by what contemporaries referred to as the "Jewish question." It is customary to put quotation marks around the Jewish question, since it was not so much a question as an exclusionary discourse about Jewish citizenship and national identity. Frequently conflated with anti-Semitism and antiliberal politics, the Jewish question actually transcended these phenomena. As recent Hungarian political analysts have suggested, at its most general the Jewish question was not just about Jewish citizenship; it was also a debate about the nature of national identity that engaged Hungarian political opinion from the extreme right to the far left.[3] The phenomenology of the Jewish question suggests not so much a coherent ideology as a highly unstable historical figure with contradictory meanings and implications that could not be disengaged from one another without shattering its unity. At times of social stress and political crisis, however, the Jewish question could temporarily crystallize into the source of radical politics, threatening not only the status of Jews but also the established liberal order itself. In the spring of 1882 such a scenario came into existence in the wake of two interrelated crises that helped transform almost overnight the status of the Jewish question from symbolic politics into full-fledged ideology.

The Political Crisis of 1882–1883

The first episode of the period of crisis was a notorious blood libel trial in which Jews were accused of murdering a Christian girl for their Passover festival; the second was an explosive immigration debate about the potential influx of Russian Jewish refugees into Hungary. The common thread that linked the two events was, of course, the Jewish question, which assumed overtly anti-Semitic tones in the months between the spring of

1882 and the autumn of 1883, radicalizing Hungarian public opinion. During this critical period, the ideological fissures within Hungarian liberalism were fully exposed and the horizon of Jewish emancipation irreversibly transformed. Paradoxically, it was the crisis of 1882–1883 that was to solidify a self-conscious strategy of assimilation and excessive patriotism that became the hallmark of Hungarian Jewry at the fin de siècle.

The catalyst for the first crisis was the disappearance of a fourteen-year-old girl, Eszter Solymosi, from the village of Tiszaeszlár on April 1, 1882, shortly before the Jewish Passover festival. Two weeks after the girl failed to return from an errand she was sent on, members of the Jewish community of Tiszaeszlár were arrested and indicted for murdering her and for using her blood for the preparation of their unleavened bread for Passover. The episode provoked one of the first and most widely publicized ritual murder trials in Central Europe. The story of the Tiszaeszlár trial, reported in minute detail in both the national and international press, was worthy of a modern murder mystery embellished with gothic details and violent folk legends. It involved insidious local officials, the intimidation of witnesses, the suppression of evidence, three inconclusive autopsies on a young female body fished out of the nearby river Tisza, a rebellious Jewish teenager turned state witness against his father, and, of course, dramatic court scenes, culminating in a seven-hour closing argument by the celebrated liberal defense attorney Károly Eötvös that resulted in the acquittal of the accused Jews in August 1883.[4]

More significant than the actual events of the trial, however, was its broad impact on political culture and its challenge to the liberal worldview. Educated opinion was shocked by the reappearance of the medieval blood libel in the midst of the century of progress and enlightenment. At a loss for rational explanations, some liberals attempted to understand the astonishing phenomenon in terms of crowd psychology, recently popularized by the French sociologist Gustav Le Bon. "In peaceful times," wrote Eötvös in his published account of the Tiszaeszlár affair, "every person denies belief in the existence of [ritual murder]. . . . But in stressful periods, peoples' minds work differently. Ten thousand people get together. All ten thousand are clear thinking, thoughtful and practical individuals. But the moment they get together as a group, one idea gains ascendancy over them, which they never professed as individuals, but which captures their imaginations one after another, until finally the entire group thinks one thought, responds to one command, is permeated by one emotion."[5]

Eötvös's intuition that the blood libel accusation was an atavistic phenomenon that brought to the surface irrational social instincts has been confirmed by the analysis of recent historians. As Hillel Kievel pointed out, Central Europe experienced a virtual epidemic of blood libel accusations against Jews in the years between 1882 and 1902.[6] These resembled in their structure and outcome the witchcraft hysteria of the seventeenth century, which also generated widespread moral panics within local communities. As with all expressions of collective violence, ritual murder charges too were passing social epidemics that ended as suddenly as they began. Yet, as Helmut Walser Smith suggested in his own analysis of the phenomenon, ritual murder affairs had a profound impact on the political temper of the age, transforming public perceptions of Jewish identity and making anti-Semitism "part of the warp and woof of everyday life."[7]

Solymosi Eszter,
Ábrányi Lajos festménye után.

Portrait of Eszter Solymosi after a painting by Lajos Ábrányi. Published in *Vasárnapi Újság* (July 15, 1883). National Széchényi Library.

As lurid details began to circulate about the Tiszaeszlár events, popular passions were provoked to the boiling point. Legends and vaguely articulated feelings about Jews crystallized with startling rapidity into public knowledge and scientific fact. Such pseudo-knowledge circulated during the summer of 1882 in a vast outpouring of sensational pamphlets about historical instances of Jewish ritual murder and other perversities. An especially notorious example of the genre was a pamphlet that presented a series of blood-curdling examples of Jewish ritual murder from antiquity to the present, culminating in a graphic depiction of the prolonged torture of a two-year-old baby whose body was ritualistically dismembered by a group of villainous Jews whose thirst for blood became irresistible during Passover.[8] So incendiary was the impact of this particular pamphlet that the prime minister issued an executive order instructing all local authorities to ban the publication of literature inciting popular passions against the

"In the fifty-seventh century" (According to the Jewish calendar). Scene of ritual murder by the Jews of Tiszaeszlár. Published in *Füstölő* (November 1, 1882). National Széchényi Library.

Jews and also to confiscate such literature wherever they found it and to deliver it to the authorities in Budapest.[9]

The inflammatory publications were accompanied by sporadic outbreaks of violence against Jews. Incidents of spontaneous demonstrations, window smashing, and written threats became commonplace in the countryside and even in large centers like Pozsony (today Bratislava, Slovakia) and Budapest. "There was no Jew," wrote Eötvös of this period, "no matter how respected or socially prominent, who was exempt from the most callous verbal insults. Sensitive individuals hardly dared to go out on the street, into public places or social gatherings. The slogan around which the general hatred crystallized was the blood libel of Tiszaeszlár. Those who could not or would not think for themselves, those who lacked all disinterested integrity, saw a murderer in every Jew."[10]

The moral panic triggered by the Tiszaeszlár blood libel affair cannot, however, be understood in isolation from a second crisis occurring at the same time and in the same geographic region of the country. This was the potential incursion of Russian Jewish immigrants to the northern counties in the wake of massive pogroms that had broken out in eastern and southern Russia in late 1881 and early 1882. By the spring of 1882 tens of thousands of Russian Jews had fled across the border into the territories of the Austro-Hungarian monarchy, where they were temporarily sheltered in the small Galician town of Brody to await resettlement in America, Palestine, or other parts of Europe.[11]

The fate of the refugees and conditions in Brody immediately became items of daily concern in the popular press of Budapest. As the number of refugees swelled to more than twenty thousand by the end of May, reports of overcrowding, infant mortality, and possible epidemics became frequent. The overall tone of the articles from Brody alternated between sentiments of pity and humanitarian concern for the victims of Russian barbarity and feelings of national superiority over the perpetrators of such acts. As a typical liberal editorial put it in mid-May:

> The unfortunate refugees, forced from their homes by a barbarous government and by wild popular passions, are arriving in growing numbers into the territory of our monarchy. . . . They cross the Galician border without food and clothing, at the mercy of an uncertain future. But they are happy, because they know their lives to be safe and their hearts become lighter because, on free soil, they already encounter signs of human empathy and brotherly love.

It is undoubtedly the glory of our monarchy that the border that separates it from Russia will now be regarded as the visible demarcation line between civilization and barbarism, between the reign of law and that of naked force.[12]

These elevated sentiments, however, were complicated from the start by another set of preoccupations that quickly overshadowed them. Since Galicia was directly adjacent to Hungarian territories, the possibility emerged that the Russian Jewish refugees would attempt to cross into Hungary and settle there. During April, May, and early June, passionate debates erupted in the northern counties, where settlement was most likely, about the desirability of such an event. These debates resulted in a flood of petitions to Budapest formally requesting that the central government take immediate legislative action to prevent the immigration of Russian Jews. But nothing in Hungarian politics was ever as it appeared on the surface. From the first it was apparent that the county petition movement was not primarily about the Russian refugees. The petitions became an occasion for challenging official liberal positions on the Jewish question by publicly rearticulating this controversial issue.

The radical populist subtext was evident in even the most carefully worded petitions, such as that of county Veszprém, which sent the following missive to Budapest: "The government, by way of Parliament, is requested to block the immigration of Russian Jews with all its strength and power, since such immigration would be harmful and even dangerous to the Hungarian people, not merely from an economic point of view, but primarily from a moral point of view."[13] Many petitions were less circumspect about the real implications of the immigration debate. County Somogy formulaically reiterated that "it has no desire to provoke a Jewish question, but it is forced to speak out against immigration ... because it considers immigration harmful from a national point of view. The influx of Russian Jews would endanger the patriotic spirit of Hungarian Jews, which is in need of strengthening and augmenting to this very day."[14] The real motives underlying the petition movement were given uncensored expression in the petition of county Nyitra, which warned that Jewish immigration should be curtailed lest "at the celebration of Hungary's millennial anniversary [in 1896], the people whose ancestors had conquered the fatherland with their blood should find themselves, to their sorrow and despair, despoiled of it by destitute aliens who had been sheltered out of charity and who repaid such charity with robbery."[15]

These county petitions gave public expression to a new kind of xenophobic, populist nationalism that brought into question the entire project of Jewish emancipations and assimilation. The radical agenda behind the movement was made explicit in the petition of county Pest, which suggested that the danger to the nation resided not only in the Russian Jews but also in the Hungarian Jews, "who are Hungarian in name and show themselves Hungarian in external appearance, but who are not Hungarian in the true sense of the word and can never be considered Hungarian patriots."[16]

Significantly, liberalism was powerless to stop this new populist movement that for the first time succeeded in linking immigration, the Jewish question, and anti-Semitism into a popular protest movement of wide appeal. The county sheriffs (*főispán*), representing official authority, used their offices to express formulaic misgivings about the content of the petitions, but they lacked the power to block them. As the sheriff of county Somogy put it: "I have pronounced the voice of the majority, but I must confess that I blush and view with a sense of deep shame that such speeches about such subjects should have been pronounced in county Somogy."[17] The same sentiments were expressed by the sheriff of county Veszprém, who made the following personal addendum to the official petition issued by the county: "Before passing the final sentence, I have to give voice to my personal opinion, which considers the accepted petition neither legal, nor constitutional, nor humane, nor practical. Having made this declaration, which I owe to my past convictions, I now reluctantly pronounce the final decision, according to which the representatives of county Veszprém, unanimously accepted the formal petition that has just been verbally presented."[18]

The grand finale of the petition movement came on June 8, 1882, when the petition of county Szatmár came before the lower house of parliament for consideration. A close textual analysis of the debate, which took place in a blaze of publicity, proves highly revealing, for it contained in microcosm the political impasse that Hungarian liberalism ran into in 1882. The liberal government of Kálmán Tisza rejected out of hand the petition of county Szatmár for immigration reform, arguing that existing laws were sufficient to keep unwanted immigrants out. "What is at issue here," began the liberal spokesman of the government, "are unfortunate victims forced into flight by the truly barbarous conditions of a neighboring state. . . . It would contradict the principles of a civilized and free nation to forcefully chase back such refugees to a state that so violently expelled them." He continued, however, that aid and temporary shelter were "not synonymous with the right to

settle." The role of the liberal Hungarian government was to help the destitute masses find new homes abroad rather than in Hungary. Having resolved
the refugee question in a way consonant with both Hungarian interests and
political values, the speaker proceeded to allude to the more delicate problem raised implicitly by the immigration petitions: the role of Hungarian
Jews within the state. The immigration issue, he noted, must be strictly distinguished from unrelated questions that had been inappropriately linked
to it. Making the issue still more explicit, he warned that the controversy
needed to be isolated from "attacks and innuendos directed against any religious group or race residing in the nation." It was the responsibility of the
Hungarian parliament, he concluded, to distance itself from the "tendency
that wants to transplant into our nation that regrettable religious and racial
hatred whose results we can observe in this very exodus."[19]

The reasonable voice of official liberalism, reinforced though it was by the
speech of Prime Minister Tisza himself, could not dominate the debate or
ultimately prevent dissenting interpretations from erupting. The most direct
attack on the liberal position came from the representative of the newly
formed anti-Semitic league, Győző Istóczy, who reformulated the parame-
ters of the debate in precisely the ways the liberals had hoped to avoid. The
Russian Jewish immigration problem, Istóczy stated, was merely a deus ex
machina whose real importance was that it brought to the fore the genuine,
until then hidden, problem of contemporary Hungarian society: the Jewish
question. He elaborated:

> I have come to the conclusion that the task of a final solution to the Jewish
> question has devolved on our generation. What is at stake here is not medi-
> eval Jew-baiting. . . . In the Middle Ages, the people of Europe faced Jews
> as individuals, whereas in our day, we have to deal with Jews as a political
> and social institution. It is an undeniable fact that modern Jewry forms
> an internal Trojan horse within the European state, a distinct ethnicity with
> political and social power, not simply a religious denomination, as Jews would
> like to claim.[20]

Istóczy's position was supported by the speech of his associate Géza
Ónódy, who for the first time explicitly linked the immigration issue with
the theme of Jewish ritual murder. Rather than addressing the Russian Jewish refugee question as a legal-constitutional issue, he reframed it as a cultural conflict in which ritual murder was assumed to be the cause of the

pogroms in Russia. "It is well known," he pointed out, "that the Jews murdered the children of the orthodox priests for ritual purposes. These actions have been historically proven and it is blood vengeance that has caused the peasants of Russia to rise up against the Jews and to chase them out of their own homes."[21]

The provocations of these anti-Semitic speeches elicited a formal reproof from the prime minister, but the actual response came from Mór Wahrmann, a Jewish member of parliament, representing the commercial, Jewish-identified district of the Lipótváros in Budapest. Wahrmann restated the official liberal position against mass immigration, but he also slightly modified it by explicitly denying its relationship with the religion of the potential immigrants. The real issue, he pointed out, was not whether Russian Jews but whether any foreign group, be they "Russian Jews or Russian nihilists, German Social Democrats or Irish Fenians, Serbians, Romanians, or Saxons," should be allowed to settle in the country. With this shift of emphasis, Wahrmann deflected the debate from the Jewish question and placed it firmly on grounds of utility and national interest.[22]

Wahrmann's clever brinksmanship was, of course, part of a larger political charade played out in parliament on June 8, 1882. As everyone knew, the ostensible subject of the debate—immigration reform—was, in fact, a pseudo-issue, since Galicia was part of the Austro-Hungarian monarchy and the power to restrict immigration did not lie within the jurisdiction of the Hungarian parliament. The real subject of the passionate exchanges that had taken place was the status of Jews in Hungary and the admissibility of the Jewish question as a subject for political discussion. The overwhelming response of parliament was "No!" The Hungarian elite categorically rejected the legitimacy of all public discussion about Jewish difference on the grounds of liberal ethics, constitutional law, national traditions, and, finally, pragmatic national interest.

Despite this seemingly successful conclusion to the immigration debate, the liberal establishment lost control of the political situation in the course of the summer of 1882. Popular passions about the Jewish question, which gradually shifted from Russian Jewish immigration to the events of the blood libel trial, refused to be put to rest. "Generally, government circles manifest the most complete confusion with regard to the ritual murder issue," reported the paper of the Independence Party, *Függetlenség* (Independence). "They do not know what to do, how to position themselves toward public opinion."[23] So volatile was the national mood that in late June the prime minister interrupted his vacation to return to the capital to consult with his advisors. For the first time, the government was becoming seriously concerned about "the increasing scale of the anti-Jewish excitement and the possible legal measures that could be taken against it."[24] An outcome of the meeting was the authorization of the minister of the interior to secure public order by the dispatch of troops to the districts where the potential for anti-Jewish violence was most likely.

The real problem with official liberal responses to the political crisis was its inability to legitimate its position in ways that could speak to the population as a whole. Hungarian liberalism failed to offer a viable counternarrative to the popular hysteria that gripped the country during these months. This failure had profoundly serious and ultimately tragic consequences. It was the anti-Semites who seized the initiative and succeeded in shaping public opinion on the Jewish question. Ironically, anti-Semitism appropriated explicitly liberal principles for defining its position, fatally disabling effective ideological opposition to their arguments. Perhaps nothing demonstrated more clearly this bizarre turn of events than the voice of the radical Independence paper, *Függetlenség*, which became openly anti-Semitic in the course of 1882. The early editorials of the paper were still uncommitted on the judicial outcome of Tiszaeszlár, pointing to the fact that the details of the disappearance of Eszter Solymosi and the circumstances of the accused were not fully known and that it was inappropriate to make political capital out of what might be a straightforward criminal case. By early June, such circumspect attitudes were replaced by a markedly shrill and bellicose tone that had not existed before. Curiously, the transformation was provoked neither by new details unearthed about the Tiszaeszlár case nor by growing certainty that a ritual murder had taken place there. The source of the new posture seems to have been outrage at Hungarian Jews' solidarity with the accused Jews of Tiszaeszlár, whose legal defense they helped organize and finance.

The Tiszaeszlár case activated visceral anxieties that had always lurked beneath the surface of Hungarian political consciousness: the fear of Jewish collective action that might overwhelm national identity and historical traditions. As the editor of *Függetlenség*, Gyula Verhovay, remonstrated, Jews refused to treat Tiszaeszlár as an ordinary criminal investigation and insisted on rallying to the cause of their co-religionists. Such gestures, he continued, resulted in a "transformation in public opinion so general and so powerful" that it resembled a raging flood that swept up in its waves "all social layers, from day laborers to the most enlightened persons."[25] Jewish solidarity was invariably seen as an unacceptable infraction against both the rule of law and the conventions of constitutional government. "Look around yourselves," Verhovay addressed an imaginary Jewish audience, "and abandon your prejudices, which are reminiscent of the religious obscurantism of the dark ages. Do not artificially make a religious and racial issue out of what is a criminal and legal case."[26] In his editorial onslaughts, Verhovay increasingly assumed the outraged posture of the man of enlightenment who watched with incredulity the reactionary activities of the Jews. "In what we had imagined to be a modern state," he thundered,

> we are subjected day-to-day to the actions of one kind of league or another, which makes a virtue of challenging the existence of a criminal case. . . . Is this possible in the nineteenth century? Can such events be fabricated by even the wildest imagination of someone educated in the modern spirit? . . . Do they want to introduce to Europe the civilization of the half-savage peoples of Africa? Do we lack the means and the force to put an end to this medieval activity? Are we afraid to beat down this league for the protection of murderers that is more despicable than the murderers themselves?[27]

The story of Tiszaeszlár was recast on the pages of *Függetlenség* into an epic struggle between superstition and civilization, atavistic collectivism and enlightened constitutionalism. Ironically, it was the Jews who were cast in the role of religious fanatics, attempting to subvert the legitimate legal and political order. In the topsy-turvy world of anti-Semitism, the Jews appeared not only as barbaric ritual murderers, indulging in religious sacrifice, but also as unprincipled obstructionists, perverting the due process of law. As a direct result of their actions, the liberal institutions of the state had come under attack. Moreover, the very reputation of Hungary as an enlightened and civilized nation was threatened by the activities of the Jews in connection with Tiszaeszlár. "How will foreigners view our culture?" asked an editorial in *Függetlenség*. "What conclusions will they form about our social conditions, when they read about the open and arrogant association of grave desecrators, corpse robbers, merchants of bloody clothes, whose whole aim is to deny the existence of a crime.[28] The world can only conclude that our country is the site of barbaric conditions, for there is no educated person, who would consider it possible to defy existing legal institutions and administrative processes in such an illegitimate way."[29]

Traditional Hungarian liberalism was powerless against the paradoxical logic of such arguments. Even the great Kossuth, hero of the revolutionary movement of 1848 and titular head of the Independence Party, was unable to restrain the radical, anti-Semitic wing of his party. Writing from exile in Turin, he repudiated the Jewish question as it played out during the summer of 1882. The debate was a source of "shame and scandal," he protested, that could no longer be considered a fit subject for individual opinion. It had become "a public issue deeply intertwined with the life of the nation that required all parties to take a stand on." He concluded with the familiar rhetorical flourish of high-minded liberalism, declaring: "I consider it unacceptable both on moral and political grounds that [the Independence Party] should deny legal equality to the citizens of the nation on any grounds stemming from racial, linguistic, or religious differences."[30] Kossuth's appeal only helped highlight the growing gap between the spirit and practice of Hungarian liberalism. The humor magazine *Borsszem Jankó* portrayed this disjunction on its frontispiece in 1883, which depicted a Hungarian patriot praising the rhetorical eloquence of Kossuth's speech while acquiescing in Jews being beaten up in the background. Kossuth's speech was nothing more than a reminder of the liberal values that had once been an integral part of the national vision. It had no restraining effect on the crisis, though it had a certain moderating impact on the extreme fringe. Thus, motions for the revocation of the political emancipation of the Jews, which were drafted by hard core anti-Semites, never found enough political support to have a national impact.

In the final analysis, however, it was not liberal principles but the political power of the state that finally put an end to the social and political crisis of 1882–1883. In August 1883 the lengthy Tiszaeszlár blood libel trial came to a close with the exoneration of the accused Jews. The unpopular verdict triggered a wave of anti-Semitic riots throughout the country, including Budapest, which on August 11, 1883, was declared to be in a state of siege. After dragging its feet for over a year, the government's decision to oppose anti-Semitic agitation and the accompanying looting finally assumed effective form. This was, as Tisza bluntly declared in parliament, an act of self-interest rather than of principles. Anti-Semitism clearly posed a threat, not just to Jews but also to the rights of property: "I would like to bring to the attention of the honorable House that yes, initially this is a Jewish affair,

"Text and reality." Kossúth's letter read by a right-wing Hungarian follower. Published in *Borsszem Jankó* (March 18, 1883). Petőfi Literary Museum.

but once the movement has achieved its first step, there follows a second step, which is the affair of the propertyless against the propertied, and then it ceases to be a Jewish affair."[31]

The anti-Semitic crisis that flared up with the immigration debates of 1882 and peaked with the blood-libel trial of 1883 came to a sudden close by the end of 1883. The appeal of anti-Semitism was temporarily halted by the combination of government suppression, public fatigue, and inner dissension and scandal within the ranks of the anti-Semitic leadership. According to contemporary liberal interpretations, the eruption of the Jewish question into the political arena had been an atavistic event or an anomaly that was fundamentally at odds with the historical trajectory and inner principles of the Hungarian nation. Like a fever or an epidemic, it had broken out, run its course, and then disappeared.

Liberal Pamphlets and the Jewish Question

Despite such reassuring assessments, the damage that Hungarian liberalism sustained in the course of 1882–1883 was irreversible. It was proven incapable of defending its self-proclaimed principles. Its progressive national traditions, rooted in the revolutionary movements of the 1840s and of 1848, had been overwritten by a new version of populist nationalism that fundamentally diverged from this historical past. The Jewish question was at the ideological vortex of this transformation, for it was on this issue that Hungarian liberalism was most inconsistent, most internally divided. According to the social theorist János Gyurgyák, no systematic history of Hungarian political theory can ignore or sidestep this issue. Referring to his efforts to write such a history, he found the Jewish question everywhere he turned. The subject, it seems, was ubiquitous and at the same time "surrounded by silences, distortions, and frequently conscious prevarications."[32]

The complex relationship between Hungarian liberalism and the Jewish question was most frequently addressed in grassroots publications rather than in official pronouncements. During the crisis of 1882–1883 in particular, the topic gave rise to an avalanche of popular pamphlets, articles, booklets, and personal reflections that struggled to define and resolve what had obviously become a central issue of Hungarian national identity. These pamphlets were formulaic in character, displaying a remarkable similarity of language, structure, and authorial persona. They resembled therapeutic discourses more than political debates in which self-appointed patriots took on the task of clarifying the Jewish question in order to contribute to the public good. The implicit assumption underlying their efforts was that the solution to the Jewish question was necessary for the very survival of the nation.

To various degrees, the authors of these popular tracts distinguished themselves from out-and-out anti-Semites, whose positions they considered inappropriate and too radical for Hungarian conditions. At the same time, however, they expressed sympathy for anti-Semitism to the extent that it acknowledged sentiments that many felt but considered impolitic to publicly express. "There are many people like this," one pamphleteer wrote. "Some are also to be found on the benches of the legislature. They feel it their cultural obligation to laugh at Istóczy, but in private, they are all the more adamant in their condemnation of the Jews. In comparison with such people, the merit of Istóczy is that at least he is honest."[33] The truth about the Jewish question, this writer claimed, lay somewhere in the middle between the radicalism of the anti-Semites, who wanted to repeal Jewish emancipation and expel Jews from the state, and the complacency of Jews and official liberals, who refused to acknowledge the existence of any problem.[34]

In trying to define a middle ground on the Jewish question, these self-styled moderates drew directly or indirectly on the historic tradition of Hungarian liberalism. Some openly dismissed anti-Semitism as a reactionary ideology, whose attempt to "delude the masses with a superstitious witch hunt" would eventually lead to the overthrow of all social authority. "Today, they threaten the 'Semites,'" this writer claimed, directly echoing Tisza's statement in parliament, "tomorrow, the 'priests,' and the day after tomorrow 'property holders.'"[35] Some simply referred to pragmatic national self-interest in their rejection of the anti-Semites. This familiar argument was presented in a series of rhetorical questions in one pamphlet: "Does anyone familiar with our conditions imagine that, were the Jews to leave, the economic activities they carry out could effectively be assumed by any other element in the nation? . . . What decline and paralysis would ensue at every level of our national enterprise, production, exchange, and industry? And this would happen precisely at the moment when growth and increase in these areas constitute the precondition of the survival of our nation!"[36]

For most pamphleteers, the core issue that defined the Jewish question was not Jewish emancipation, as the anti-Semites claimed, but rather the lack of or insufficient Jewish integration within Hungarian society following emancipation. "We just have to look around our society," claimed one author, "to immediately recognize that in actual fact, Hungary has two societies. The first is Hungarian and the second, foreign."[37] Proofs of Jewish failure to blend in with the customs of the nation were multiple and depended on the individual perspective of the observer.

Many pointed to the continuing existence of Jewish social and charitable organizations and to Hungarian Jewry's stubborn refusal to change its everyday language from German to Hungarian. According to others, the ultimate reason for the continuation of Jewish separatism lay in the structural problems of Hungarian society itself, which was economically too weak and politically too disorganized to absorb the Jews. "Hungary," in this vision, was "unable to exert sufficient pressure to counter the tenacious separatism of Jewry because of the chaotic state of its public and private finances and its economy, and more generally, because of its cultural backwardness and lack of political unity."[38] According to still others, the problem of Jewish difference was to be sought not just in obvious external factors but also in invisible spiritual attitudes. "While our Jews have demonstrated sufficient progress in respect to their patriotism," wrote one author, "the same cannot be said in the area of their assimilation [*magyarization*] which still requires improvement." Explaining the fine nuances between "patriotic" and "national," the author pointed out that the first term involved an act of conscious political choice, while the second was the result of a more complex process of inner transformation.[39]

Some writers acknowledged that the real obstacle to Jewish integration lay not in the attitudes of the Jews themselves but in the host society, which refused to accord Jews the same terms of acceptance as other groups. The Jews of Budapest in particular, one writer claimed, had rapidly assimilated to Hungarians in terms of their language, their names, their customs, and their sentiments, but still more effort was required. The reason for this was to be found in the unique situation of Jews, who were "obliged to overcome such strong prejudice, to break down such deep-seated hostility in their efforts to claim national identity, which other groups such as the Germans, the Slavs, or the Romanians do not have to face. This may not be fair, but it is a fact that needs to be reckoned with."[40] The full implication of this comment was completed in a later pamphlet on the Jewish question, written by the legal scholar Peter Ágoston. Judaism, Ágoston wrote here, cannot be considered a religion like others, because it involved a deeper degree of otherness, a more fundamental kind of foreignness, than other religions. "Jews," he claimed, "do not constitute the same kind of entity as the Lutherans, the Calvinists, or the Catholics. Jewry forms a much tighter community than these groups. For this reason, it is wrong to believe, as the Jews seem to do, that Jewry is nothing more than a religious denomination."[41]

At the core of these pamphlets on the Jewish question was a fundamental ambivalence about the terms of emancipation and the very possibility of Jewish assimilation within the nation. On the one hand, they argued for the necessity of full Jewish integration in the national community and reproached Jews for remaining separate. On the other hand, they saw Jewish difference as so intractable as to make integration virtually impossible. The Jew simultaneously appeared as the potential native as well as the inadmissible stranger. What made this contradiction so lethal in the Hungarian context was that it was linked from the beginning to the broader question of Hungarian political survival and national identity. This interconnection was implied in most of the popular pamphlets, but its centrality to the liberal outlook was fully articulated in a pamphlet of 1884, titled *Társadalmunk és nemzeti hivatásunk* (Our society and our national mission). The author of the pamphlet was Gusztáv Beksics, one of the most prominent liberal journalists of the age, who was a member of Prime Minister Kálmán Tisza's inner circle and a contributor to the semi-official government paper, *Nemzet* (Nation).

Beksics's "anxiety about the fate of the nation" was no vague metaphysical attitude but rather based on hard demographic facts. "With the exception of Austria," he pointed out, "Hungary is in the most endangered position among the larger European states. In Germany, Italy, France, and Spain, there exist only one nationality and one ethnicity. . . . In Hungary, Magyars form only 45 percent of the population. What guarantee does this number provide for the survival of the ethnic nation? What goals should guide Hungarian society in order to increase its ethnic weight?"[42] The answer was self-evident to the generation of Hungarian liberals that Beksics belonged to: the creation of a strong Hungarian middle class capable of helping the Magyars achieve demographic and economic superiority in the multi-ethnic state. "Hungarian society cannot be saved without the help of a bourgeois middle class," Beksics declared. "Only with the cooperation of the middle class can we bring into existence the great national middle class that can incorporate all social layers and fuse within itself their best elements. Only the bourgeois middle class is capable of providing the much-needed blood transfusion for our national body.[43]

Beksics's usage of the concept of the "middle class" was deliberately ambiguous, containing two conceptually distinct formulations: a "national

middle class" and a "bourgeois middle class." The first was a utopian concept, referring to a future class that would reconcile the anomalies of
Hungarian historical development and unify tradition and modernity in
a new, national class. The second was an empirical reality, associated with
an actual Jewish, entrepreneurial middle class that existed in the nation
and was presumed to become the source of the future, national middle
class. The potential conceptual and ideological conflict between these two
distinct concepts of the middle class was profound, though deliberately
underplayed in Beksics's account.

The "bourgeois middle class" was entrusted with the urgent task of reju-
venating Hungarian national existence. According to Beksics, Jews' well-
known business proclivities and assimilatory tendencies made them ideal
candidates for the role of reinforcing the beleaguered Magyar ethnic group,
which was in need of blood transfusion from outsiders. The "national middle class" that was to emerge out of the fusion between "traditional" Hungarian and "modern" Jewish elements would theoretically benefit both groups.
Yet, as Beksics made clear, the Jews were expected to play a subordinate,
specifically "feminine," role in the new national middle class that would
miraculously emerge out of the fusion of their opposite virtues. "The Hungarian gentry," Beksics pointed out, "possesses a proud manliness, elevated
principles, and traditional honor, but lacks the spirit of commerce and economic initiative, and most especially, a work ethic. The bourgeois middle
classes and the new landowners, by contrast, possess these valuable traits
that the gentry lacks, without, however, the genuine virtues of the gentry."
While the fusion between these two groups "can only be to the advantage
of both parties," Beksics concluded, it was never in any doubt which group
would contribute the defining element in the synthesis. "Even while the
gentry gains a little commercial spirit," Beksics argued,

> the middle classes will be enabled to rise beyond their narrow pursuits and
> the gaudy parvenu will gain substance and modesty. They will learn from the
> gentry a dignified and manly deportment, will stop flaunting their tasteless
> and ostentatious homes, and will cease worshiping before the altar of the
> Golden Calf. They will realize that there exists something nobler than money
> and that the manly spirit contains characteristics that are incommensurable
> with even a fortune of millions and cannot be acquired even at the expense
> of the greatest of treasures. Only this nobler, elevated, spiritually integrated
> middle class will be capable of solving the collective tasks of the nation.[44]

This vision of a future Hungarian middle class found possibly its most fantastic, yet compelling, articulation in an article written in 1917 by the great symbolist poet Endre Ady. The article was probably too provocative to pass wartime censorship and it only came out in 1924, five years after Ady's death. Ady's essay recast the political conflict of the Jewish question into a primitivist allegory, called the dance of the "Korribori," in which Jews and Hungarians were depicted engaged in a deadly mating ritual that could never be consummated. The rules of the "Korribori" involved the female members of the tribe, who wielded the musical instruments, and the male members, who danced to the music until they dropped in deathly exhaustion. "Why not finally end our cowardly denials," Ady asked,

> and acknowledge that we Hungarians have been dancing the Korribori here in the Danube-Tisza region for a number of decades? Two mongrel races, equally strangers among the European nations, have been engaged in an erotic struggle here according to the rules of the Korribori. The Jews wield the musical instruments, which they have copied from more advanced cultures. And we, Hungarians, dance to their tune with hatred and longing. Caught in a stranglehold of love and hate, we either produce a new race or we destroy each other.[45]

The seductive myth of a modern national middle class, created out of the fusion between Jews and Hungarians, had contradictory implications not easily disentangled from each other. The myth was simultaneously the source of Hungarian liberalism's generous receptivity to Jewish assimilation but also of its fanatical intolerance toward even the hint of Jewish difference. In the final analysis, it was also the grounds for Hungarian liberalism's tragic inability to sufficiently distance itself from anti-Semitism. Both subscribed to the notion of an existentially threatened national community whose very survival hinged on the presence or absence of Jews in its midst.

This common assumption gave rise to a profoundly paradoxical political culture where genuinely progressive goals could be articulated in terms of anti-Jewish rhetoric and explicitly anti-Semitic polemics could be advanced under the banner of liberalism. The ideological borders between Hungarian liberalism and anti-Semitism were real, yet also disturbingly porous, subject to frequent border crossings that undermined Hungarian liberalism's ability to distinguish its own national goals from anti-Semitism. Formulaic references to liberal principles could not make up for the lack of a genuine counternarrative to the assaults of anti-Semitism and radical nationalism. Under the circumstances, the Jewish question became the dark underside of Hungarian liberalism, its disreputable other, which could neither be fully acknowledged nor completely rejected. In 1896 a Hungarian liberal survey of Jewish contributions to the state and economy expressed this divided state of mind in the following words: "There exist topics about which an enlightened man of our century is embarrassed to speak, or speaks of only in private. Yet, these things cry out to be discussed in public. I am referring to the Jewish question, which continues to haunt our society."[46]

One of the few Hungarian liberals willing to articulate these contradictions was Péter Ágoston, whose pamphlet on the Jewish question caused a scandal when it appeared in 1917. "Those contemporary Jews," he wrote here, "who, in spite of their emancipation, insist on giving expression to the fact that they are Jews, that they always want to remain Jews, and want to publicly display their Jewishness, have failed to understand the goals that emancipation had hoped to achieve. Emancipation was not for making possible the retention of [Jewish] differences, but for creating the means for them [Jews] to become equal citizens."[47] As Ágoston made clear, the unconditional ethnic and cultural absorption of Jews into Hungarian society was the implicit, if unacknowledged, political agenda behind Jewish emancipation. This agenda was never openly stated because of its dissonance from the universalistic values of liberalism, but Jews were expected to understand it nevertheless. Ágoston bluntly summarized the case in the following words: "Jewry does not understand its situation, and up until now, the non-Jews have failed to enlighten them about it."[48]

It is questionable whether more enlightenment on the subject would have significantly altered Jewish attitudes. The secular and religious leaders of the Jewish community insisted on seeing assimilation in terms of the publicly articulated principles of Hungarian liberalism and defined its place in the nation exclusively in terms of legal rights, civic freedoms, and contractual obligations. They chose to ignore the fact that these abstract rights were intertwined with deeply held notions of Hungarian national solidarity, which tacitly excluded Jews as a recognizable entity in the nation. The very meaning of emancipation was at stake in these different readings of liberalism. After 1882 in particular, an increasingly self-confident and economically powerful Jewish bourgeoisie insisted on seeing emancipation as a legal contract between equal parties rather than as a cultural metaphor in which Jews were cast in a subordinate, "feminine" role, to the dominant, "masculine" role of the Hungarian political elite. The conflicted interpretations resulted in two different narratives of Hungarian national identity—a Hungarian one and a Jewish one—that coexisted without substantially intersecting with each other.

Hungarian Jewish Liberalism after 1882

The political trauma of 1882–1883 unquestionably played a role in the bifurcation between a specifically Hungarian Jewish and a generically Hungarian version of national identity. The new Hungarian Jewish narrative emerged in the context of a network of Jewish publications that proliferated in the years immediately after the Tiszaeszlár events.[49] In 1882 the political weekly *Egyenlőség* (Equality) came into existence with the aim of creating a specifically Jewish political forum; in 1884 the scholarly journal *Magyar Zsidó Szemle* (Hungarian Jewish review) was established on the model of the German *Wissenschaft des Judentums* in order to modernize Jewish religious teachings and ethical traditions; in 1894 the Izraelita Magyar Irodalmi Társaság (Israelite Hungarian Literary Association) was established with the goal of translating and popularizing Hebrew literary texts in Hungarian. Different as these enterprises were, they were motivated by similar goals. On the one hand, they wanted to create cultural models for a new generation of assimilated Hungarian Jews who were quickly forgetting the religious and cultural traditions of Judaism. On the other hand, they wanted to spread knowledge about the tenets of Judaism among Hungarian society at large in order to reassure it of the compatibility between Judaism and Hungarian culture. As the editors of *Magyar Zsidó Szemle* phrased it in their introductory remarks, "We have shared this homeland with our Christian compatriots for a thousand years, yet it is questionable whether they actually know who we are."[50]

One of the earliest and most comprehensive formulations of the new, more assertive Jewish public identity emerged in a pamphlet of 1883 titled *Zsidó és nemzsidó magyarok az emanczipáczió után* (Jewish and non-Jewish Hungarians after emancipation). The author was Ignácz Acsády, a journalist, novelist, and professional historian, whose original training in law was clearly reflected in the argumentation of the work. Though popular in tone and anecdotal in style, the text fundamentally reinterpreted the meaning and implication of Jewish emancipation and assimilation in Hungary. According to Acsády, the political crisis of 1882–1883 had brought Hungarian Jewry to a turning point that required a rethinking of its previous strategies. "I used to be among the most vocal advocates of the need to adjust to new conditions," he claimed, "and urged Hungarian Jews to speed up the tempo of their assimilation. These urgings and inducements, which took both serious and satiric forms, were appropriate for a peaceful age. Today, however, we are living through a period of the most vicious political conflict, when the human dignity, the civic rights, and the physical security of Hungarians of the Jewish faith have come under direct attack."[51]

Surprisingly, Acsády counseled not a retrenchment but an intensification of the process of assimilation. However, the theoretical grounds and legitimating principles for the new effort were conceived in radically different terms from the past. Directly challenging liberal discourses on the Jewish question, Acsády asserted that the right to determine who was to be considered a Hungarian resided exclusively in the individual seeking admission to the nation rather than in the existing national community. "To be Hungarian," he declared, "is not the exclusive privilege of particular classes or religions. Anyone who identifies himself as Hungarian on the basis of language, nationality, and affiliation, is de facto a Hungarian."[52]

Even more surprisingly, Acsády went on to argue that the assertion of this principle was not made arbitrarily or capriciously but in the true spirit of Hungarian national culture, which was by nature receptive to newcomers and hostile to exclusivist tendencies. "To declare Hungarian nationality the exclusive privilege of a particular denomination," he pointed out, "is not only a glaring injustice, but also a crime against the fatherland, a transgression against the very concept of what it means to be Hungarian. It is to contradict the thousand-year-old history of the nation; it is a distortion, an arbitrary disavowal, of the actual state of contemporary life."[53]

Acsády offered nothing less than a wholesale reformulation of Hungarian liberalism. He set out to correct its inconsistencies and to reinterpret its tenets from a specifically Jewish perspective. He held up a normative vision of Hungarian liberalism against its less than perfect practice, urging Hungarians to live up to their own ideals. In a distinctively didactic turn, Acsády presented what he considered the appropriate narrative for Hungarian liberals to assume on the subject of Jewish citizenship:

> Having made the Jews into citizens with equal rights, the state must demand of them the dignified self-esteem of free men. *Civis Romanum sum*—these three words express the Roman citizen's uncompromising dignity. Emancipation intended to make the Hungarian of the Jewish faith into a true Hungarian

citizen, into an equal son of the fatherland, not into the obedient servant of petty tyrants. Hungarian society has not yet recognized this inherent demand of emancipation, and this is the cause of today's reaction against the Jews. Equality of rights, once it has become law, cannot be regarded as a mere platitude, such as "liberty, equality and fraternity," often used to string along the masses. . . . Emancipation is not an empty precept, but a concrete reality, or at any rate, it aspires to become one."[54]

While investing emancipation with new political content, Acsády also generated an explicit counternarrative to anti-Semitism that Hungarian liberalism had singularly failed to create on its own. In this formulation, Hungarian history was seen as the site of a Manichean struggle between the forces of good and evil, progress and reaction, emancipation and anti-Semitism, in which liberalism was accorded a central mediating role. The battle for enlightenment was first engaged during the reform movement of 1848, continued with the Compromise Agreement of 1867, and temporarily halted by the anti-Semitic reaction of 1882. "The anti-Semites," Acsády asserted, "lost the first battle, because the majority of the Hungarian parliament is, after all, made up of thoughtful patriots. But the war is not yet over, the conflict will more than once be renewed, and every defender of the liberty of the nation will have to stand guard with weapons in hand on the battlement of our constitution, in order to defend it against the attacks of the modern barbarians."[55]

Notably absent from Acsády's reinterpretation of Hungarian liberalism were some key features that had defined the liberal pamphlets of the period. There was no hint of apprehension regarding the nation's survival, nor references to a national middle class whose mission was to save the nation by incorporating the Jewish bourgeoisie into its ranks. In Acsády's version of the Hungarian story, Jews were already integrated into the nation, rooted in its history and institutions through centuries of coexistence. Far from being rootless outsiders or newcomers in Hungary, the Jews were portrayed as natives: "Their memories of the past, their interests in the present, and their hopes for the future all tie them here." Acsády's text raised for the first time one of the most curious historical myths of late nineteenth-century Hungarian Jewish historiography, that of the Khazars, who supposedly established the crucial link between the Jews and the original Hungarian tribes who settled in the Hungarian plains. "There had always been Jews in this nation," Acsády reiterated. "They had accompanied the

Hungarian tribes of Árpád and they found Jews already among the native population here."[56]

The kind of historical mythmaking that Acsády and other contemporary intellectuals engaged in was not unique to Hungarian Jews. The custom, which Eric Hobsbawm tellingly labeled the "invention of tradition," was among the most common practices of the late nineteenth century, which witnessed the erosion of traditions and the need for stabilizing narratives and cultural myths.[57] What was perhaps unusual in the Hungarian Jewish case was the remarkable success of its mythmaking. The image of the patriotic Hungarian Jew, emotionally and historically integrated within the nation, became a psychological reality in the course of the late nineteenth century. It was the source of a powerful collective identity that gave self-definition, security, and political direction to Hungarian Jews. Only in the realms of humor and popular entertainment were these attitudes systematically questioned and ironically deflated. In the public arena, however, Hungarian Jewry became unambiguously identified with the myth of its own creation, gaining a reputation, at least among fellow European Jews, for fanatic nationalism and a zealous advocacy of all things Hungarian.

The early Zionist leadership famously denounced the Hungarians as an "ultra-assimilationist community" that had become a "desiccated branch" of European Judaism.[58] In 1887 the Viennese Jewish newspaper *Neuzeit* leveled a similar critique against the Neolog establishment of Budapest, whom it reproached for excessive haste in its eagerness to become Hungarian. Hungarian Jews, claimed the article, were in danger of losing both their distinct Jewish traditions and their mooring in general European culture. Such comments brought impatient rebuttal from the Hungarian Jewish side. József Bánóczi, the principle of the Jewish Theological Seminary, curtly dismissed the *Neuzeit* critique in the following words: "We consider the tendency of Austrian and German newspapers to spread scurrilous rumors about us among their readership directly harmful. . . . We request our European colleagues to allow us to take care of our internal affairs according to our own views. We thank them for their advice, but we have no intention of hiring them as professional consultants."[59]

Bánóczy's spirited debate with his meddling "European colleagues" was more than a passing disagreement. It was the expression of a new kind of collective identity that Hungarian Jewry typically reenacted through its cultural rituals and religious ceremonies at the fin de siècle. An impressive example of such a ceremony took place in 1889, on the occasion of the death of Crown Prince Rudolf. The occasion provided an ideal opportunity for patriotic gestures as well as for collective self-portraiture. The details of the mourning ceremonial were published in a series of articles that appeared in *Egyenlőség* under the general title "How Hungarian Jewry Mourns." The articles reflected a Jewish community united in common grief for the dead prince and in filial sympathy for the aged father, Franz Joseph. Ignoring years of acrimonious disagreement between the Orthodox and Neolog religious communities, the article enumerated without distinction all the commemoration services held in the major synagogues of the city, including the Rumbach Street synagogue, where the rabbi spoke in German, and the Orczy House synagogue, where there was no rabbi and services were conducted by the congregation itself.[60]

The climactic event in this collective mourning ritual took place in the magnificent Dohány Street synagogue, the second largest synagogue in Europe and an appropriate symbol of the social ambitions of the Budapest Neolog community. Ten thousand mourners crowded into a space that was built to accommodate three thousand, and hundreds more stood in the courtyard fronting the building. Inside, all the lamps, the pulpit, the altar, and the sacred arc were draped in heavy black cloth, and all the mourners wore black as well. A choir of forty singers, with the celebrated tenor Mór Friedman at their head, gave emotional renditions of the Jewish prayer for the dead, as well as of the nineteenth psalm. At the conclusion of the service, Chief Rabbi Samuel Kohn rose to address the congregation, whose hushed silence was broken only by the occasional sound of hysterical weeping.

The speech was a classic summary of the politics of assimilation, as interpreted by the Jewish elite of the fin de siècle. According to this narrative, which was recorded in the *Egyenlőség* and artfully combined the language of patriarchy with the rhetoric of equality, the central meaning of Jewish history in the modern world was the transition from slavery to freedom, from the status of a pariah people to that of free citizens. It is for this reason, Kohn claimed,

> that Hungarian Jews assume a larger share in the general mourning and grief than any other religious group. Franz Joseph is dearer to us than to any other religion, for Franz Joseph is not only our lord, our king, but also our benefactor. He is the object of our most fervent prayers, of our heart's unending gratitude. It is under his rule that we regained what the dark centuries have deprived us of: our most precious treasure, our freedom and legal equality.[61]

Dohány Street synagogue, ca. 1880. Courtesy of Budapest History Museum, Museum Kiscell.

The explicit goal of these public expressions of collective grief was undoubtedly to proclaim the solidarity of Hungarian Jewry with its political rulers at a moment of national trauma. But its implicit message was to celebrate the institutional strength and social accomplishments of the Jewish elite. This message was visually enacted in the seating arrangement of the Dohány Street synagogue, which faithfully reflected the corporate rank and professional status of those in attendance. Seated in the front row were the lay and religious leaders of the synagogue, testifying to the institutional strength of Neolog Jewry. In adjourning rows were to be found

the Jewish members of parliament, two appeals court judges, the Jewish university professors and middle school teachers, the ambassadors of the Jewish faith, the faculty of the religious schools and its instructors; the professors and students of the Rabbinical Institute, the representatives of the twenty-seven Jewish charitable foundations and cultural organizations. In the galleries were to be seen almost every member of the Budapest Women's Association,

Interior of Dohány Street synagogue, ca. 1930. Courtesy of Budapest History Museum, Museum Kiscell.

unparalleled for its charitable activities. Down below in the first rows were seated the Jewish army officers and junior officers and a troop of the National Guard.[62]

This idealized portrait of Budapest Jewry was not an expression of actual social and political conditions. It was rather a visual and emotional affirmation of the principles of civic equality first articulated by Acsády in 1883 and subsequently popularized by the Jewish press of the late 1880s. The same principles were reenacted five years later in another highly publicized public performance, the inauguration of the Israelite Hungarian Literary Society (Izraelita Magyar Irodalmi Társulat) in 1894. The occasion, attended by the Jewish social and cultural elite of the capital, was only partially a literary event. The society's stated objective, to "disseminate Jewish scholarship and literature in the Hungarian tongue,"[63] had an acknowledged ideological agenda. As Chief Rabbi Samuel Kohn explained in his keynote address, the overwhelming enthusiasm generated by the literary society was due to its identification with the ideals of assimilation. The essence of its message was contained in the title of the society, which linked in indissoluble unity the words "Jewish" and "Hungarian." "We know ourselves to be Hungarians body and soul," Kohn declared. "We are Hungarian even within the framework of our religious lives. And yet, we are also Jews; we identify ourselves as such, even within the framework of our Hungarian lives. The Jewish word is an adjective to the Hungarian word and means this: we are Hungarians, what is more, Jewish Hungarians, or if you like, Hungarians of the Jewish faith.[64]

These heartfelt assertions seemed superficially born out by developments taking place within the larger Hungarian political world. In the early 1890s the Liberal Party introduced a series of ambitious secularization laws, which included the separation of church and state, the introduction of civil marriage, and the "Reception" of Judaism as one of the official religions of the state. Hungarian Jews celebrated these measures with nothing less than euphoria, seeing them as the culminating achievement of Hungarian liberalism and the completion of the process of Jewish emancipation that began with the Emancipation Decree of 1867. "In almost every state on the European continent," exulted in 1895 an editorial in *Magyar Zsidó Szemle,*

> the flame of liberalism has been dimmed or snuffed out. . . . Yet, in Hungary, Europe's easternmost constitutional state, the sun of liberalism continues to

Rabbi Samuel Kohn. Courtesy of Hungarian Jewish Museum and Archive.

shine with undiminished brightness and warmth. While everywhere in Europe we witness the growth of reaction and anti-Semitism, in Hungary—only recently and sometimes even today regarded as part of "darkest Asia"—politicians have deliberately and jubilantly torn down the last barrier . . . dividing Jews from non-Jews."[65]

The contrast between Hungary's flourishing liberalism and the resurgence of reactionary conservatism in Europe became the dominant theme of the Hungarian Jewish press. Accounts of French politics, where the Dreyfus Case was polarizing society, or of neighboring Vienna, where anti-Semitism was beginning to dominate city politics, were implicit arguments for Hungarian exceptionalism. Characteristic of this mood was the following article about Viennese politics, filed in 1890 by the prominent Hungarian Jewish politician Vilmos Vázsonyi. "The political life of Austria," he observed, is coming close to the point where political commentary needs to be supplemented by psychiatric analysis. The political aberration demonstrated in Vienna at the moment is impossible to imagine without a corresponding aberration of the spirit. A kind of collective madness has taken possession of the population of the imperial city. Its obsession is that the Jews are the cause of Austria's every problem and this obsession has given rise to an active paranoia that has brought into question the social existence and physical safety of Viennese Jews. . . . Today, Vienna is in a virtual state of siege.[66]

In Vázsonyi's presentation of Viennese right-wing politics, the subject of Hungarian anti-Semitism was conspicuously absent. The fact that only seven years earlier Budapest, too, had been the site of anti-Semitic rioting was conveniently forgotten. Despite evidence to the contrary, Hungary was proclaimed to be a unique place where anti-Semitism was an aberration, an atavism from an earlier age, or at most an alien import from Germany or Austria. Jewish belief in the exceptionally progressive nature of Hungarian political culture can be explained in part by the pervasiveness of official liberal propaganda, which liked to drape itself in the mantle of constitutionalism and liberty. But Hungarian Jews themselves were in collusion with the creation of such narratives. It was in their interest to see Hungarian conditions in idealized terms, since their collective identity was intricately tied up with Hungarian liberalism's self-proclaimed values.

The Hungarian Jewish ideology of assimilation, based on a reinterpretation of Hungarian liberal values, turned out to be far more fragile and fraught with anxiety than its public rhetoric would suggest. Despite its sincere and vehement affirmation of Hungarian patriotism, it could not abolish the Jewish question from Hungarian public life. Indeed, the very effectiveness and visibility of Jewish cultural institutions and newspapers promulgating the creed of assimilation served as irrefutable proof to Hungarian society of continued Jewish autonomy and separatism. The political crisis of World War I would once again rekindle the passions and resentments surrounding this unresolved issue, causing another rehearsal of the Jewish question.[67]

The *Huszadik Század* Inquiry into the Jewish Question

The immediate occasion for the national debate was the publication in 1917 of yet another analysis of the Jewish question, Péter Ágoston's *A zsidók útja* (The path of the Jews). The book professed to explain from a specifically Hungarian liberal perspective the reason for the intensification of anti-Jewish sentiments during the Great War. Ágoston posed the question: "Why has the Jewish question suddenly become of such burning urgency at this particular time?" His answer reiterated the familiar theory of a crisis of social solidarity and an intensification of nationalist sentiment at times of collective danger. "In the course of the World War," he wrote, "every race and community whose sense of mutual interdependence is rooted in causes deeper than mere convenience will be bound to one another in even tighter and more exclusionary ways than could previously be imagined. People will be suspicious of strangers to a greater extent than in the past. . . . This is the reason why the Jewish question has generated such a huge literature during the war."[68]

To an audience familiar with the terms of the debates about the Jewish question, there was nothing particularly novel about Ágoston's thesis. The uproar provoked by his book was caused not so much by its content as by the intellectual stature and political credentials of its author. This was not the work of a semiliterate pamphleteer or an anti-Semitic hack but of a respected professor of law with impeccable left-wing credentials. Ágoston was a regular contributor to the radical *Világ* (World), the Social Democratic *Népszava* (People's voice), and the innovative sociological review *Huszadig Század* (Twentieth century). His decision to break with a long-established practice of refraining from engaging in public discussion of the Jewish question was unprecedented. For the first time, Ágoston brought into the conversation reputable intellectuals and cultural leaders, who had traditionally kept silent on the sensitive subject. Even the high-minded *Huszadik Század*, dedicated to dispassionate social research, could not afford to remain on the sidelines in this debate. "Since Péter Ágoston's book gave rise to such vehement controversies in both the specialized as well as in the daily press," the journal's editor conceded, "the *Huszadik Század* considers it its responsibility to engage with this problem, even though it would have considered it wiser to postpone the debate till less agitated times."[69]

A special issue of *Huszadig Század* was published in 1917 with the explicit goal of providing a comprehensive and respectable intellectual forum for the discussion of the Jewish question.[70] The professed aim of the project was to clarify the self-understanding of contemporary educated opinion on what had become the central, undeclared issue of Hungarian political life. A questionnaire was sent out to more than 180 "luminaries of Hungarian science, scholarship, literature, and public life," eliciting frank and objective discussion of the Jewish question in Hungary. The goal, according to the questionnaire, was to "gain as faithful an image as possible of the radically opposing perspectives and attitudes that have developed within Hungarian society in relationship to Jews."[71] The respondents, who included both Jews and non-Jews, were asked to organize their answers around three seemingly clear-cut yet ultimately elusive questions: Is there a Jewish question in Hungary? What are the causes of the Jewish question? What are its solutions?

Of the roughly sixty responses that were sent in, all were published in unabridged form on the pages of *Huszadik Század*. One of the curious features of these opinions was their failure to directly address the arguments presented in Ágoston's book. Instead, they proceeded to generate their own, independent definitions of the subject. What emerged from this representative cross-section of educated opinion on the Jewish question was the infinite elasticity and ultimate indefinability of the subject. For many of the self-identified Jewish respondents, the very act of posing the question was illegitimate, since assimilation had supposedly erased the cultural or ethnic differences of Jews, making the Jewish question irrelevant. Others refuted the existence of a Jewish question on purely legal and political grounds. In Hungary, one writer maintained, where "the law does not acknowledge differences among its citizens," there could be no Jewish question. The possibility of speaking of a Jewish question existed only in societies like Russia and Romania, where "Jews are oppressed and lack equality of rights."[72]

In contrast to these recognizably Jewish voices, the majority of respondents opined that a Jewish question did exist in Hungary, though they were far from united in defining its substance, much less its solution. Some argued that the roots of the Jewish question were ultimately religious in nature, having to do with "the eternal question of whose is the true religion."[73] For others, the Jewish question was ultimately economic in nature and was connected to the fact that "in Hungary, Jews are the virtual incarnations of the spirit of capitalism."[74] Still others contended that Jews were scapegoats and the Jewish question was merely a smoke screen for unsolved social and economic antagonisms between "agriculture, industry, trade, capital, and labor."[75] Others argued that the Jewish question was a cultural issue having to do with the survival of traditional prejudices that blocked the emergence of progressive ideas on "the position of women, the raising of children, and the choice of professions."[76] According to still other views, the Jewish question was a symptom of modern alienation and of the metaphysical uprooting of the individual. It expressed "a solitary, intimidated, offended, self-centered, and at the same time self-effacing neurotic sensibility, which is deprived of every form of earthly or otherworldly consolation."[77] Some maintained that there actually existed two Jewish questions: the first centering on assimilated Jews, who had become so Hungarian that they could be regarded only as a denomination; and a second, embodied in the "orthodox, strongly oriental Jew, who speaks a degenerate form of German and is colloquially called Galician."[78]

When the final statements and contributions had been compiled, the editors confronted an unexpected dilemma rooted in the very assumption underlying their enterprise. How could objective patterns of causality be determined on the basis of such heterogeneous, mutually exclusive narratives? Was the Jewish question capable of becoming an object of social scientific investigation in the first place? Oszkár Jászi, one of the founders and editors of *Huszadik Század*, and a passionate advocate of the scientific method, tentatively answered in the negative. In his own contribution to the survey, Jászi admitted that the Jewish question was different from the usual problems social investigators encountered in their research. It lacked the kind of empirical foundation one finds in "the agrarian question, the nationality question, or the administrative question. In these instances, it is possible to define the problem to be solved and the concrete practical means for solving them. In the Jewish question, however, there is no such clearly definable content or administrative remedy that could be directly applied to achieve a solution."[79]

The ambitious and well-meaning inquiry launched by *Huszadig Század* had been singularly unsuccessful in bringing clarity to the state of the Jewish question in Hungary. It ended up reproducing the very contradictions it hoped to solve. The editors ultimately decided to transfer the burden of interpretation to future historians, with presumably more empirical material at their disposal. Their goal, they modestly concluded, could naturally not be "the final, scientific definition of the question, but simply the compilation of opinion from a wide variety of people with interesting observations and experiences who lived this problem in a genuine way."[80]

The deferral to future historians for an explication and solution of the Jewish question was more than an admission of failure. It was a recognition that the ideological stakes in the conflict were beyond the objectivist and dispassionate methods of the social sciences. At the same time, however, this admission also represented a curious evasion of responsibility and failure of imagination on the part of privileged observers and scientific experts. For the Jewish question did not preempt the spirit of pragmatic coexistence and cooperation among the ordinary masses of the city. The realms of contemporary popular culture and commercial entertainment offered countless examples of creative engagement with its seemingly intractable issues. Indeed, it could be argued that these realms developed the social antibodies to the dogmatic spirit and essentialist assumptions that sustained and fueled the Jewish question. It is true that these popular cultural practices posed their own challenges and difficulties for respectable society. They failed to provide the kind of stability and intellectual foundations that were generally expected to offer a workable solution. They confronted the Jewish question not with political treatises, scientific surveys, and historical theories but with the unstable gestures of humor, parody, and inversion.

3

A Jewish Politician in a
Divided Public Space

The Funeral

On November 29, 1892, the citizens of Budapest were witnesses to an elaborate state funeral, staged according to the grandiose, theatrical traditions of
the fin-de-siècle monarchy.[1] The funeral was to honor Mór Wahrmann, the
first Jewish Member of Parliament, who had represented the Lipótváros for
almost a quarter century.[2] Wahrmann's unexpected death provoked an outpouring of tributes in the national press. The prominent politician, who was
also a wealthy banker and the president of the Neolog Jewish Congregation
of Budapest, was presented as the ideal type of assimilated Hungarian Jewry.
"The Jews of Hungary," proclaimed the liberal daily *Pesti Hirlap* (Budapest
daily), "possessed in Mór Wahrmann their virtual chief and leader."[3] Wahrmann's exemplary status, however, transcended the Jewish community. He
was also celebrated as a symbol of Hungarian liberalism and one of the
mainstays of the Compromise Agreement of 1867, which had established
the constitutional frame of the Austro-Hungarian monarchy.

Wahrmann's funeral was conducted under the auspices of the Budapest
Jewish Congregation, which collectively assumed responsibility for bury-
ing its illustrious president. Given Wahrmann's political stature, however,
the ceremony could not be restricted to the protocols of a traditional Jewish funeral. The event took on the form of an urban spectacle that artfully blended Jewish religious motifs with secular political symbolism. On
the morning of Tuesday, November 29, the city was transformed into a
stage where the rituals of public mourning were performed according to a
carefully choreographed script. In the Lipótváros, all the public buildings

Ceremonial portrait of
Mór Wahrmann, 1892.
Hungarian Jewish Museum
and Archive.

and many of the private residences flew black flags in honor of the district's departed deputy. Streetlamps were draped in black, storefronts shuttered, and crowds restrained by mounted police in ceremonial uniforms who lined the path of the funeral procession. Wahrmann's coffin was carried from his home by the leading officials of the Budapest Jewish Congregation and transferred to a six-horse carriage accompanied by an honor guard. The procession itself was led by a platoon of mounted policemen, followed by massed representatives of charitable and professional organizations, and three carriages with the official funeral wreaths donated by political associates and friends. Among the mourners who followed immediately after the funeral carriage were to be found not only Wahrmann's family and relatives but also the leading political figures of the age, without "consideration of religion or denomination."[4] No fewer than forty thousand people took part in the official funeral procession, which made a brief stop in front of the black-draped Dohány Street synagogue. Here, the rabbi pronounced a prayer and the synagogue choir sang a psalm before the procession proceeded on to the Jewish section of the Kerepesi Street cemetery, where the

Politisches Volksblatt.

| Achtzehnter Jahrgang Nr. 331. | Einzelnummern in Budapest 3 kr., in der Proviuz 4 kr. | Mittwoch, 30. November 1892 |

| Redaktion: Budapest, 5. Bez., Waiszner-Boulevard Nr. 34. | Erscheint täglich, auch nach Sonn- und Feiertagen. Inserate und Eingesendet billigst nach aufliegendem Tarif. | Abonnement für Budapest u. die Proviuz: Jährlich . . fl. 10.— Vierteljährl. fl. 2.50 Halbjährlich . 6.— Monatlich „ —.85 mit Zusendung. | Administration: Budapest, 5. Bezirk, Waiszner-Boulevard Nr. 34. |

Das Leichenbegängniß Wahrmann's.

Mór Wahrmann's funeral procession, 1892. Hungarian Jewish Museum and Archive.

final, more intimate stage of the funeral ceremony was performed before immediate family members and friends. Miksa Falk, a close friend of the deceased, who had also once been a political rival, delivered the eulogy, whose emotional tone left no eyes dry at Wahrmann's graveside.

Wahrmann's funeral was more than a public celebration of one of the most successful political careers of Dualistic Hungary. It was also the swan song of nineteenth-century Hungarian liberalism, increasingly under attack from clerical and anti-Semitic mass movements on the right. The event was a summation and reenactment of the progressive principles that had defined the liberal party and much of Hungarian political opinion during the previous quarter century. More specifically, the funeral served to showcase a series of highly controversial secularization laws recently introduced in parliament by the liberal party that became the fulcrum of political battles for years to come. Since the crowning achievement of these measures was the so-called Law of Reception, granting Judaism equal status with other religions of the state, Wahrmann's figure was a particularly charged symbol for the liberal establishment. There was no attempt to disguise the political agenda that formed the subtext of the funeral. As an editorial of the illustrated family magazine V*asárnapi Újság* (Sunday paper) acknowledged the week after the ceremony:

> In these days of deepening religious antagonism and strife, the general sympathy manifested at the funeral of this veteran figure of our public life has a virtually symbolic importance. Present at the funeral were members of the ruling party and officials representing every branch of our state and national institutions. Even the man of the street, usually indifferent to such things, made an attempt to express his condolences by his participation in the event. This was the emblem of our national solidarity, an encouraging sign for the future, and a rebuttal of hundreds of dark prophesies and thousands of disquieting fears.[5]

The political hopes proclaimed by *Vasárnapi Újság* were echoed in the hundreds of obituaries published in the wake of Wahrmann's funeral. The defining themes of these obituaries were already sounded at a special session of parliament convened on the Monday after Wahrmann's death. Sándor Hegedűs, speaking on behalf of the finance committee that Wahrmann headed for years, touched on Wahrmann's remarkable abilities as an economic and financial expert. "No one had a more impressive capacity to harmonize practical life with abstract considerations," he pointed out. "Thus, he never supported a practical measure without theoretical and principled justification, and he never put forth a theory or principle, without practical illustration." Károly Eötvös, a member of the opposition Independence party and the former defense attorney of the Jews of Tiszaeszlár, singled out Wahrmann's contributions to the Budapest Jewish Congregation, and Count Albert Apponyi stressed Wahrmann's exemplary role in the transformation of the national capital into an increasingly Hungarian-speaking city.[6]

In these accounts, Wahrmann was presented as a larger-than-life figure, whose sheer force of character allowed him to transcend the myriad contradictions threatening the unity of the liberal state. Successfully balancing economic pragmatism with political idealism, Hungarian national interests with the imperatives of Dualism, Wahrmann became the symbol of an ideal liberalism that increasingly eluded political practitioners. His greatest and most frequently cited achievement, however, was his ability to align and harmonize his Jewish and Hungarian identities. In the words of a deputy who identified himself as a political opponent of Wahrmann's, no other member of the Jewish elite possessed a comparable ability to "reconcile— we would say even fuse—a genuine love of his native land with an equal devotion to his religious denomination."[7]

Perhaps not surprisingly, it was the Hungarian Jewish press that produced the most effusive narrative on the theme of reconciliation embodied in Wahrmann's figure. He exemplified, wrote *Magyar Zsidó Szemle* (Hungarian Jewish review), "all the characteristic traits of Hungarian Jewry: enthusiasm for the Hungarian state, striving for economic modernization and prosperity, a fervent liberalism and clear-sighted religious consciousness."[8] Wahrmann's death, proclaimed the Jewish liberal weekly *Egyenlőség* (Equality), affected all segments of Hungarian society: "Charitable institutions mourn the loss of their benefactor; the representatives of political life, their hard-working colleague; business and industrial interests, their leader; the creators of scholarship and art, their patron; Jewish organizational life, its column of fire."[9]

These idealized images of Wahrmann bear only slight resemblance to the actual politician who was at the center of Hungarian political life for over a quarter century. Indeed, the obituaries, like the funeral itself, were less about Wahrmann than about the ideological self-representation of Hungarian liberalism. The very grandiosity of the funeral was an attempt to bridge the disjuncture between normative ideals and political realities that characterized the system. The historian Andrew Handler correctly identified this gap when he remarked that "perhaps the most misleading clue to understanding the position of the Jews in nineteenth-century Hungary is provided by the writings and speeches of politicians and social philosophers."[10]

Yet it would be wrong to consider Wahrmann's funeral as nothing more than political theater or a cynical manipulation of the mass media. The ceremony and its characteristic rhetoric expressed, even if in hyperbolic terms, the symbolic categories in which Jewish political identity was conceived and understood throughout the late nineteenth century. It also suggested through Wahrmann's example the conditions of possibility for a particular kind of Jewish public self that found its enabling conditions in Hungarian liberalism but its characteristic expression in the soil of urban popular culture. Wahrmann was an exemplary figure not because he transcended the contradictions of Hungarian liberalism but precisely because he embodied them in a more acute and self-conscious form than his contemporaries. His political career exemplified both the possibilities and limitations of the liberal political world that came into existence in 1867 and remained more or less in place until the fall of the Austro-Hungarian monarchy in October 1918.

The Paradoxes of Hungarian Political Culture

The narrative of inclusiveness enacted at Wahrmann's funeral was almost immediately challenged by segments of Hungarian society beyond the liberal establishment. Predictably, the most common objection raised was the appropriateness of according a mere Jewish politician the honor of a state funeral, something usually reserved for prominent national figures. The Catholic conservative *Magyar Állam* (Hungarian state) voiced these concerns in their most explicit form. Wahrmann, suggested its editorial, was hardly equal to such political luminaries as the former prime minister Gyula Andrássy or the prominent railway developer Gábor Baross, who had been given similar funerals in 1890 and 1892, respectively. What had been enacted in this ceremony, suggested the writer, was a defense of Jewish interests, not of Hungarian values. "At such times," it concluded, "the true face of the famous Hungarian liberalism is revealed: it is nothing more than Jewish liberalism!"[11]

The attempt to incorporate Wahrmann into the Hungarian national pantheon typically found more muted and indirect forms of opposition. One of the most curious examples was reported in the Viennese liberal paper the *Neue Freie Presse*, which never missed an opportunity to embarrass the

Hungarian political establishment. The episode, described in a postscript to an otherwise respectful obituary for Wahrmann, had to do with the size of the black flag raised above the Hungarian Lower House at the time of Wahrmann's death. The flag in question, it turns out, was smaller than the one ordered on the occasion of the death of Archduke Rudolf in 1889 and of Dániel Irányi, a hero of the Revolution of 1848, who had died only weeks before Wahrmann. The smaller flag hoisted to honor Wahrmann presumably denoted a lesser degree of respect than the larger one accorded to Rudolf and Irányi. The incident in all its triviality seems to have been taken seriously by the liberal leadership. When Dezső Bánffy, the President of the House, found out about it, "he called to task the responsible official, explaining that he would not tolerate even the hint of anti-Semitism and ordered that the larger flag be raised."[12]

These episodes exposed fundamental and unresolved questions about the relationship of Jews to Hungarian public life. Significantly, these questions transcended party lines and posed as much of a dilemma to liberals as to conservatives and anti-Semites. What political role should Jews play in the liberal state? Under what conditions could Jews appear as Jews in the public realm? In theory, these issues had been rendered irrelevant by emancipation, which had granted Jews full legal and political equality. With the rights of citizenship, Jews had presumably gained equal access to a disinterested and transparent public sphere, where they could articulate their interests in the same way and under the same conditions as other citizens. In the context of liberal ideology, the discussion of a distinctly Jewish political identity made no sense, since Jews were by definition citizens indistinguishable from others in the state.

In practice, however, the ideal of a neutral public sphere was a fiction and Jews never became transparent, unmarked selves within the modern Hungarian state. Their stigmatized status remained an unspoken and inadmissible fact of liberal society, creating unceasing tension between official ideology and everyday practice. The solution to the problem was the repression of all expressions of Jewish identity or difference in public life.[13] Far from disappearing from view, however, Jewish difference was rendered hyper-visible in everyday culture. Satiric representations of Jewish characteristics became staples of commercial entertainment, popular culture, and of course the Jewish joke, which was ubiquitous in Budapest. It was impossible to navigate public life without encountering representations of Jews. Significantly, however, there was nothing haphazard or improvised about these representations. They were governed by protocols that functioned as internalized reflexes, making some kinds of public statements about Jews acceptable and others not.

The Jewish Ambassador in Budapest

Perhaps no one was a more adroit practitioner of these unwritten rules than Wahrmann himself, who through much of his life managed to be the consummate political insider as well as the ultimate cultural outsider. His true skills were those of the performer who could function in different social settings and play in different cultural registers at the same time. It is not surprising that during his life Wahrmann was far better known for his wit and humor than for his elevated public sentiments. *Borsszem Jankó*, the major humor magazine of the age, paid him the ultimate professional compliment by writing his obituary in Wahrmann's own distinctive voice. "I have to admit," wrote Wahrmann about his own funeral, "that the speech Miksa Falk pronounced at my graveside was brilliant. But I can't help feeling that I would much have preferred my own speech at his gravesite."[14] A connoisseur of jokes, Wahrmann frequently used the double-edged weapon of humor to deflate official ideologies and to give expression to the actual conditions of Jews in a fractured political culture. He was, in fact, the author of arguably the most famous witticism on the subject of Jews in public life, which came to be known as the "Jewish ambassador" joke. It provides an appropriate point of entry into our analysis of this tangled subject.

The joke, which circulated in Budapest as late as the 1890s, assumed the classic question and answer format, with Cohen representing the archetypal Jewish protagonist. Question: "Why does Cohen support the establishment of a Jewish state in Palestine?" Answer: "So he can become Jewish ambassador to Budapest."[15] On the surface, the joke was a witty parody of Hungarian Jewry's well-known patriotism and excessive devotion to Hungarian culture. The origins of the joke, however, had a more specific political context. The joke reached back to the late 1870s when a new brand of political anti-Semitism was introduced into Hungarian public life by Győző Istóczy and his followers. Istóczy single-handedly radicalized the Jewish question by demanding the revocation of the emancipation decree of 1867 and the physical expulsion of the Jews from Hungary. The actual reference to a Jewish state in Palestine came from one of Istóczy's more notorious parliamentary speeches, in which he suggested that the solution to the Jewish question would be the forced emigration of Jews to Palestine.

It was Wahrmann who formulated the most memorable rebuttal to this proposal. Several versions of the joke were passed from mouth to mouth at the fin de siècle,[16] but the most reliable was probably the following. Wahrmann was accustomed to visit the home of Cardinal Lajos Haynald, a prominent Catholic cleric and good friend of Wahrmann's, whose afternoon teas were attended by the political luminaries of the age. At one of these gatherings, the conversation turned to Istóczy's recent parliamentary speech about deporting the Jews to Palestine. Haynald jokingly turned to Wahrmann with the remark: "If they establish a Jewish state in Palestine, all Jews will be expected to go there, including you, Moric, no matter how great a patriot you are." "I have no intention of going," replied Wahrmann. "I cannot live anywhere but here." "And if you have to?" persisted his host. "If I have to, I will go," shot back Wahrmann, "but I would hope to have enough influence to have myself immediately appointed Jewish ambassador to Budapest."[17]

The significance of Wahrmann's quick-witted response was that it redefined the narrowly ideological problem of anti-Semitism as posed by

Wahrmann Mór saját kérelmére Budapesten marad mint zsidó főkonzul s annyira vallásossá lesz, hogy nem áll meg födetlen fővel még Királyi Pál előtt sem.

Mór Wahrmann portrayed as Jewish ambassador in Budapest. Published in *Borsszem Jankó* (June 23, 1878). Petőfi Literary Museum

Istóczy. It addressed the larger cultural issue of the Jewish question, which had invaded not only political life but even private spaces of sociability like Haynald's salon. Wahrmann's offer to return to Budapest in the guise of Jewish ambassador from Palestine was more than a clever ploy to regain his previous status. It was actually a proposal to renegotiate the terms of his identity as a Hungarian Jew. By accepting the existence of a hypothetical Jewish state, he implicitly recognized what advocates of the Jewish question had always claimed, that Judaism was not just a religion but also a collective ethnic and political identity. His rejection of an essentialist definition of national identity meant in effect his withdrawing from the contested terrain of Hungarian politics, where Jews were considered strangers in fact, if not in law. In return for this concession, however, he gained the existential right to live in Budapest as an insider/outsider with the freedom to craft his identity according to his own creative vision.

The Jewish ambassador joke was, in a sense, the unacknowledged root metaphor for the much-acclaimed Hungarian Jewish symbiosis of the fin de siècle. It functioned on different symbolic and analytic levels at the same time. On the most obvious level, it provided a brilliantly subversive reformulation of the liberal ideal of emancipation that continued to define official Jewish narratives of assimilation throughout the fin de siècle. It offered a sly parody of the idealized self-representation of Jewish officialdom, which refused to acknowledge the ambiguities of liberal politics, mistaking political rhetoric for reality. At a different level, however, it was also a daring thought experiment that used the utopian conventions of humor to reimagine the relationship between Jews and politics under the changed conditions of late nineteenth-century nationalism. It supplied an explicitly cultural as opposed to a social definition of Jewish identity in an attempt to bypass the deadly and irresolvable conflicts of the Jewish question. At the most general level, however, the Jewish ambassador joke was what Kenneth Burke called a "representative anecdote" that provided an abstract model of actual social relations between Jews and non-Jews. According to Burke, the representative anecdote was a condensation or distillation of social realities that made no pretense at formal realism. It was, he suggested, "summational in character . . . wherein human relations grandly converge."[18]

Viewed as a representative anecdote, the Jewish ambassador joke offered a blueprint of an empirical world that was far closer to the hypothetical logic of the joke than to the ideological formulae of politics. It suggested that in the world of social relations and collective experience, Jews did in fact function as ambassadors from a nonexistent nation, with a status defined by informal rules and unspoken conventions. Within this world, Jews alternately played the roles of insiders and outsiders, natives and foreigners, depending on the context they found themselves in. Their dual status may not have been formally acknowledged in politics or the legal system, but it was imprinted within the informal cultural codes of society. This explains why the representation of Jewish themes became such a highly charged matter, in constant need of supervision and discipline. In official politics, in respectable society, in high culture, the formal principle of Jewish equality prevailed, and the presentation of Jewish difference, or even references to individuals as Jews, was considered bad form and strictly banned. In popular culture, however, especially in commercial entertainment and the realm of humor, Jewish difference was not only permitted but encouraged and given unchecked expression.

Representation of Jews in Literature, Society, and Politics

One of the striking features of this bifurcated cultural system was its unofficial character. There were no publicly acknowledged codes or formulae that defined the appropriate representation of Jews in public life. These matters were a part of an elaborate set of internalized cultural reflexes that were surrounded by a peculiarly illicit underground quality. The subject could not be openly broached and analyzed without exposing the ideological inconsistencies and even hypocrisy of the liberal order. The very definition of cultural competence at the fin de siècle presumed the mastery of the codes for talking about Jews in public life.

Ignorance of these codes could have serious consequences. As the naturalist writer Lajos Nagy discovered, his initial attempts to break into the literary life of the capital ran aground precisely on his lack of understanding of the unwritten rules for representing Jews in literature. He apparently submitted a short story to the modernist literary journal *Nyugat* (West), modeled on a Polish Jewish immigrant family living on Király Street. The point of the story was to explore the complicated linguistic practices and cultural identities of a typical, lower-middle-class Jewish family in Budapest. To the astonishment and indignation of the author, his short story was published in a severely truncated form. Ernő Osvát, the powerful editor of *Nyugat*, had unilaterally expunged all references to the Jewish origins of the characters and to the ethnic features of their milieu. Even the original title, "The Schvarczes" (The Schwarz family), was changed to the nondescript "Este van" (It is evening).[19] As this painful introduction to contemporary literary life illustrated, the political shadow of the Jewish question could not be exorcised from even the most innocent and well-meaning literary enterprises.[20]

The discrepancies between legitimate and illegitimate expressions of Jewish identity provided a virtual gold mine for the humor mills of Budapest. Indeed, central to Budapest Jewish humor was the paradoxical status of Jews, who were considered simultaneously equal but also unequal in society. The problem found a wonderfully economical illustration in a caricature of *Borsszem Jankó* that focused on the common dilemma of children of mixed marriages but implied a much broader kind of experience as well. "Imagine, Papa," asks the little girl of her father, "Mama says that you are Jewish!" "I am, darling," responds the father, "and it is not something to be ashamed of. But I don't want to hear you ever talking about it again!"[21]

The Jewish humorist Adolf Ágai provided an astute parody of the same phenomenon in one of his urban essays published in *Utazás Pestről–Budapestre 1843–1907* (Travels from Pest to Budapest 1843–1907). The essay, which focused on commercial entertainment in Budapest, sardonically commented on Jewish middle-class attitudes to parodic representations of Jewish themes in Orpheums and music halls. "Strange," he mused. "If our Israelite fellow citizens are made fun of in Hungarian—be it on stage, in literature, or in art—he is full of indignation. But if the Jew is represented through the characteristic dialect and disjointed gestures of Szerecsen Street [a particularly impoverished street in the Terézváros] or in the Polish Jewish inflections of 'Ingvar' [probably refers to the Yiddish dialect of Ungvar], his amusement is without bounds."[22] Ágai's mock surprise at the apparent hypocrisy of Jewish elites who seemed unwilling to acknowledge their Jewish identity in official culture but were more than willing to laugh at it in popular venues was only rhetorical. He was perfectly aware of the cultural codes that constrained public articulations of Jewish identity in fin-de-siècle Budapest. Ágai's readers, no less sensitized to these codes, recognized their own self-portrait in Ágai's imagined Orpheum audiences. They were all Jewish ambassadors in Budapest, who had learned the art of monitoring their performance and self-presentation in the public sphere.

The imperative for Jewish self-censorship in public life could lead to paradoxical results, especially in the realm of politics. In 1884, when the Lower House publicly condemned anti-Semitism in the wake of the election of sixteen anti-Semitic members to parliament, the Jewish deputies conspicuously recused themselves from taking part in the debate. *Magyar*

Zsidó Szemle praised their action in the following words: "The Jewish deputies in the House displayed enough tact to refrain from participating in the pre-advertised debate, and enough self-esteem to refuse to enter into dialogue with the anti-Semitic gentlemen."[23] The same strategy of noninvolvement was repeated in 1895, during the final phase of the controversial Law of Reception debate.[24] The ten Jewish deputies in the Lower House, including Wahrmann himself, agreed not to speak to the question individually but to have their voices represented by the liberal Hungarian leadership as a whole. Their reasoning was that the Reception of Judaism was not a parochial Jewish issue but a universal liberal principle, and therefore best represented by Hungarian liberal politicians. The actual reason, however, was the old fear of being perceived to act collectively in Jewish interests. "The deputies of the Jewish faith in both the Lower and Upper Houses," explained the reporter in *Magyar Zsidó Szemle*, "abstained from addressing the matter for reasons that, in my opinion, can be understood. They were concerned that if they engaged the question as Jews, their words might be construed by the nation as the collective voice of Hungarian Jewry. For this task, however, they did not feel empowered by their charge."[25]

The Code of "Tactfulness"

As these random episodes illustrate, the very act of representing Jewish identity in the public arena—be it in literature, in society, or in politics—was surrounded by anxiety and uncertainty. The special skill needed to navigate the treacherous waters of this realm was commonly referred to as "tactfulness" (*tapintat*). Wahrmann, for instance, was praised for his "discretion and tact" in dealing with the conflicts of party politics.[26] The Jewish deputies who chose to remain passive during the parliamentary initiative that condemned anti-Semitism in 1884 were commended for showing "tact" in refusing to engage with their opponents. Perhaps most puzzling of all was the frequent use of the word in the context of the Tiszaeszlár blood libel affair in 1882–1883. Jews who manifested solidarity with the accused Jews were reproached for showing "tactlessness" and thus provoking public opinion. When in the summer of 1882 the Jews of the Tokaj region purchased guns to defend their property against anti-Semitic vandalism, they were sharply rebuked for their "tactlessness." "Their first tactless act," declared the anti-Semitic paper, *Függetlenség* (Independence), "was their open decision to purchase weapons from Zákó's gunsmith . . . and this was far from the only tactless action they committed."[27]

Why were these manifestations of Jewish self-interest or self-defense invariably described as "tactless"? The word was obviously derived from the realm of etiquette rather than politics. The notion of "tactless behavior" suggests not a transgression against impersonal rules used to regulate political society but a breach of appropriate behavior or social courtesy in an intimate setting such as a salon or the closed circle of friends. In fact, the most fraught interactions between Jews and non-Jews often did take place in the semiprivate spaces of professional life and urban sociability, where the identity and social legitimacy of the Jewish participants were by definition ambiguous or imperfectly articulated. One of the paradoxical results of the success of Jewish integration within Hungarian society was the growth of opportunities for social tensions and misunderstandings between Jews and non-Jews.

The predicament could result in excruciating situations, poignantly depicted in an essay published in 1890 in *Egyenlőség*. Simply titled "Zsidók a társaságban" (Jews in society), the article examined the common situation of individual Jews finding themselves in social settings where the general topic of conversation turned to the "Jewish question" or the negative character of the Jews, without the company being aware of, or concerned about, the presence in their midst of a member of the group under discussion. The explicit goal of the article was to provide Jewish readers with practical guidelines for dealing with such awkward encounters. According to the author, the extremes of silent acquiescence or open confrontation were both to be avoided. "Let us admit quite openly," he illustrated the point, "that there are Jews, who, on occasions when the 'Jewish question' is raised as a general topic of conversation prove themselves quite capable of listening with external calm, though with inner disquiet, to even the most insulting details, as if they had nothing to do with the subject." Such behavior was condemned as both ethically contemptible and socially unrealistic. Yet the alternate strategy of open affirmation of Jewish difference was also rejected as disruptive of social harmony. "The tendency," concluded the article, "to fall into the other extreme and exercise a kind of terrorism on the relaxed good cheer of the company would also be a pity. The Jew should have self-respect, but should be selective about the occasions where he chooses to express it."[28]

The suggested solution for the inherent ambiguities of Jewish presence in public life was, of course, "tact," that elusive quality capable of resolving the intractable contradictions between equality and difference, self-effacement and self-assertion. The actual recipe for "tactful" behavior remained sketchy in the article, whose aim was essentially didactic, pointing out behavior to avoid rather than practices to adopt. Its general concern, however, helps illustrate the everyday dimension of the problem of Jewish and non-Jewish interaction in the public realm. "Tact" was an essential requirement of everyday life, as well as of politics, which were inseparably associated with each other. The "tactful" Jew was not just an individual who had learned to avoid embarrassing confrontations in the public realm but one capable of mastering distinct discursive realms for the appropriate articulation of his Jewishness.

The Janus Face of Wahrmann/Börzeviczy

One of the reasons the attribute of "tact" proved so difficult to define lay in the fact that to be truly successful it had to become virtually invisible. Tactfulness was both a social skill and a political attribute that was seamlessly incorporated into one's everyday actions and public persona. It was perceived and experienced as part of the inevitable order of things. Perhaps this is why the idealized portrait of Wahrmann produced at the time of his death appeared so unsurprising and "realistic" to the general public. Wahrmann's remarkable ease in the clubby atmosphere of the Hungarian Lower House, where he enjoyed genuine popularity, was perhaps the surest sign of his skill in this difficult art.[29] Shortly before his death, he expressed deep satisfaction with his daily routine in parliament, which he claimed "had become part of my second nature, so that I could not imagine my life without it, especially now, when I am disheartened and dissatisfied with my general condition."[30]

Wahrmann's successful public role as a politician was crafted out of the inner contradictions of a highly fractured self, whose conflicting elements could still be read between the lines of the respectful obituaries of 1893. It is worth returning to these tributes in order to more fully analyze the meaning of "tact" in the life of one of the consummate practitioners of the genre. As most of the obituaries directly or obliquely acknowledged, Wahrmann was not a typical Hungarian politician. He was, for one thing, a poor orator, whose skepticism toward great ideals deprived his speeches of all theatricality. "His arguments," one observer admitted, "often fizzled into mere cleverness."[31] Wahrmann avoided the political limelight, suggested another, preferring to express himself through "silent, tireless and successful work." He stood outside the conflicts of party politics and "wore the honorable mantle of independence . . . with discretion and tact."[32]

Mór Wahrmann in the Lower House among fellow politicians, 1886. (Wahrmann is standing on the extreme left.) Published in *Vasárnapi Újság* (March 27, 1892). National Széchényi Library.

Wahrmann's personal background was well suited for the role of the dispassionate financial advisor and banking expert that he fulfilled most of his life under Dualism. The son of a successful textile retailer, he amassed an enormous fortune in his own right during the economic boom of the 1850s and '60s.[33] He came to the attention of the Hungarian political leadership in 1867 with a series of articles on banking reform, published in the German-language liberal paper the *Pester Lloyd*. Articulating the interests of the Jewish financial elite, Wahrmann made the case for an independent national credit bank that would protect Hungarian autonomy from Viennese control.

The concerns sounded in the *Pester Lloyd* articles contained the major themes of Wahrmann's future economic policies and political philosophy. He was a classic liberal modernizer who placed rationality, pragmatism, and moderation at the core of his worldview. While a passionate supporter of economic growth and a jealous protector of Hungarian autonomy, he was also an eloquent and consistent defender of the benefits of the Dualistic system, which he felt provided the best guarantee of Hungary's long-range interests and welfare. His economic pragmatism and distrust of ideology were strikingly summarized in the following remark: "Political interests are always transient, economic interests, however, are permanent; political mistakes can always be corrected, but economic miscalculations are often difficult to undo even after long years of effort."[34] He was also a shrewd judge of the political world, and his intuitions proved remarkably prescient. During the American Civil War, when no one could predict the outcome of the conflict, he purchased Union bonds, believing in the northern victory.[35] In 1879 he was one of the few delegates to oppose the annexation of Bosnia-Herzegovina, arguing that it was not in the long-term interest of Austria-Hungary to dominate the region.

Wahrmann's remarkably consistent political creed found eloquent summation in his "Electoral Speech to the Voters of the Lipótváros" in 1884. The speech, which blended high principles with pragmatic considerations, was perfectly suited to the worldview of the Hungarian Jewish commercial elite that formed Wahrmann's constituency. His defense of liberalism was pitted against an increasingly polarized European political world, with conservative reaction on one side and socialist and anarchistic movements on the other. Avoiding both extremes, he invoked the liberal struggles of the 1840s as the true source of Hungary's progressive traditions, which had found legal and constitutional incarnation in the Compromise Agreement of 1867. Despite evidence to the contrary, he rejected contemporary claims that the stars of liberalism and parliamentary democracy were in decline, affirming the political and economic achievements of Dualism during the past decades. "By nature I do not belong to the tribe of optimists," he admitted, "but since the resurrection of our constitution, we have made significant, scarcely expected or hoped for, progress in all directions."[36] Hungary's political standing among the European powers had been established and its relationship with Austria regulated and systematized. Above all, the economy was expanding and showing the beneficial impact of free competition and personal initiative. Wahrmann's speech concluded with the following ringing words of affirmation: "From the preceding, you can see that I sincerely support the teachings of liberalism and democracy; my unchanging conviction is that these principles represent a humanistic politics that can embrace at one and the same time the interests of our nation and of mankind."[37]

The image of the competent financial expert and principled politician evoked by this passage does not exhaust the persona of Wahrmann. From all accounts, Wahrmann's public role was equally defined by his irresistible sense of humor and tendency for sharp repartee and irony. Almost every obituary made extended reference to Wahrmann's wit, which apparently enjoyed universal acclaim, both in and out of parliament.[38] Indeed, Wahrmann's claim to fame was not simply as a politician but also as a humorist, who found incarnation as W. M. Börzeviczy, one of the satirical social types of *Borsszem Jankó*. Börzeviczy was Wahrmann's fictional alter ego, who gleefully transgressed the boundaries of tactful behavior and confronted questions such as anti-Semitism and his own Jewish identity, which lay beyond the boundaries of conventional behavior.

Wahrmann's relationship to Börzeviczy is complex, not easy to define in any direct or causal way. The figure was not entirely his own creation and eventually acquired a life of its own independent of the empirical Wahrmann. There is, however, no question that Wahrmann was the direct inspiration for Börzeviczy, the rotund, wisecracking Jewish businessman/politician whose puns and aphorisms amused Budapest audiences for decades. Börzeviczy's physical characteristics, as well as his habit of punning in Hungarian and commenting on his own wit in German, were closely modeled on Wahrmann himself. It is also probable that most of the jokes published on the pages of *Borsszem Jankó* under the title "The Witticisms of W. M. Börzeviczy"

Recurring image of W. M. Börzeviczy in *Borsszem Jankó*. Petőfi Literary Museum.

were actual transcriptions of Wahrmann's famous jokes that circulated in Budapest. At the same time, however, Börzeviczy as a social type unquestionably owed its broader symbolic power to the editors of *Borsszem Jankó*. It is they who assigned the Wahrmann caricature the satiric name "Börzeviczy," which gestured to Wahrmann's complex relationship to the Hungarian political elite and to the public realm in general. While the initials "W. M." unambiguously pointed to Wahrmann, "Börzeviczy" was a comic distortion of the name of the liberal politician Albert Berzeviczy, a descendant of an illustrious Hungarian noble family. With the substitution of only one letter, the original historic name gained an entirely new connotation, since "börze" meant "stock exchange" in Hungarian. "Börzeviczy" thus became not only the shadow of the liberal politician but also a commerce-minded transformation and usurpation of his historic name, something that Jews were frequently accused of doing.

In Börzeviczy, Wahrmann found the physical incarnation and genial symbol of the radical otherness of his Jewish identity. The following anecdote, included in one of Wahrmann's obituaries, serves to illustrate the point. The story reached back to the time when Gyula Andrássy was prime minister and Hungarian politicians, including Wahrmann, were frequently invited to dinner at the imperial court in Vienna. On these occasions, the protocol was for the Hungarian delegation to make its appearance in national costume, with a ceremonial sword attached at the side. Needless to say, Wahrmann, who was small and corpulent, did not appear to advantage in this outfit. More distressing for Wahrmann was the fact that the silk material of his jacket (*attila*) caused his dinner napkin to constantly slip off his lap. Being a practical and resourceful man, he found a solution to the problem by attaching his napkin to the point of his sword and thus saving himself the trouble of having to retrieve the napkin from the floor. At the end of the dinner, when the emperor and his guests rose from the table and began to move toward the smoking room, Andrássy noticed that Wahrmann's napkin still hung from his sword. Alerting the emperor to this comic oversight, Franz Joseph smilingly turned to Wahrmann with the following remark: "My dear Wahrmann, you are welcome to eat my dinner, but at least you could leave the table linen behind."[39]

The anecdote, which was more than likely apocryphal, provides revealing insight into the contemporary political imagination and the acute discomfort associated with the presence of Jews in high public places. Börzeviczy's comic persona functioned as a means for humorously representing the reality of Jewish difference that could not be otherwise acknowledged in public. Wahrmann/Börzeviczy was frequently depicted on the pages of *Borsszem Jankó* in ill-fitting and comical Hungarian costume to signal his ambiguous relationship to national traditions. A particularly famous example featured Wahrmann and a fellow politician, both wearing national costumes and swords, trying to pass each other in a narrow space. As his companion apologizes to Wahrmann for the nuisance of his sword, Wahrmann politely responds that his own sword bothered him far more than that of his colleague. The visual focus on the Hungarian national costume helped establish the conceptual links between public life, national culture, and historic traditions, which Jews could not enter without appearing ridiculous and inappropriate.

Börzeviczy was a brilliant analyst and devastating critic of the conventions that defined the role of Jews in Hungarian public life. Indeed, Börzeviczy's self-defined task was to expose and ridicule the contradictions of official political culture and the artifice of tactful behavior. Unlike Wahrmann the politician, Börzeviczy the humorist openly acknowledged his Jewish identity and wittily commentated on the paradoxes of Jewish collective life. In one of his most succinct formulations, he characterized Hungarian Jews as plaintiffs in a prolonged paternity suit filed against the Hungarian nation, which refused to acknowledge them as legitimate sons.[40]

In many respects, Börzeviczy was the mirror image of Wahrmann, making explicit and public what Wahrmann kept implicit and private. While Wahrmann envisioned Jewish identity as invisible and universal, Börzeviczy made it visible and distinctive. Börzeviczy's satirical remarks equally encompassed the contradictions of the external world and the follies of his fellow Jews. In fact, his comments even extended to the delicate issue of his own self-erasure in public life. On one occasion, he admitted that his reluctance to openly engage with Jewish issues in parliament drew criticism from certain quarters. He added, however, that the opposite course of action would provoke recrimination from the very same quarters. He characterized his decision to withdraw from public activity in the House with the following witty pun: "Up till now, I had a standing in the House; now I have a seating."[41] His irony was particularly trenchant on the question of anti-Semitism, which never failed to provoke him, especially when it involved longtime friends like Franz Liszt, who regularly performed at his home. "That Liszt!" he proclaimed in exasperation. "I can't calmly accept his dalliance with anti-Semitism when he had been invited to so many soirees in so many Jewish salons. To a surprising degree he lacks rhythm [in Hungarian, the word for rhythm is "taktus" and therefore echoes the overcharged word "tact"], and therefore offends against good tone! [*Wird ihm wehtun!*]."[42]

The dichotomies encoded within the twin personae of Wahrmann/ Börzeviczy were responses to a radically bifurcated political culture whose official principles were increasingly at odds with its informal values and actual practices. Already anticipated in the Jewish ambassador joke, the project of Jewish public participation required mental agility, discernment, and, of course, tact. It presupposed the ability to distinguish between the realms of political rhetoric and cultural discourse, between the appropriate venues for expressing Hungarian identification and Jewish difference. Wahrmann, the consummate political performer, rarely made the mistake of confusing the discursive territory of the two realms. Only once did the carefully constructed walls between Wahrmann the politician and Börzeviczy the humorist temporarily break down. The result was an astonishing and ultimately mock-heroic duel between Wahrmann the discrete parliamentarian and Istóczy the flamboyant anti-Semite. The highly publicized social drama provoked by the duel was played out on the streets of Budapest in June 1882, only a decade before Wahrmann's state funeral in 1892. The two events form appropriate bookends for the assessment of Wahrmann's political legacy.

The Duel

The duel was precipitated by the controversial parliamentary debate about Russian Jewish immigration to Hungary in the wake of massive anti-Jewish pogroms that had broken out in Russia in early 1882. Despite his previous resolution to keep silent, Wahrmann decided at the last minute to speak to the issue after the inflammatory speech of Istóczy, who insisted on connecting the immigration discussion with the status of Hungarian Jews. Wahrmann began his speech with the familiar Jewish parliamentary gesture of refusing to recognize the anti-Semites as debating partners. "A man," he repeated, "who incites to unlimited internal warfare within this house may have the right to such expressions as a representative enjoying the privileges of parliamentary immunity, but he can have no right to claim me as a participant in debate."[43] Having rejected political dialogue with anti-Semitism, Wahrmann then proceeded to express his own views as to why mass immigration on the part of Russian Jews was undesirable.

Wahrmann concluded his speech with a rhetorical flourish that seemed to point toward Istóczy. The gesture set in motion a sequence of implausible and melodramatic events that were to culminate in the much-publicized duel between the two deputies. The steps leading to the duel were exhaustively reported in the daily press and had the appearance of inevitability. The overall logic of the confrontation, however, is less apparent, especially in light of Wahrmann's well-known cautious and skeptical temperament. It appears that Istóczy took offence at Wahrmann's concluding gesture and immediately left the floor of the House in seeming agitation. Within minutes, two of his friends approached Wahrmann with the demand of satisfaction in the form of a duel for the recently inflicted insult on Istóczy. Reasonable bourgeois that he was, Wahrmann refused the challenge, explaining that his were oratorical gestures not intended for Istóczy personally and that, in any case, parliamentary immunity would preclude his talk from being construed as a personal affront. After the message was relayed to Istóczy, he decided to confront Wahrmann in person. Overtaking his antagonist in the midst of conversation with a group in the parliamentary library, Istóczy accused Wahrmann of cowardice for refusing to accept the duel. Wahrmann repeated his previous claim that he had not insulted Istóczy and that he was, in any case, not obliged to offer satisfaction for words spoken in Parliament. After an exchange of unflattering epithets, physical violence suddenly erupted, as Istóczy lounged toward Wahrmann in an attempt to slap him. Bystanders intervened just in time to deflect the blow from Wahrmann's face to the back of his neck.[44]

This unconventional confrontation in the parliamentary library actually transgressed two different sets of social rules or conventions, held equally sacred at the time. The most obvious was the affront to parliamentary codes of behavior manifested in Istóczy's physical outburst. The House, in fact, met in closed emergency session that very afternoon to discuss and censure the incident, which by common consensus had offended against the dignity of the House. But in the course of the debate, several oblique remarks about Wahrmann's cowardice in rejecting the duel indicated that another equally binding breach of conduct had occurred when Wahrmann refused Istóczy's challenge. The infraction against the nobility's code of honor seemed, among some circles, to carry even more weight than the offense against parliamentary etiquette. At the very time that Parliament was debating the incident, another emergency meeting was being prepared at the Noble Casino, an exclusive social club to which Wahrmann belonged, to consider a motion to expel Wahrmann for actions showing "lack of chivalry and cowardice."[45]

It is easy to lose sight of the carefully crafted political choreography behind the accelerating events and passions surrounding the impending duel. Istóczy, who was a frequent object of ridicule in parliament, was not motivated by the supposed insult he had suffered at the hands of Wahrmann. The real reason for his physical provocation was tactical. Having failed in his efforts to trigger a full-scale debate on the Jewish question in parliament, Istóczy was determined to take the controversy out to the street. He correctly calculated that the aggressively populist rhetoric of anti-Semitism would generate more support among the masses than among the political elite. His ultimate goal, however, was to unmask Wahrmann, to force him into the role of the public champion of Jewry, a role Wahrmann consistently rejected to play in Parliament.

Wahrmann's motivation for agreeing to the duel is more difficult to guess at. The obvious explanation frequently offered is that he capitulated to social pressure, especially after the threat of expulsion from the Noble Casino, which meant, in effect, social ostracism by the Hungarian nobility. Such a consideration, however, seems oddly out of character in a man as deeply ironic and as clear-sighted about his relationship with the Hungarian establishment as Wahrmann. A more likely cause was pressure from his Jewish constituents in the Lipótváros, who had been urging him for months to take a more active and aggressive stance on the question of Russian immigration to Hungary. Impatient with Wahrmann's cautious strategies and preference to work behind the scenes, his electors were elated by the prospect of open confrontation with the anti-Semitic Istóczy and assumed a vicarious engagement with the duel. In a revealing gesture of support, they sent the following ceremonial greeting to Wahrmann: "We the citizens of the 5th district of Budapest [the Lipótváros], consider the insult that has befallen our deputy tantamount to our own mistreatment. We would like to use this unfortunate occasion to offer renewed assurance to our beloved deputy of our unconditional respect and patriotic support."[46] The petition was signed by two hundred supporters, which included some of the most powerful names of Jewish finance and industry.

The Wahrmann-Istóczy affair, as it rapidly came to be known, took the form of a social drama enacted in the public arena of the nation. It was the anthropologist Victor Turner who coined the phrase "social drama" to refer to certain kinds of collective conflicts or crisis that tend to be acted out in patterns strongly resembling—indeed, anticipating—aesthetic drama and theatrical performance. The social drama as Turner describes it has two distinguishing features that are of particular relevance to the events that erupted in Budapest in the aftermath of the immigration debate on June 8. The first is that it takes place outside the boundaries of normal, institutional social action. It has, to use Turner's word, "'liminal' characteristics since each is a 'threshold' [*limen*] between more or less stable and harmonious phases of social processes."[47] The social drama, thus, represents a breach in the public norms and values of a collectivity, exposing precisely those fault lines that underlie existing social consensus. The social drama, to return to Turner, "takes up its menacing stance in the forum or agora itself, and as it were, challenges the representatives of order to grapple with it."[48]

The second characteristic of the social drama is that it is "processually structured"; that is, it unfolds according to a fairly coherent sequence of events or moments that Turner considered inherent in the very nature of human agonistic behavior. Beginning as an infraction in the rules of social norms, the social drama opens up a deeper cleavage in social relations. After attempts to adjudicate the breach fail, the conflict is ritually enacted between the conflicting parties. The social drama ends, Turner claims, with the reintegration of the disturbed groups or the recognition that an irreparable breach had occurred that could only be resolved by separating the hostile parties.[49]

Applying Turner's model to the Wahrmann-Istóczy conflict, it is clear that a symbolic breach had occurred within the dominant liberal order, which had ordinarily kept such conflicts under check and outside the public arena. As was apparent to all participants, the confrontation between Wahrmann and Istóczy was not simply between two individuals but between Jews and anti-Semites, who enacted their hostility within a public arena outside of liberal institutions. The transformation of the initial breach of parliamentary conventions into generalized social crisis was well under way by Friday afternoon of June 8, when a crowd of four or five hundred people gathered outside Parliament in hopes of finding first-hand information about the rumored conflict between Wahrmann and Istóczy. As excited groups collected throughout the city, on street corners, in coffee houses, in stores and offices, contradictory versions of the story circulated, especially concerning the crucial issue of who had insulted whom. One popular rumor held that Wahrmann had initiated the provocation and that the House, bribed by the Jews, had supported him. Among the majority of Jews, on the other hand, it was Wahrmann who was perceived as the victim, and fears of anti-Semitic violence, ever present under the surface of liberal society, were flamed into new life.[50]

The affair rapidly divided the capital, and eventually the nation, into two antagonistic camps, cheering on their respective champions in a ritualized confrontation minutely reported, embroidered upon, and analyzed by the popular press. According to one report, "Every layer of society was feverishly preoccupied with the affair."[51] The process of polarization continued over the weekend, which proved unsuitable for the duel for religious reasons: Wahrmann refused to fight on Saturday and Istóczy on Sunday. Each side found dramatic public gestures through which to express its commitment to its cause. Wahrmann's constituents in the Lipótváros planned a torchlight procession with music, to show their support for their champion. As one article reported, "In this well-to-do neighborhood, every individual feels himself personally affronted. . . . Several members of the younger generation want to ask for personal satisfaction from Istóczy, since they strongly condemn an action that forces a half-blind man to fight a duel. [Wahrmann had very poor eyesight and wore thick glasses.] Calmer elements, fearing possibly dangerous consequence, are scarcely able to restrain them."[52]

Istóczy, too, was overwhelmed by gestures of support from all over the country. On Sunday, his apartment was thronged with visitors and inundated with letters and telegrams "commending his true cause under the protection of God." Typical of the overheated atmosphere was his associate's formal petition to the prime minister for guards to ensure the safety of Istóczy, for rumors were rife that Jewish army officers were planning to assassinate Istóczy if Wahrmann should be injured in the duel.[53]

The much-awaited and highly publicized duel was to take place on Monday morning at 6:00 a.m. on the site of the old racetrack at the edge of the city. The antagonists, their seconds, and their respective physicians were all ready at 5:50; and the formalities of the duel were scrupulously played out. Perhaps the most important participants were the representatives of the press, who were present in full force, ready to inform the nation of the antagonists' every move. After the space had been measured out and the pistols filled, one of the seconds undertook the traditional role of attempting to reconcile the parties. Both refused any thought of reconciliation, Istóczy curtly, with the words, "Let's get down to business," Wahrmann, more expansively, with, "After such an insult, there is no room for reconciliation."

At this critical juncture, the figure of a mounted police officer suddenly appeared from behind the bushes; he trotted up to the duelers and declared that his mission was to "prevent the enactment of illegal deeds."[54] (Dueling was technically illegal in Hungary, through in practice it was never interfered with.) This sudden intervention by the liberal government initiated what Turner called the third phase of the social drama: the application of "redressive or remedial procedures" by the collective authority of the community, in order to contain the contagion and prevent the crisis from spreading. The liberal government had intervened in the final moment to stop the conflict, but typically, the redressive mechanisms that were brought into play were only symbolic and entirely ineffectual. Instead of behind-the-scenes negotiations, influence, or pressure, which were well within their means, the liberal authorities chose to intervene through a highly theatrical gesture that could have had no impact on the events.

The police interruption only delayed the duel by a few hours. The participants and their entourages reassembled near the estate of Count Brunswick outside of Budapest to finish what they had started in the morning. "The two shots went off almost simultaneously," Budapest audiences could read a few hours later in the evening papers, "and to the question, did anyone get hurt, both parties answered in the negative. At this point, the seconds shook hands with the duelers. The duelers, however, remained cool and distant from each other. Ónódy, Istóczy's second, briefly suggested reconciliation, but Wahrmann shook his head, and Istóczy said, "Let everything remain as before.""[55]

The two parties drove separately to the nearby town of Ercsi to await the midnight train back to Budapest. Istóczy and his friends spent the intervening hours in a tavern, where they were joined by local intellectuals; they drank wine and sang anti-Semitic ditties to the accompaniment of a Gypsy band. Wahrmann and his party retired to the private home of a coreligionist, where they were greeted by an official delegation of the local Jewish community. The contrast between the patterns of social interaction characteristic of the two groups could not have been more revealing. As readers of these accounts would have been quick to grasp, the duel had ritually enacted not only collective grievances but also different ways of life, different modes of being Hungarian. Graphically juxtaposed were the traditional habits of the Hungarian gentry on the one side and the culture of the newly assimilated bourgeoisie on the other.[56]

The social drama, with its collective enactment of breach, crisis, attempted redress, and final resolution, seemed over by Tuesday morning, when editorials scrambled to clarify the implications of what had taken place. In the words of one summary, "The Jewish question, in the sense that it was defined by the movement against Russian immigration, is now over. It began quietly, it rapidly generated public passion, and it ended with pistol shots. After the nerve-wracking excitement of the past few days, moods are ready to return to normal."[57]

The assessment that the duel had somehow put to rest the Jewish question, or in any case made it retreat from the public forum to the recesses of private opinion, proved to be a mistaken conclusion. Indeed, the final phase of the social drama did not play out according to the classic pattern suggested by Turner. It brought about neither "the reintegration of the disturbed social groups" nor "the social recognition of irreparable breach between the contending parties."[58] What happened instead was a radical reinterpretation and transformation of the meaning of the duel itself accomplished by the humor magazine *Borsszem Jankó*. The week after the confrontation between Wahrmann and Istóczy, it published as its frontispiece a satirical depiction of the recently concluded duel, titled "The end of the comedy." The caricature portrayed Wahrmann and Istóczy, holding hands on stage, smoking pistols in hand, taking self-satisfied bows in front of a wildly enthusiastic audience, half of whom were cheering Wahrmann, the other half Istóczy. Between the two actors on stage was the prompter's box, conspicuously labeled "Noble Casino," to symbolize the highly ambiguous role of the Hungarian liberal establishment in the affair.

By reframing the Wahrmann-Istóczy affair and placing it within the realm of the melodrama, the *Borsszem Jankó* image trivialized the event and made explicit what seems to have been common knowledge among its contemporary spectators; namely, that the duel had been rigged and the guns had been fixed to fire awry, so that the participants would not sustain injuries. The confrontation that had held the capital spellbound for days was, after all, only a theatrical production that did not need to be taken overly seriously. The mock-heroic image of Wahrmann and Istóczy, united by the professional bonds of actors though divided by the popular passion of their followers, repudiated not only the political legitimacy of anti-Semitism but of all ideological interpretations of the Jewish question. The duel, which had briefly threatened to disrupt public life and transform politics into popular action, could once again be returned to its appropriate place: the nonserious realm of humor and parody.[59]

The final assessment of the Wahrmann-Istóczy duel came a year after the event, from one of the wittiest novelists and parliamentary reporters

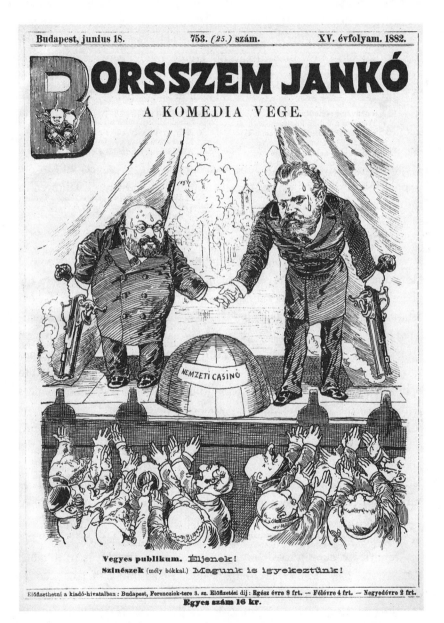

"The end of the comedy." Published in *Borsszem Jankó* (June 18, 1882). Petőfi Literary Museum.

of the age, Kálmán Mikszáth, who was famous for his ironic parliamentary vignettes in the *Pesti Hirlap* (Budapest daily). "Gentlemen," he wrote in an article recounting the court decision to revoke the fines leveled against the participants of the duel, "let us not condemn all duels, since there are some that are, by their very nature, convivial affairs, which bring a smile to people's faces, or even cause gales of laughter among those hearing about it. Such was the duel fought by Wahrmann and Istóczy, which needs no detailed description, since its entire text conforms perfectly to the conventions of the classic operetta."[60] What had apparently taken place was not a social drama but a farce, a comic reenactment on the streets and in the popular press, of a dangerous social conflict that had been disallowed in the official forums of political life.

The Possibilities of Jewish Politics in a Liberal State

How are we to assess the long-range implications of this political operetta? How does it fit into the larger problem of the relationship of Jews to the liberal state? Such questions cannot avoid confronting Hannah Arendt's devastating critique of Jewish assimilation in Central Europe, most fully articulated in *The Origins of Totalitarianism* but already anticipated in her Jewish essays of the 1940s. According to Arendt, secular Jews showed dangerous myopia and unwarranted indifference toward politics when they failed to oppose anti-Semitism directly. Lacking political traditions or experiences of their own, she contended, Jews placed excessive faith in the liberal state that had protected them since emancipation.[61] In this respect, even Heine, that most astute observer of the limitations of assimilation, manifested the kind of "worldlessness" commonly displayed by traditional Judaism. His "attitude of amused indifference," she claimed, was inadequate "when measured by the standards of political realities." "When one comes down to earth," she concluded, "one has to admit that laughter does not kill and that neither slaves nor tyrants are extinguished by mere amusement."[62]

Arendt's critique, infused by tragic historical hindsight, is irrefutable. Yet it is also historically inaccurate. It fails to take into sufficient account the limited political options available for Jewish political practice within the liberal state. Given the contradictory impulses of Central European liberalism, which simultaneously granted Jews the roles of legal insiders and cultural outsiders, the possibilities for an autonomous Jewish politics were severely circumscribed. Wahrmann was fully aware of these limitations and illustrated their consequences in his famous Jewish ambassador joke. As Jewish ambassador in Budapest, he provided an example of how to wield influence through indirection and how to use humor to confront, and even triumph, over ideology. This practice can hardly be called "worldless" or indifferent to political affairs. It was, on the contrary, highly pragmatic and brilliantly calibrated to the paradoxical realities and possibilities of liberal politics.

4

The Jewish Humor Magazine
and Collective Self-Parody

Borsszem Jankó and the Tradition of Judenwitz

The humor magazine *Borsszem Jankó* may not have invented the Jewish joke, but it undoubtedly helped transform it into the lingua franca of fin-de-siècle Budapest. Under the magazine's auspices, Jewish humor became the common currency of an urban culture that was notoriously lacking in other unifying elements. In 1887, after almost twenty years of unprecedented success, the magazine's editor, Adolf Ágai, playfully complained of the lack of even a hint of a worthy competitor to his venture. *Borsszem Jankó*, he boasted, had single-handedly created "the genre of the new humor magazine" in Hungary.[1]

The assessment appears somewhat hyperbolic at first glance, seeming to ignore the rich tradition of commercial humor magazines that preceded the establishment of *Borsszem Jankó*.[2] In fact, the genre had flourished in Hungary since the decade following the failed Revolution of 1848, when Habsburg occupation and censorship made humor the main source for coded political expression and public debate. Humor continued to play a significant role in public affairs after the lifting of direct Habsburg rule in the 1860s, when constitutional debates about a compromise with Austria and the implications of Jewish emancipation preoccupied general attention. Superficially at least, there was little to differentiate *Borsszem Jankó* from the politically oriented humor magazines of the period.

Ágai, for his part, did his best to define his project in terms that resonated with contemporary expectations. Drawing on well-established historical precedent, Ágai affirmed that the humor magazine was an integral part of the political world, acting as a mirror that reflected and corrected the ideological distortions of official culture. "Whoever writes one day the history of this age," he claimed, "cannot do without the humor magazine, where he will find the amusing criticism of its characteristic features. Even if distorted, as in a curved mirror, reality is reflected on its pages, with the exaggeration of its true qualities."[3]

The problem with this theory is that it did not correspond to Ágai's actual practice as a humorist. There was something startling and provocative about his comic discourse that was hard to reconcile with traditional ideas of social reflection. The novelty of his enterprise was obliquely suggested by the explicitly military metaphors he used to describe its impact. The new magazine, he claimed, took rival humorists by surprise, "when they realized that we were shooting with live ammunition from the other side. What is more, we were using the new technology of machine guns . . . against their old-fashioned, sluggish, smoky muskets!"[4] Ágai's image of humor as military warfare suggests not simply the modernity of his discourse but also its explicitly adversarial nature. Whether he fully realized it or not, the biting social satire and brilliant caricature of everyday life that became defining features of *Borsszem Jankó* did more than simply reflect the political world. They also challenged it, creating an alternative discursive space where official politics were parodied and reconstituted according to the conventions of private life and individual desire.

The comic tradition that Ágai inaugurated with *Borsszem Jankó* was what contemporaries referred to as *Judenwitz* or the Jewish joke. Freud famously relied on it in his theoretical masterpiece *Wit and Its Relation to the Unconscious*, which explored the subversive and creative potential of humor in human affairs. While Freud implicitly postulated an overlap between the universal significance of humor and its specifically Jewish manifestations, this was by no means a general assumption in the culture of his time. As Jefferson Chase has pointed out, in German-speaking Central Europe throughout the nineteenth century, a distinction was made between general humor, which was considered part of the national culture and served to integrate individuals into the community,[5] and a specifically Jewish form of humor, which was seen as subversive and leading to cultural negation and instability.[6] *Judenwitz* implied more than simply jokes by or about Jews. It was identified with the nihilism of the Jewish spirit itself that found characteristic expression in irony and malicious laughter. *Judenwitz* was thought to be the creation of rootless outsiders who could never fully master the native idiom or contribute to the collective values of the nation. Inimical to the practices of both folk culture and high art, *Judenwitz* was closely aligned in popular imagination with the commercial press and modern journalism.[7] "Along with the smear of tawdriness and illegitimacy," Jefferson Chase elaborated, "the tag *Judenwitz* also carried the promise of the sensational and the exotic. This represented a major source of popular appeal."[8] In the final analysis, *Judenwitz* came to embody a compendium of trends directly or indirectly associated with the destructive forces of modernity. The connotations of *Judenwitz* included such diverse and seemingly distinct gestures as "satiric humor, frank acknowledgment of the commercial basis of cultural production, frivolous wordplay, banking persiflage, and oppositional stance toward established political and social authorities."[9]

The historical concept of *Judenwitz*, with its implicitly ideological and polemical implications, has more or less vanished from contemporary theoretical debates about humor.[10] Nevertheless, unmistakable traces of the tradition persist in the common association between humor, opposition, instability, and ambiguity. The anthropologist Mary Douglas, for instance, has incorporated many aspects of *Judenwitz* into her own conceptions of humor.[11] The joke, she has suggested, was by definition subversive, challenging social control, objectivity, and established conventions. Echoing classic definitions of *Judenwitz*, she saw the essence of humor in terms of "the leveling of hierarchy, the triumph of intimacy over formality, of unofficial values over official ones."[12] It is no accident that Douglas singled out two Jewish theorists of humor, Henri Bergson and Sigmund Freud, as the exemplary nineteenth-century voices of the subversive implications of humor.[13] "For both," she explains, "the essence of the joke is that something formal is attacked by something informal, something organized and controlled, by something vital, energetic, an upsurge of life for Bergson, of libido for Freud. The common denominator underlying both approaches is the joke seen as an attack on control."[14]

Douglas went beyond Freud and Bergson in one important aspect, however. She claimed that humor was not only subversive but also socially embedded. "As I see it," Douglas famously declared, "all jokes are expressive of the social situation in which they occur. . . . If there is no joke in the social structure, no other joking can appear."[15] Douglas's insight that jokes were the expressions of contradictions within the social order suggests inescapable connections between *Judenwitz* and the Jewish question. Indeed, it could be argued that the two were mirror images of each other, reflecting the ideological crisis of Central European modernity that thrust Jews into the epicenter of the conflict. Surprisingly little is known about the theoretical and empirical interconnections among *Judenwitz*, the Jewish question, and modernity.[16] The difficulty of integrating *Judenwitz* into serious scholarly discussion can be explained in part by its compromised status as a cultural practice. Associated with negative Jewish stereotypes and crude self-deprecating humor, *Judenwitz* has proven to be deeply controversial and has given rise to divergent interpretations among historians of modern Jewry. Was *Judenwitz* a gesture of Jewish self-hatred and masochism or an act of self-assertion and cultural emancipation? Was it a reflection of the degradation of Jewish life in the Diaspora or, on the contrary, a sophisticated alternative to its established cultural codes?[17]

The difficulty with these questions, as with the debates they generate, is their tendency to recapitulate the very categories and intellectual frames that *Judenwitz* set out to challenge and destabilize. For the defining feature of *Judenwitz* was not the affirmation of any particular social, political, or moral agenda but the ironic deflation of all such agendas. *Judenwitz* was the voice of the disengaged individual who saw the world in absurdist terms. It gave rise to a relativistic and modernist state of mind that reflected the instability of human experience and the fragmentary nature of human identity. The tradition relied on irony and comic doubling in order to repudiate the dogmatic political traditions of ultranationalism and anti-Semitism but also the universal ethical claims of Jewish culture and identity.

The modernity of *Judenwitz* explains both its wide appeal and its contested status. It was a tradition, writes Jefferson Chase, that carried social stigma and intellectual allure at the same time. Ágai himself characterized audience reactions to *Borsszem Jankó* in terms of unavoidable ambivalence. "Those who loved it most," he confessed, "were also the ones who berated it most."[18] Conceptual ambiguity was inseparable from the creative function of Jewish humor and holds the secret to its central importance in the cultural life of fin-de-siècle Budapest.

Contemporary observers frequently pointed to a dangerous moral relativism inherent in the comic spirit of *Borsszem Jankó*. Jewish religious leaders themselves were troubled by the implications of Ágai's subversive humor, which they feared undermined Jewish solidarity and challenged religious authority and cultural traditions. They maintained a decorous silence on the subject, failing to even acknowledge the existence of *Borsszem Jankó* in official Neolog publications such as *Magyar Zsidó Szemle* (Hungarian

Jewish review). *Judenwitz* clearly did not belong among the accomplishments of Jewish culture these intellectuals wished to encourage or to celebrate. Yet there was never an open breach or direct confrontation between Ágai and the Jewish religious establishment, which did not want to add its voice to the chorus of anti-Semitic and nationalist detractors already attacking the Jewish-identified magazine.

The objections of the extreme right were, not surprisingly, the most violent and uncompromising. Anti-Semitic humor magazines such as *Füstölő* directly identified *Borsszem Jankó* with the nefarious influence of *Judenwitz* and called upon Hungarian society to resist it in the name of its national self-preservation. "We maintain," the editors of *Füstölő* declared in 1881, "that any person who continues to subscribe to this magazine [*Borsszem Jankó*] is not a true Hungarian. This simple-minded publication is the enemy of Christian Hungarians and celebrates our most hated enemies, its own tribe, the Jews.—Let's burn the copies of *Borsszem Jankó*!" Ágai was singled out as the chief culprit in the cultural pollution of Jewish humor. "We consider it our responsibility to declare," continued the article, "that Adolf Ágai should long ago have been expelled from the ranks of Hungarian literature. The reason for this is not simply because he is a literary plagiarist . . . but above all, because for years, he has been spreading messages . . . that we should not tolerate in the interest of our national self-esteem."[19]

The protests of anti-Semites were joined by the more subdued opposition of conservative nationalists who also worried about the impact of *Judenwitz* on the cultural and linguistic tradition of the Hungarian people. As late as 1903 Ágai was still engaging in polemics about the compatibility of jokes and word plays with the "majesty of the Hungarian language." His self-defense was that many of his jokes were taken from the lips of the common people themselves, and that "Hungarians are just as likely to engage in word plays as the stupid English, the idiotic French, and the ignorant German." Yet, as Ágai well knew, the polemic was not about national humor in general but about Jewish humor in particular, which was automatically associated with destructive tendencies. Referring to this implicit assumption, Ágai posed the ironic question: "Are the enemies of the word and the carriers of linguistic contagion perchance to be discovered among the Hebrews? Never!"[20]

Significantly, such fears about the potential cultural and moral damage caused by Jewish humor remained mostly confined to intellectuals and ideologues. They failed to make a deep impact on the larger society, which seemed highly receptive to the scandalous appeal of *Judenwitz*. The interesting question, thus, is not why certain groups and individuals objected to *Juden-witz* but rather why such large segments of the population were open to its attractions. For there is no doubt that Ágai's humor magazine, after some initial technical difficulties, was hugely successful among the general public. Starting with a subscription base of five hundred in 1868, the magazine increased its circulation to four thousand by 1870. Its popularity was to decline by the late 1890s, when newer kinds of humor magazines emerged, but during the first two decades of its existence, it provided the template for modern humorous discourse in Budapest. The characteristic readership of *Borsszem Jankó* was undoubtedly recruited from the Jewish urban middle classes, but it was by no means restricted to this audience. The magazine generated strong support and interest among educated non-Jewish readers as well, people who recognized their own social concerns and linguistic peculiarities in its parodic voice.

The comic idiom of *Borsszem Jankó* was inclusive, rather than exclusive, and its satiric attacks were applied with equal measure against Jews and non-Jews, urban and rural groups, elites and non-elites. In time, the recurring social types published in *Borsszem Jankó* became well-loved public figures, defined by idiosyncrasies of manner, speech, and appearance, which generated loyal followers. "For me, nothing serves as a source of greater satisfaction," Ágai wrote in his reminiscences of 1887, "than the fact that these types have acquired a life of their own among our readers, their idiomatic expressions becoming a part of the slang of our time."[21] Remarkably, *Borsszem Jankó* managed to single-handedly transform the scandalous tradition of *Judenwitz* into an acknowledged national tradition. Its centrality to the culture was confirmed by its status as the official humor magazine of the new liberal government that came to power with the Compromise Agreement of 1867.

The Foundational Narrative of *Borsszem Jankó*

The unlikely circumstances that brought this alliance into existence became part of the founding myth of the magazine, which Ágai first elaborated in his reminiscences of 1887 and later extended in different versions. Like all narratives of origins, this, too, had the appearance of serendipity. "On a gray November afternoon—exactly nineteen years ago this autumn," Ágai began with the leisurely pace of the practiced anecdotist, "I encountered on the corner of the Nádor Street a familiar face smiling at me from the upturned collar of his fur coat."[22] The face was that of Mór Ludassy, an insider of the

Deák Party and a member of the official press office at the foreign ministry in Vienna.[23] The conversation turned to the Deák Party's current difficulties in recruiting an editor for a pro-government humor magazine. None were to be found for the task in Pest, Ludassy complained, while in Vienna "one can hardly shake off the crowds of applicants."[24] At this point, the conversation took an unexpected turn that transformed the casual exchange into a life-altering event. Ágai, who had only recently returned to the Hungarian capital from Vienna, identified himself as the writer working under the pseudonym Csicseri Bors, known for his caustic essays and caricatures on the pages of the popular humor magazine *Bolond Miska* (Mike the fool). Ludassy's interest was immediately awakened, and he tentatively raised the possibility of Ágai assuming the editorship of the prospective humor magazine. A series of unofficial meetings followed that brought Ágai and members of the Deák Party into contact with one another. The exploratory conversations culminated with the titular head of the party, Ferenc Deák, and his prime minister, Gyula Andrássy.

The interview with Deák took place the next morning at the politician's favorite coffee house, the Angol Királyné (English queen). Deák seemed already acquainted with Ágai's work and was receptive to collaboration between the government and the Jewish humorist. He ended the interview with the following encouraging, though tentative, words about the projected magazine: "If you can do it my friend, you should give it a try."[25] The meeting with Gyula Andrássy was more substantive and took place at the prime minister's residence that evening. Perhaps for reasons of discretion, Ágai waited until Andrássy's death in 1890 to provide a full account of their conversation. More than simply encouraging, Andrássy was directly involved in formulating the details of the projected magazine, including its possible name. After several options were rejected, they finally agreed on the name of *Borsszem Jankó* (Johnny Peppercorn), which of course echoed Ágai's own pseudonym, "Csicseri Bors," but also suggested the figure of an imaginary folk hero. Most importantly, the emphasis on *bors* (pepper) implied qualities of sharpness and assertiveness that Andrássy considered an essential attribute of the planned humor magazine. To Ágai's objection that the name might be difficult to pronounce, Andrássy responded: "The harder the better. It should twist people's tongues and burn their palates."[26]

Ágai's central concern in the course of his negotiations with the political representatives of the Deák Party revolved around the question of the independence of the projected humor magazine. On this issue, Andrássy apparently gave him complete reassurance. "You should rest at ease on this count. You are not joining the government's pay role in the role of a servant. I have never liked intellectuals clothed in livery. To be a supporter of the Deák Party means to be a servant of liberalism. Believe me, whatever little liberalism exists in this country is to be found on our side. The opposition, despite its revolutionary poses, is at heart threadbare and atavistic."[27]

There is no reason to doubt the factual accuracy of Ágai's narrative of these events, but they nevertheless seem puzzling and raise a number of questions. Why should Ágai, the relatively obscure *Judenwitzler*, only recently relocated to Pest, be so eagerly courted by the venerable politician Deák and the powerful aristocrat Andrássy? What was the reason for the interest these political leaders took in the kind of radical humor associated with Ágai's journalistic persona? Ágai's implied answer, that the new government found it hard to recruit Hungarian supporters for their pro-Habsburg political enterprise, goes only so far to resolve the puzzle. The real reason for the alliance between Ágai and the Dualistic leadership was the fact that the Jewish humorist fit into the larger vision on which Dualism was founded. Deák had articulated this vision in another context, when he maintained that the new liberal government needed to actively recruit what he called the "intelligent and patriotic elements of Hungarian Jewry" to assist in the building of the new nation.[28]

Ágai fit perfectly the profile of the Hungarian Jewish patriot that the Hungarian liberals were hoping to attract. The son of a Polish Jewish immigrant who had changed the original family name from Rosenzweig to the more Hungarian sounding Ágai, the humorist grew up in a secular household committed to assimilation.[29] Like many Hungarian Jews coming of age in the 1840s, Ágai, too, assumed the existence of a historically inevitable convergence between Hungarian nationalism, political liberalism, and Jewish emancipation. The crushing defeat of the Hungarian revolution in 1849 seemed only to deepen the alliance between reform-minded Jews like Ágai and the Hungarian national cause.[30]

During the repressive decade of the 1850s, Ágai became part of what he later called the "great student migration" from "the banks of the blond Danube to those of the blue Danube: from Pest to Vienna."[31] As he explained, the attractions of Vienna over Pest lay in the fact that "academic standards were higher, and police vigilance laxer" in the Austrian capital.[32] Following in the footsteps of his physician father, Ágai also decided to pursue the study of medicine at the University of Vienna. He spent most of his free time, however, in the coffee houses of the Alserstadt, the student quarter around the university's medical facility, fraternizing with fellow Hungarians, who read newspapers, talked politics, and dreamed of the liberation of their homeland. Ágai automatically viewed the world through the heroic lenses of Hungarian nationalism. He dismissed the vaunted *Gemütlichkeit* of the Viennese as the characteristic product of "cultural Philistinism, unearned prosperity and political immaturity."[33] Along with his fellow émigrés, Ágai donned the Hungarian national costume as a sign of his political and cultural allegiances. He admitted that the historic attire was highly impractical, failing to keep out the chill of the Viennese winter. Moreover, the high boots with spurs that went with the costume were ill suited for walking along cobblestones. Nevertheless, symbolism outweighed practicality. Ágai summarized the meaning of his gesture through the mock-heroic paraphrase of Horace: "It is sweet to suffer for the fatherland."[34]

The ironic depiction of assimilated Jews strutting around in ill-fitting Hungarian national costume was to become one of the iconic images of *Borsszem Jankó*, reflecting the irresolvable dilemmas of assimilation and acculturation. Significantly, the spirit of irony and self-parody projected by these images did not cancel out the genuine patriotism that Ágai continued to feel for his homeland. Indeed, Ágai's student days in Vienna helped crystallize the possible coexistence of such antithetical attitudes and perspectives. They found expression in a new kind of cultural identity and journalistic practice associated with the creative possibilities of the feuilleton and *Judenwitz* and with the exemplary figures of Heine and Börne. Ágai returned to Pest in 1862 with freshly minted medical degree in hand but no intention of practicing medicine for a living. He joined the bohemian journalistic world of the Hungarian capital and assumed the role of the *Judenwitzler* in what proved to be an unusually receptive cultural environment for the genre. "The persona that he single-handedly presented to the public," wrote a reviewer of his urban essays in 1879, "was virtually a new phenomenon in Hungarian literature."[35]

It was in the role of editor and cultural impresario that Ágai was to realize the full potential of this new cultural role. *Borsszem Jankó* was, in many respects, his personal creation, which reflected the novel attitudes and practices of the *Judenwitz* tradition. Although the editorial staff of *Borsszem Jankó* was by no means entirely Jewish, the magazine itself was Jewish-identified through the very symbolic space it occupied in the culture. From the 1870s this identification found informal confirmation through the ironic appellation of "Kagál" that the editorial staff playfully adopted for its enterprise. The name was first used by the anti-Semite Győző Istóczy in a parliamentary speech of 1882, in which he expounded on the theory that world Jewry was striving for global domination through a secret society he called the Kagál. On discovering that the original meaning of Kagál was Hebrew for "community," the editorial staff of *Borsszem Jankó* immediately appropriated it as a badge of honor.

For much of the life of the magazine, the name Kagál was applied to its regular editorial meetings on Monday evenings, when the content of the week's number was thrashed out. These meetings invariably took place in a coffee house and were followed by supper, billiards, card games, and the spontaneous exchange of jokes and witticisms that often ended up on the pages of the magazine. The concept of the Kagál became a synonym for the extensive network of sociability and camaraderie that came to surround the enterprise of *Borsszem Jankó*. There even emerged by the early years of

"The coffee spring." First meeting place of the editorial staff of *Borsszem Jankó*. Published in *Borsszem Jankó* (April 10, 1887). Petőfi Literary Museum.

the twentieth century a Ladies' Kagál, which presumably recruited the wives and female relatives of the contributors into a social club of their own. As one participant of these meetings observed with a note of Schadenfreude: "Poor Istóczy could most certainly not have anticipated this turn of events."[36]

Ágai's own references to the Kagál suggest the unique character of his magazine, which seemed to be a cross between a semibohemian community of friends and acquaintances and a highly successful commercial and journalistic venture. The contributors were not all professional writers but often had middle-class careers. There were among the regular members a banker, a lawyer, a theater director, as well as a smattering of doctors, professors, government officials, and landowners. In Ágai's view, the Monday evening meetings of the Kagál provided for this group a "restful oasis" in the midst of "their busy and tiring schedules."[37] At times, the Kagál was also seen as a refuge from the hostility of a dangerous and inhospitable world. In a letter of 1884, at the peak of anti-Semitic political agitation, Ágai likened his circle to "the company in the Decameron during the plague in Florence [who found refuge] in that beautiful park outside the city."[38]

Ágai's abiding models for his literary and journalist practice were Heine and Börne, whose names he frequently invoked in the course of his long career. There was only one area where he rejected their example, and that was their conversion to Christianity.[39] In a reported conversation with the Archbishop of Esztergom,[40] Ágai gave the following response to the cleric's tentative exploration of the possibility of his conversion: "This would not be advantageous for a writer such as myself. As the great Heine himself confessed, no one bothered him on account of his Jewish faith before his conversion. After that, they never ceased to throw this in his face. . . . The same fate befell his contemporary Börne. Those who make their living through criticizing and irritating others, whose profession is to point out people's weaknesses and mistakes; cannot afford to display weakness that will inevitably be turned against them."[41]

Ágai's insistence that the viability of the *Judenwitzler* depended on his moral independence from established authority seems to be contradicted by his close association with the political establishment of the Dualistic system. In fact, however, the brand of radical journalism that Ágai pioneered in *Borsszem Jankó* was fully compatible with the political vision of the Deák Party. Its leaders entrusted Ágai with the editorship of a pro-government humor magazine with the expectation that he would establish the kind of innovative modern press capable of attracting wide popular support for the enterprise of Dualism.

Ágai, for his part, viewed the backing of the Deák Party as a source of much-needed legitimacy and national visibility for his magazine. The financial aspects of the arrangement were never made transparent in the official record, but there is little doubt that *Borsszem Jankó* received some kind of government subsidy, especially in the early years of its existence, before it became a self-sustaining commercial enterprise. It is also evident, however, that the implicit relationship between the magazine and its official sponsors was based on more than mutual exchange. It was in fact a unique instance of the broader historic alliance between Jewish modernity and Hungarian liberalism that defined the period.[42] Hungarian liberals promised to allow Ágai full intellectual freedom to develop the satiric potential of *Judenwitz*, while Ágai agreed to use the tradition to advance the causes of Dualism, Hungarian modernity, and Jewish assimilation.

Years after the original agreement, Ágai claimed to have fulfilled his end of the bargain with unswerving consistency. "*Borsszem* Jankó was the organ of the Deák's Party," he wrote in 1890, "and, twenty-three years after it came into existence, [the magazine] continues to profess the party's ideals and to fight for its principles."[43] Ágai's declaration of fidelity, however, was more complicated than appears on the surface. It implied continuing identification with the critical spirit of liberalism that the Deák Party had embodied in the 1860s, but it did not mean automatic support for the policies of the Liberal Party itself, which came into existence in 1875.

An implicit differentiation between the generic ideals of liberalism and the political ideology of the liberal establishment was central to the identity of *Borsszem Jankó*. The former was the necessary precondition for its very existence as a humor magazine; the latter was a frequent target of its satire. These cultural premises were spelled out early in the life of the magazine in a foundation story titled "A 'Borsszem Jankó' látogatói" (The visitors of *Borsszem Jankó*). The narrative evokes a string of imaginary and more-or-less unsavory visitors with diverse ideological agendas, who ask for admission to the pages of *Borsszem Jankó*. The unwelcome intruders included ultranationalists, ethnic minorities, aristocrats, Catholic clergy, and even an Orthodox rabbi. All are denied entry, with the exception of Count Szelleméri, an imaginary figure who stood for nothing more serious than the spirit of French wit and intellectual independence.[44]

Borsszem Jankó's Satiric Humor

Borsszem Jankó's repudiation of ideology by no means implied a retreat from daily politics. On the contrary, its independence gave it greater scope and latitude for political satire. *Borsszem Jankó* was famous for its inventive and cutting parodies of the political leadership of Dualistic Hungary. A characteristic example of its wit was the notorious caricature of Count Albert Apponyi, the leader of the moderate opposition, whose prolonged exclusion from power was wickedly depicted as a never-ending Yom Kippur fast. The caricature appeared on the pages of *Borsszem Jankó* every fall around the time of the Jewish New Year, with Apponyi and his political allies dressed as Orthodox rabbis hungrily watching for the appearance of the three evening stars that signaled the end of the fast. The refrain was always the same: "The three stars have still not come up and so we continue to fast." Apponyi, apparently, was outraged by these recurring images, which not only exposed his political frustrations but did so in what he considered a particularly undignified way.[45] *Borsszem Jankó's* political satire did not spare liberal politicians either. Among its characteristic practices was the depiction of liberal politicians in drag, with extravagant finery and effeminate gestures that served to deflate their authority and pretensions to dignity.

Political satire represented the most visible and directly confrontational aspect of *Borsszem Jankó*. The magazine's more enduring, and ultimately more radical, innovation, however, crystallized around its regular social types, which became its defining features from the mid-1870s on. Based on stereotypes of existing social groups or individuals, these recurring figures were not simply puppets or intellectual mouthpieces of the editors. In many cases, they were full-fledged artistic creations, whose letters to one another and to the editors of *Borsszem Jankó* were linked in a noncontinous narrative based on the common themes of everyday life and politics.[46] In his reminiscences, Ágai gave a revealing account of the birth of his comic types. "I could not reconstruct their origins," he wrote. "Often a voice, a form of expression, was enough to bring alive for me the incarnation of a particular type. . . . The conception of these types is often hidden in mysterious obscurity, just like that of the human being. There is a small seed here, another is brought to me by the breeze, and, arbitrarily, I sow them, to see if anything will come of them."[47] The success of the figures often depended on the response of the audience, which occasionally intervened in the development of a type, supplying details that were incorporated into the general formula. Each of the characters acquired a loyal following of its own, and if any of

A MEGTÉRT.

W—n M—r. Én vagyok, Kálmánkám! Nem ismered a te Muczidat?

"Returned home." Satirical depiction of Mór Wahrmann and Kálmán Tisza in the role of a newly reconciled couple. Published in *Borsszem Jankó* (April 17, 1881). Petőfi Literary Museum.

them remained absent from the pages of the magazine for any length of time, letters of protest arrived, testifying to dissatisfaction with editorial policies.

Ágai apparently conceived his social types as documentaries of the age, meant to showcase the enormous diversity and heterogeneity of fin-de-siècle Hungarian society. Writing to a friend in the late 1880s, he proudly proclaimed that with the completion of the thirty-ninth type, the "gallery of *Borsszem Jankó*" was virtually complete, offering a comprehensive cross-section of ethnic, religious, occupational, and cultural differences in the nation.[48] The collective impact of these social types, however, was not simply documentary. Their very diversity helped expose the deep disjuncture between official ideology and social reality in the multinational state. *Borsszem Jankó*'s types spoke in a cacophony of voices, accents, dialects, and mixtures of languages, testifying to a far different reality than the one reflected in nationalist rhetoric. They challenged the very conception of Hungary as a unitary nation-state based on an essentialist historical culture reflected in a unified national language. The social types of *Borsszem Jankó* gave expression to a rich and hilarious world of cultural difference that overrode the abstract vision of cultural uniformity propagated by official culture.

Given the centrality of language in Hungarian national discourse, it is hardly surprising that the impulse to express difference found its primary representation in the satiric depiction of language use among the types. Almost every figure expressed itself in parodic versions of Hungarian. The figure of the aristocrat, appropriately named "Monocles," spoke Hungarian with a heavy French accent and invariably mixed French and English phrases in his comic disquisitions on "High Life." The embodiment of the reactionary Catholic clergy, Pater Povadik Hyacinthus, spoke with a Czech accent and mixed his anti-Semitic tirades with Latin platitudes. The representative German burgher, Tobias Kraxelhuber, was equally deficient in Hungarian, invariably reverting to Schwabian dialect in his xenophobic outbursts against foreigners in general and Jews in particular. Even the type of the Hungarian gentry, Berczi Mokány, spoke with a local country accent that marked him as an outsider in the sophisticated cultural environment of the capital.

In this colorful gallery of idiosyncratic social types, the linguistic and cultural peculiarities of the Jewish figures hardly appeared exceptional. Indeed, their class and social diversity was more striking than their supposed cultural or ethnic solidarity, which politicians were perennially declaiming. The Jewish grocer Salamon Seiffensteiner was originally depicted as a naïve enthusiast and gullible follower of nationalist politics who was

"The history of *Borsszem Jankó*." Collective portrait of social types for commemorative issue of magazine. Published in *Borsszem Jankó* (April 10, 1887). Petőfi Literary Museum.

easily manipulated by flattery and ideology. The Jewish banker W. M. Börzeviczy, on the other hand, was a skeptic whose comments on the affairs of the world and parliament were invariably made in both Hungarian and German. He was prone to punning in Hungarian and then commenting on his own wit in German. The Jewish landowner Dávid Vöröshegyi spoke his own version of hybrid Hungarian, which he employed in letters to his steward containing harebrained instructions for the improvement of his estate. The moneylender Kóbi Blau was perhaps the least appealing of the Jewish types, one whose unsavory legal wrangling introduced yet another side of Jewish urban life. Significantly, the sizable Orthodox population of Budapest and the countryside found only indirect recognition in the comic figure of Reb Menachen Czicizbeiser, whose inventive curses against assimilated Jewry offered no end of amusement to his readers.

Borsszem Jankó's symbolic rearticulation of national identity in terms of social difference and cultural diversity found genial expression on the frontispiece of the magazines celebrating the holiday season of December 1875. The image depicted an elegantly furnished bourgeois interior with the different social types of the magazine, often represented at odds with each other during the year, united in friendly conversation and amicable interaction. At the center of the tableau was the icon of the magazine, the tiny figure of Borsszem Jankó (Johnny Peppercorn), raising his glass to the complex world of the humor magazine, where social and political differences coexisted in apparent fellowship and harmony.[49]

Not surprisingly, the cultural message articulated by *Borsszem Jankó* had its most direct and consequential implication for the ideology of the Jewish question. Its comic vision denied the central tenet of this ideology, which focused on the need to erase Jewish difference as the precondition for social acceptance and equality. Such expectations found characteristic expression in the following liberal editorial of 1889: "If [Jews] want to be regarded as completely equal, they must not differ in any detail from the other inhabitants of the nation. . . . They have to alter their external appearance, their clothing, their way of life, their occupations. We acknowledge that, in themselves, these details are trivial, but collectively, they nevertheless become important factors that isolate Jews from the majority of the nation."[50] What made this demand for Jewish identification with Hungarian culture so problematic was its implicit subtext that saw Jewish identity in essentialist terms. Thus, no matter how meticulously Jewish external differences were erased, traces of otherness inevitably remained, making it impossible to bring about a perfect alignment between Jewish identity and national culture. The internal contradiction of the Jewish question was that it both acknowledged and denied the legitimacy of Jewish presence in the nation. It held out the promise of equality in the name of a perpetually deferred identity that was ultimately unreachable. In fact, the Jewish question was the perfect embodiment of what Mary Douglas referred to as a joke in the social structure that was the precondition of all other joking.

Borsszem Jankó mirrored the paradox at the heart of the Jewish question, exposing and deflating its seemingly coherent ideological claims. Using the indirect techniques of irony and comic exaggeration, it punctured all foundational claims about Jews. It spoke through negative Jewish stereotypes circulating in society in order to expose their absurdity. Such comic gestures were undoubtedly double-edged swords that ended up discrediting not only the tenets of the Jewish question but also formal visions of assimilation articulated by Jewish cultural elites and religious leaders. The ultimate goal of *Borsszem Jankó*, however, was not to repudiate assimilation or to reaffirm negative Jewish stereotypes developed by anti-Semites or opponents. On the contrary, it was to discredit all stereotypes, including their positive and normative formulations suggested by the Neolog establishment.

The Phenomenology of the *Judenwitzler*

The most witty and sophisticated advocate of *Borsszem Jankó*'s cultural agenda on assimilation was Itzig Spitzig, the fictional Jewish journalist associated with Király Street in the Jewish Terézváros neighborhood. Spitzig, who became Ágai's acknowledged alter ego in *Borsszem Jankó*, first appeared on the pages of an earlier satiric paper called *Bolond Miska* in 1865. He made his entrance to the world of Jewish humor with the following memorable introduction: "Dear Mr. Editor, I am, if you please, a Jew, a Hungarian Israelite, and I am proud of it, for even if I were not proud of it, I would still remain a Jew."[51] The essence of Spitzig's message was the imperative to affirm rather than deny Jewish difference, which he consistently associated with external identity rather than inner conviction. Spitzig's Jewishness was, in fact, independent of religious, cultural, or ethnic content. It was situational, based on the cultural codes and social interactions that defined Jewish everyday life in society.

Spitzig's paradoxical Jewish self-identification was not a sign of disenchantment with the outcome of assimilation. His figure was conceived in 1865, two years before the emancipation of Hungarian Jewry, when the promise of liberalism was still undiminished. Spitzig's cultural persona expressed Ágai's essential optimism about the possibilities of assimilation, but it was an optimism tempered by powerful reservations. He was convinced that conditions for the social integration of Jews had not yet arrived but needed to be created through the critical task of the humorist. Through the voice of Spitzig, Ágai attempted to imagine a novel cultural space and social terrain that would make genuine assimilation possible. His voice was both normative and utopian and motivated by the desire to bring into existence a new kind of Jewish identity capable of confronting with dignity and creativity the challenges of modern, secular life.

Spitzig's "Letters from the Király Street," which became a regular feature of *Borsszem Jankó* between 1868 and 1882, were primarily directed at Hungarian secular Jews and focused on a wide-ranging critique of their attempts to translate literally the terms of assimilation. The delusion of trying to appear Hungarian and the futility of denying Jewish difference became the leitmotifs of his letters. He had a sharp eye for the foibles and vanities of the

Recurring image of Itzig Spitzig in *Borsszem Jankó*. Petőfi Literary Museum.

parvenu Jewish bourgeoisie, whose propensity to purchase noble titles and ape the customs of the Hungarian nobility were frequent objects of his ridicule. This "stock exchange of vanity," as he called it, would eventually bring about a situation "where Hungarian noblemen would petition the ministry to be able to get rid of their titles of nobility and be declared peasants." He reprimanded his audience by reminding them, "You are descendants of the oldest and purest aristocrats and you abandon the ancient parchment to run after the Hungarian nobility's dog skin."[52]

Spitzig denounced his fellow Jews for their political naïveté in confusing the legal formula of emancipation with the social reality of assimilation. He ironically invoked the example of his neighbor from Király Street, a certain Moritz Mandelbogen, who was so overwhelmed with enthusiasm on learning that the Jews had been emancipated that he immediately set out for a stroll in the city's fashionable promenade, Váci Street, to celebrate his new status. He hoped to be greeted by the distinguished strollers and to be invited to their homes for dinner or a reception. Spitzig's commentary on Mandelbogen's futile expectations was a combination of understated wit and genial empathy: "He waited, but the invitations never came. And in my humble opinion, he can wait two weeks—what am I saying, even three weeks!—for an invitation for a soiree at Count Károlyi's to materialize."[53]

In 1875 the same theme provoked one of Spitzig's most mocking denunciations against the Jewish community of Aszód, which apparently petitioned the government to have its official title changed from "Hungarian Jews" to "Hungarian Israelites." "My dear brothers in Israel," Spitzig thundered. "Are you *meshuge*? I am embarrassed that you are Jews, because till now, people thought of us as a clever people. You no longer want to be Jews and appeal to parliament to be declared 'Israelites'? *Wie heisst?* ... If we are called ten thousand times 'Israelites,' we will still remain nothing else than Jews. And I don't want to be anything but a Jew, a brave Moses hussar, who fights, not for a name, but for a cause. The word 'Israelite' is an empty title, like calling an ass a negative wise man. Why do you need such negative wisdom?"[54]

Spitzig's critique of the delusions of assimilation was both compelling and astute. At the same time, it was profoundly paradoxical. His unceasing exhortation for Jews to assert their unique qualities as Jews lacked empirical content. What, after all, was the formula for Jewish difference that could replace the ideology of assimilation? How were secular urban Jews, who had given up their traditional religious practices and social roles, to affirm a distinctly Jewish identity? What were the physical, cultural, and linguistic markers that differentiated the Jewish from the non-Jewish self in the public spaces of modern life? There were no obvious answers to these questions, which reflected the very ambiguities of the modern condition. Insofar as there was a solution to the problem of Jewish difference, it came into existence within the realm of humor. According to the paradoxical tenets of *Judenwitz*, Jewish difference lay in the very stereotypes that characterized society's ingrained views of Jews. Its comic representation of Jews became inseparably intertwined with the parodic manipulation of negative Jewish stereotypes that circulated in society.

Itzig Spitzig was a master of this technique in his capacity as *Judenwitzler*. He not only preached the need to acknowledge Jewish difference but also performed it in numerous disconcerting ways. The graphic image that accompanied his "Letters from the Király Street" invariably portrayed him with the characteristic hooked nose, dark curly hair, and crafty expression that were supposed to betray the inherent traits of the Jewish character. More significantly, Spitzig spoke a scandalously ungrammatical form of Hungarian, which betrayed his linguistic and cultural foreignness. Spitzig's language resembled, but was not identical with, the Yiddish-inflected *Mauschel* commonly associated with caricatures of Jewish speech.[55] It was a novel invention of Ágai's, who single-handedly created a uniquely Hungarian version of *Mauschel* based on humorous misspellings, awkward syntaxes, reversed word orders, and mangled grammatical structures that suggested an imaginary Jewish self incapable of mastering the linguistic conventions of Hungarian.

Ágai's invention of Hungarian *Mauschel* was not only an act of linguistic virtuosity but also a complicated expression of his love for the Hungarian language, whose beauties and expressive qualities he celebrated throughout his adult life. In a tribute to the lives of his parents, delivered at a prestigious Jewish literary association in 1900, Ágai did not hesitate to link the language with his most intimate family relations. "I bless the innate warmth of the Hungarian tongue," he claimed, "which, unlike other languages, uses the preface 'sweet' [*édes*] rather than 'natural', to designate the biological relationship between family members. It makes possible terms such as 'sweet father', 'sweet mother', 'sweet child', and 'sweet sibling', without the danger of falling into sentimentality."[56] Ágai's intense relationship to the Hungarian language was inseparable from cultural choices and affiliations that he had made early in life. Like most Central European Jews, Ágai was a polyglot who spoke many languages beside Hungarian. He used German and presumably Yiddish at home and often relapsed into stylized Yiddish at moments of exasperation. Hungarian was not even his second language, for he began his early education in Croatian, which was the language of southern Hungary, where his family had originally settled. Only after moving to a Hungarian-speaking district at the age of four did Ágai learn Hungarian, apparently under the influence of the great national poet János Arany, who happened to be his high school teacher. "The language that he was forced to acquire from the outside," claimed his biographer, "becomes flexible in his hands, he daily shows it off in new light; he does not cease to analyze and wonder at it; to turn it round and round in his mind; to explore and admire its beauty."[57] In the course of his early education, he also became fluent in French, which he used interchangeably with German in his frequent travels in Europe.

Ágai's affirmation of Jewish difference through the linguistic distortions of *Mauschel* was obviously a self-conscious artifice rather than a reflection of his own or his contemporaries' linguistic incompetence. It was an integral part of the comic repertoire of the *Judenwitzler*, whose figure Ágai so successfully reinvented in the Hungarian context. The practice of *Mauschel*, however, raises an interpretive conundrum that has still not found resolution among historians of European Jewry. What exactly was the significance of *Mauschel* in the context of Jewish emancipation and assimilation? How did it function as a tool of comic discourse and cultural self-fashioning? There is no unambiguous answer to these questions and no consensus about its different, paradoxical meanings.

The majority interpretation is that *Mauschel* simply mirrored and re-enacted the general prejudice that Jews were incapable of mastering the linguistic conventions of their host country because they lacked access to its inner spirit and history. From this observation it is only a short step to the psychological conclusion that *Mauschel* was essentially an act of self-hatred based on masochism and self-alienation. This argument found its most cogent articulation in a statement by the Hungarian literary scholar Aladár Komlós, who in 1944 defined *Judenwitz* as a pathological product of assimilation and something fundamentally alien to the intellectual and spiritual traditions of Judaism. "The Talmud," he claimed, "does not acknowledge plays on words, *bon mots*, anecdotes, or anything that is reminiscent of the Jewish joke. Only the modern Jew can tolerate laughing at himself. But if we think about it, it becomes clear that it is the stranger alone, who is capable of seeing us, and that the Jewish joke can only be invented by Jews who look at themselves through the eyes of strangers. . . . It is one of the more painful moments of Jewish history when the son of the ghetto first laughs at himself."[58]

Komlós's critique recapitulated a long tradition of Jewish polemics against *Judenwitz* in general and *Mauschel* in particular. Indeed, it was Theodore Herzl who first explicitly characterized *Mauschel* as the expression of Jewish degradation and humiliation in the Diaspora. "Who is this *Mauschel* anyway?" he asked rhetorically in an article of 1897 published in the Zionist weekly *Die Welt.*

> A type, my dear friends, a figure that keeps reappearing over the ages, the hideous companion of the *Jew* and so inseparable from him that the two have always been confused with each other. A *Jew* is a human being like any other—no better and no worse, possibly intimidated and embittered by persecution, and very steadfast in suffering. Mauschel, on the other hand, is a distortion of human character, something unspeakably low and repugnant. Where a *Jew* feels pain or pride, *Mauschel's* face shows only miserable fright or a mocking grin. In hard times, the *Jew* stands tall, but *Mauschel* cringes even more ignominiously.[59]

Herzl's deep distaste for *Mauschel* was widely shared by progressive Jewish opinion throughout Europe. Ágai himself was frequently subjected to the kind of condemnation voiced by Herzl. As early as 1866 the reformist Jewish publication *Ben-Chananja* expressed reservations about the characteristic comic techniques that Ágai was in the process of developing. In particular, the article strongly objected to Spitzig's use of *Mauschel*, which it considered unnecessarily demeaning to the dignity and image of Hungarian Jewry.[60]

While such critiques of *Mauschel* are well known and have tended to dominate historical debates, counterarguments justifying the phenomenon are more difficult to find. One obvious reason for this is the notorious difficulty of analyzing the experience of humor. Audiences who laugh at jokes cannot usually explain why they do so, and humorists who create them usually lack the capacity or inclination to theorize about them. During his long career as a humorist, Ágai often found himself involved in bitter controversies about his work, but he never explicated his actual practice as *Judenwitzler*. Insofar as he provided clues to its cultural meanings, they were through the voices of his comic creations themselves, who were often highly self-conscious about the broader implications of their gestures.

In the case of the *Ben-Chananja* article, it was Spitzig, not Ágai, who responded to the objection that *Mauschel* was detrimental to the dignity of Hungarian Jews. Spitzig defended the practice as a technique he consciously devised in order to capture the attention of audiences who otherwise might not have been interested in reading about specifically Jewish characters. Humor, according to this claim, was not only a simple or unproblematic act of communication but also a calculated strategy on the part of the humorist, who needed to obtain the audience's direct or indirect complicity with his discourse. *Mauschel*, as presented by Spitzig, was a linguistic bait to compel attention from a potentially reluctant or uninterested audience.

Spitzig's explanation, however, does not exhaust the scope and complexity of the subject. In particular, it fails to touch on the fact that Ágai's use of *Mauschel* was highly selective and associated with some of his Jewish characters, but not with others. *Mauschel* was almost exclusively reserved for comic figures like Itzig Spitzig and his successor, Salamon Seiffensteiner, whose voices were invested with the authority of the Jewish community as a whole. The other Jewish social types all had their idiosyncratic speech patterns, often linked to the eccentricities of their character or social position, but none spoke the excessively distorted and humorously stylized version of *Mauschel* that Ágai first invented for Spitzig and then passed on to Seiffensteiner. Just as significantly, characters closely associated with the domestic realm, such as women and children, were automatically excluded from *Mauschel*. Spitzig's wife, Regina, and his son, Árpad Spitzényi, for example, who made occasional cameo appearances in his "Letters from the Király Street," were always presented speaking correct Hungarian. The same strategy was later used for representations of Seiffensteiner's wife and daughters, who were also assigned impeccable Hungarian diction. Ágai's discriminating use of *Mauschel* provides important clues about its cultural function. Rather than being an automatic reflection of Jewish collective degradation, it was a consciously manipulated tool that came to signal cultural authority and the right to speak on behalf of the Jewish community at large. In the satiric, topsy-turvy world of *Judenwitz*, *Mauschel* implied the "mastery of discourse," rather than its opposite.[61]

This interpretation is borne out by the humor traditions of other ethnic minorities as well. According to contemporary cultural theorists, most minorities have used linguistic self-parody to depict themselves in the context of the national community. Such humor, Homi Bhabha contends, constitutes a "minority speech act" that helps reconcile ethnic differences with majority identity by promoting inclusion within the larger discursive community. In his view, the notion of a "self-critical community" is based on a performance of difference, which "neither disavowed nor suppressed [alterity] but worked around" it.[62] Jefferson Chase reiterates essentially the same idea when he argues that the nineteenth-century tradition of *Judenwitz* was "both stereotype and strategy," allowing Jews to acknowledge difference even while laying claim to cultural inclusion within the larger community. It was a sign of superior discursive competence that successfully repudiated

Recurring image of Salamon Seiffensteiner in *Borsszem Jankó*. Petőfi Literary Museum.

mainstream efforts to exclude Jews from the discursive community of the nation. "By being funny," he elaborates, "outsiders gain access to and purchase over a social mainstream from which they are otherwise excluded. Even if the audience is predisposed toward rejecting minority bids for inclusion, a display of humor can overcome resistance by eliciting a reflexive response not under the audience's full control."[63]

As indicated by Spitzig's self-reflections about his use of *Mauschel*, Ágai was fully aware of the discursive possibilities of self-deprecatory humor, and he used them to full effect on the pages of *Borsszem Jankó*. At the same time, however, his practice of *Judenwitz* went beyond such purely pragmatic considerations. For him, *Judenwitz* was not simply a strategy for gaining recognition of Jewish difference within the popular public sphere. It was also the expression of a radicalized sense of self that could no longer be represented through stable or conventional professional identities. Itzig Spitzig gestured toward this possibility in one of his earliest letters, in which he explained why he chose to become a humorist rather than a journalist. "It came to me," he announced in hilarious *Mauschel*, "that I would most like to write about important public affairs, not in ordinary newspapers, but in comic newspapers, because, as you will agree with me, it is always far better if a clever man plays the fool, than if a fool plays the clever man."[64]

In laying claim to the role of the fool over that of the serious man, Ágai/Spitzig was gesturing toward a new kind of cultural authority that Mary Douglas associated with the mythic role of the joker. Such a figure, she wrote in her analysis of the social meaning of jokes, "appears to be a privileged person who can say certain things in a certain way which confers immunity." At the same time, however, the joker does not resemble "a taboo breaker whose polluting act is a real offence to society." Unlike marginal or transitional types, who are "held to be dangerous to themselves and to others until they have gone through the whole ritual of redefinition," the joker was never truly an outsider and never exposed to actual danger. "He has," Douglas suggested, "a firm hold on his own position in the structure and the disruptive comments, which he makes upon it are, in a sense, the comments of the social group upon itself. He merely expresses consensus. Safe within the permitted range of attack, he lightens for everyone the oppressiveness of social reality, demonstrates its arbitrariness by making light of formality in general, and exposes the creative possibilities of the situation."[65]

Itzig Spitzig closely resembles Douglas's typology of the joker. As his "Letters from the Király Street" suggest, he was geographically associated with the Terézváros, which was also the major locus of Jewish life in the city. At the same time, he maintained his independence from social or class affiliations of all kinds. He spoke in the name of the community as a whole and was equally critical of the vanities of the Jewish bourgeoisie and the gullibility of the Jewish masses, of the antimodernity of religious Jews and the hypermodernity of Jewish capitalists. Elusive both socially and ideologically, the joker appealed to the unstructured experiences of readers, giving definition to their collective perceptions and concerns.

The joker's unique cultural and historical perspective found graphic illustration through a series of seemingly puzzling caricatures regularly published on the pages of *Borsszem Jankó*. Titled "Then and Now" or "Before and After," these were paired images juxtaposing typically modern and traditional tableaus of Jewish life, activities, and occupations. In a characteristic example of the genre, two parallel frames were presented, with the first showing a group of religious Jews praying before the Wailing Wall, and the second depicting the same group, now fashionably dressed in contemporary clothes, worshiping before a new version of the Wailing Wall, the modern music hall.[66] Despite appearances, the image was not meant to be a direct critique of the frivolity of modern culture. Like all the tableaus characteristic of the genre, it failed to offer a clearly legible moral lesson or ideological conclusion. It was neither an idealization of the past nor a celebration of the present but an ambivalent illustration of the flux of historical experience. The juxtaposed images gave expression to the destabilized perceptions of an urban population that had been uprooted from its past but had not yet found anchorage in the present.

The joker or *Judenwitzler* gestured toward the creative possibilities of an unstructured self that had liberated itself from the rules of social conventions and political assumptions. Spitzig's "Letters from the Király Street" gave humorous expression to multiple combinations of these possibilities. He fancifully personified the icon of *Borsszem Jankó* as his "unbaptized godson" and addressed him through the affectionate Yiddish phrase "Jankó Leben," suggesting the hybrid nature of the magazine, as well as its producer. In a more serious vein, he adopted the habit of signing his letters as "Spitzig, the well-known Jew and patriot," or alternatively, as "Spitzig, the well-known family man and patriot." The first signature poked fun at anti-Semitic discourses, which insinuated that Jews were incapable of being good citizens as long as they remained self-identified as Jews. The second problematized liberal axioms, which typically held that social stability required the separation between private and public functions. Spitzig's unique freedom lay in his ability to transcend the binaries of modern ideology, which produced not only the lethal contradictions of the Jewish question but also the alienation of modern liberalism. As *Judenwitzler*, he affirmed a new, radicalized version of modern identity that prioritized difference over identity, change over stability, and everyday life over universal rules.

Anti-Semitism and Jewish Humor

The tradition of *Judenwitz* provided assimilated Jewry with a paradoxical form of personal authority and cultural integrity in its conflicted encounter with postemancipation society. There was, however, a price to be paid for this essentially cultural solution to the Jewish question. The Achilles heel of Jewish humor was politics. As Hannah Arendt famously pointed out in her Jewish essays of the 1940s, the playful irony of Jewish pariahs like Heine did not constitute a viable response to the world of power and politics. The exclusive valorization of creativity and subjectivity, she concluded, proved to be dangerous, if not irresponsible, in the context of the threatening political realities of late nineteenth-century Central Europe.[67]

While the tragic outcome cannot be disputed, the actual relationship of Jewish humor to the political world was more complex than Hannah Arendt implied. Indeed, looking closer at the *Judenwitzler* as a cultural type, it emerges that he was not entirely divorced from the political world he satirized. He may have rejected the ideological premises of liberalism, but he was intimately tied to its structures, which provided the very condition of possibility for his freedom from politics. It is thus entirely appropriate that the comic figure of Itzig Spitzig came into existence during the heyday of Hungarian liberalism, when the compatibility between Jewish identity and Hungarian nationalism was a genuine possibility shared by wide segments of both Hungarian and Jewish intellectuals. The relevance of Spitzig's unique brand of cultural politics was intimately tied to these conditions and gradually dissipated as these conditions changed. By the 1880s, the values of official liberalism were under attack from the ranks of chauvinistic nationalism closely linked to the rise of organized political anti-Semitism. In the new political environment, the role of humor in opposing anti-Semitism was far from self-evident, and the problematic relationship between Jewish humor and politics came under scrutiny.

One of the most revealing expressions of this self-scrutiny was a remarkable caricature published on the frontispiece of *Borsszem Jankó* on April 25,

1875. The image showed Győző Istóczy, the notorious leader of the anti-Semitic movement, in the role of a wild man at a circus performance, with Itzig Spitzig, the *Judenwitzler*, in the role of his handler. The contrast between the two figures dramatized their incommensurability as cultural symbols. Istóczy was presented half naked, covered with a wild boar's pelt, clutching a sword in one hand and a cluster of tiny, stereotyped Jewish figures in the other. Spitzig, by contrast, was depicted half the size of Istóczy, wearing Hungarian national costume and holding in one hand a thick rope attached to Istóczy's waist and in the other a conductor's baton, used to illustrate the exotic features of the dangerous savage on display.

The overall impact of the tableau is disorienting. Overtly, it seemed to be a demonstration of the superiority of humor over naked force, of the power of wit and intelligence over hatred and rage. Yet the subliminal message of the image was more threatening and ambiguous. It suggested that the power relations on display were far more complicated than they appeared and might at one point be reversed. Istóczy's crazed expression and hulking size raised the possibility that the latent violence of the wild man might be no match for the smiling civility of his diminutive handler. The inevitable question hovering over the image was what would happen if the rope around the waist of the wild man were to snap and he were to escape from the contained environment of the circus into the real world?

The potential for violence implicit within the image became a political reality in the spring of 1882, when a fourteen-year-old girl disappeared from the village of Tiszaeszlár and the Jewish community in the village was accused of the medieval crime of ritual murder (see chap. 2). Although the Jews of Tiszaeszlár were eventually cleared of the charge, between 1882 and 1883 anti-Jewish riots broke out throughout the countryside, and Budapest itself was briefly placed under a state of siege. Tiszaeszlár became Hungarian Jewry's "Mohács," the disastrous battle of 1526 when Hungarians were defeated by the forces of the Ottoman Empire and lost control of their political destiny for a century and a half. The political analogy suggested by *Borsszem Jankó* may not have been exact, but the comparison was apt, illustrating the sense of collective trauma and historic breach that Tiszaeszlár represented for Hungarian Jewry. Their optimism associated with the possibilities of Jewish emancipation in 1867 was forever altered by the events of 1882.

The symbolic marker of the seismic shift in Hungarian political culture was the formal withdrawal of Itzig Spitzig from the pages of *Borsszem Jankó*. His departure from the magazine was characteristically understated and

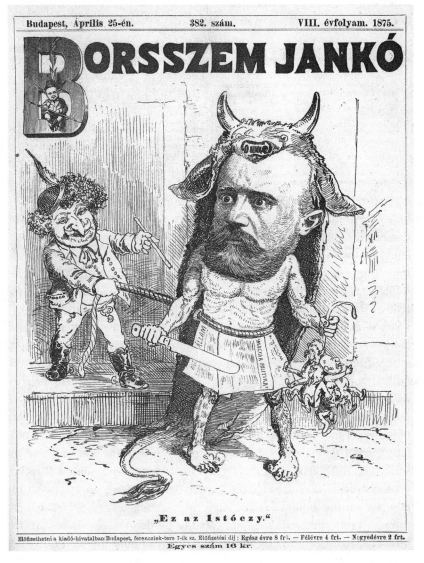

"This is Istóczy." Spitzig and Istóczy as circus performers. Published in *Borsszem Jankó* (April 25, 1875). Petőfi Literary Museum.

without ideological fanfare. It was, however, unmistakably connected with the events of Tiszaeszlár. The announcement was made public through a letter sent by Spitzig to his brother-in-law, Salamon Seiffensteiner, about his decision to absent himself from Seiffensteiner's Passover seder:

> Dear Brother-in-law!
>
> Thank you for the invitation. But I cannot accept it. I am a little indisposed and I do not like large gatherings. I will slaughter my own Eszter Solymosi at home in the circle of my own family.
>
> Good-bye,
> Itzig Spitzig[68]

Spitzig never resumed his letters to *Borsszem Jankó*, whose satiric spirit he helped shape for over fifteen years. Only twice did he make a brief return appearance in the 1890s, significantly without using *Mauschel*. The distinctive linguistic marker of *Mauschel* was passed on to Salamon Seiffensteiner, who became not only Spitzig's successor but also the unofficial mouthpiece of Budapest Jewry in the magazine. The invention of Seiffensteiner was generally attributed to Ferencz Székely, a self-made man a generation younger than Ágai, who was an active member of *Borsszem Jankó*'s editorial board, even while holding down a day job as the president of a bank. The figure of Seiffensteiner was originally conceived as the garrulous grocer from number 3 Dob Street, who embodied the political mood and limited perspective of the Jewish lower-middle classes of the Terézváros. By the 1880s Seiffensteiner had undergone a process of gentrification, no doubt reflecting the career path of his creator as well as the social mobility of Budapest Jewry itself. While retaining the graphic features of the round-faced, jovial shopkeeper clutching a moneybag with the Star of David inscribed on it, Seiffensteiner metamorphosed over the years into a skeptical urban observer who attended the theater, read the newspapers, and wittily reflected on the follies of politics and international affairs. Seiffensteiner's primary preoccupation, however, came to be defined by Tiszaeszlár, the problem of anti-Semitism, and the inadequacy of official Jewish responses to the phenomenon.

He offered a distinctively pessimistic narrative of anti-Semitism that implicitly rejected the inherited vision of Jewish liberalism. Rather than seeing anti-Semitism as an atavistic remnant of medieval prejudice bound to disappear with social progress and political enlightenment, Seiffensteiner perceived it as an essentially modern phenomenon with no political meaning or solution. It was an irrational projection of populist politics in which Jews were cast as symbolic scapegoats for Hungarian failures. "For the past fifteen years," he illustrated, "we have been bombarded with stories that our troubles and miseries are caused by the joint affairs, the quota, the delegation, the camarilla, the nationalities, and since we like to have as many enemies as possible, we have added the Germans, the Russians and the Croats into the mix. Then suddenly, it turns out that all these grievances were based on a misunderstanding, since the real cause of every problem was to be found exclusively in the Talmud, the Schulchan Aruch, matzos, payots, challah, and cholent."[69]

Equally sardonic was his reaction to the continuing efforts of contemporary Jewish scholars to provide incontrovertible proof of Hungarian Jews' historic roots and longstanding identification with the nation. One such effort—based on the supposed connections between the prehistoric Magyars and the Jewish tribe of the Khazars—drew the following skeptical assessment from Seiffensteiner: "That Dr. Kohn, our rabbi, has just discovered that Árpád's mother was a Khazar Jewess. And he hopes that this discovery will advance the cause of Hungarian Jewry and stop the cholera of anti-Semitism. Strange idea! Jesus Christ himself was Jewish and it has been of no help to us at all!"[70]

The characteristic technique that Seiffensteiner developed for reflecting on the anomalies of anti-Semitism was a kind of absurdist humor that was frequently associated with the issue of ritual murder. It involved the ironic appropriation of the accusation by symbolically performing the role of ritual murderer in the realm of everyday life. A typical example of such black jokes was the question posed by Spitzig's young son about why the Passover matzo had no taste that year. The answer was that the Jewish community had been unable to find a young Hungarian girl to slaughter and was forced to make do with the blood of an old Czech woman. Another illustration was Seiffensteiner's explanation for the advantages of remaining Jewish in face of the option to convert: "I was asked recently whether I would consider converting. I answered I would be crazy to do such a dumb thing. Now at least I know that the Jewish butcher will leave my daughters alone, but if they were to become Christian girls, then they would probably be in danger of being slaughtered by him."[71] Twenty years after the events of Tiszaeszlár, traces of such grim joking were still to be found in Ágai's personal correspondence. In a letter to the famous actress Mari Jászai, Ágai presented a gift of cholent, apparently the culinary specialty of his wife, with the explanation that the dish had become the ritual food of the Jews ever since the slaughter of Christian girls had become outlawed in Hungary.[72]

The ironic self-presentation of Jews in the roles of ritual murderers betrays many of the characteristics of *Judenwitz*, which was also based on the creative appropriation of hostile or unfavorable stereotypes. The purpose of these jokes, however, was inherently polemical. They mobilized a cognitive technique that Arthur Koestler called "bisociation," which juxtaposed two different logical codes or types of behavior, or conversely, presented the same situation through "two self-consistent, but habitually incompatible frames of reference."[73] For Koestler, the process of bisociation was the unique precondition for all creativity and originality, allowing existing reality to be reimagined in radically new ways. The technique, however, was also suited for the production of absurdist humor, in which the world of common sense is presented through the distorted fantasy of political paranoia. The implicit assumption behind these jokes was the transposition of anti-Semitic claims into a different social or cultural context in order to expose their flawed logic or incompatibility with reality. The cultural performance of bisociation redirected anti-Semitic aggression back to its source, deliberately using role reversal in order to deliver a moral or political indictment.

One of the most extended uses of this technique was a curious counter-narrative about ritual murder published in the midst of the popular violence that erupted after the Jews of Tiszaeszlár were pronounced innocent of ritual murder in August 1883.[74] The story, whose protagonist was Salamon Seiffensteiner, took place in Palestine, where Jews, including Seiffensteiner, had settled and now constituted the majority surrounding a tiny Christian minority. The ritual murder accusation in the story unfolded as a mirror image of the Tiszaeszlár case in Hungary. It was the Christian minority that was accused of crucifying a Jewish girl, Moczele, to "celebrate the resurrection of Christ with mysterious rituals."[75] The fomenters of the violence against the Christians were called the "Anti-Christian League" rather than the "Anti-Semitic League," and they were led by the disreputable Kobi Blau, transformed into the demagogic editor in chief of the anti-Christian *Jeruzsálemi Függetlenség* (Jerusalem independence), modeled on the major anti-Semitic Hungarian journal *Függetlenség* (Independence).

The Jewish authorities in Jerusalem proved to be as inapt in suppressing the anti-Christian mob as the Hungarians were in suppressing the anti-Semitic crowds. Börzeviczy, in the role of the minister of justice, indulged in his usual witticisms; the mayor of Jerusalem, his Excellence Karolojos,[76] was busy with affairs of protocol; and the head of the police made excuses that he could do nothing until official orders were issued. Under the circumstances, it devolved on Seiffensteiner to address the angry mob and to speak on behalf of the persecuted Christians. His words echoed the normative discourse of the contemporary Jewish press. "Dear brothers!" he began his speech. "In the holy name of Jehovah, I implore you not to listen to the promptings of evil instigators; do not allow yourselves to be seduced by racial hatred and destructive appeals against our fellow Christian citizens. (Clamor.) Remember, my brothers, that in the dark days of the not too distant past, we too were subject to accusations of such terrible crimes. Do not, therefore, be hasty in bringing charges against the Christians. (Noise. Down with the philo-Christian!) But are the Christians not similar to us? . . . Why should they not be loyal citizens of the nation in whose midst they make their lives?"[77] Just as Seiffensteiner was about to be lynched by the outraged mob, he woke up in Budapest to the concerned voice of Itzig Spitzig, who happened to be visiting and decided to wake his brother-in-law from what was obviously a nightmare. "Thank you, Itzig," Seiffensteiner responded. "You did well to wake me. What a strange world! When I am awake, anti-Semites want to beat me to death; when I am asleep, anti-Christians want to do the same thing."[78]

This rather obvious morality tale raises intriguing questions about the function of humor in times of social and political crisis. Who was the target audience of this narrative and what was its likely effect? It was obviously not Jews but the vast majority of Hungarian society that needed to be persuaded of the injustice and absurdity of the Tiszaeszlár accusation. It is questionable, however, how many of this potential audience were likely to change their attitudes toward ritual murder after reading the story. In the case of convinced anti-Semites, the task was obviously hopeless. Among moderate observers, the urgency of the appeal was also likely to be lost. Average educated Hungarians were more likely to get their information about the Tiszaeszlár affair from popular magazines, tabloids, and political journals than from *Borsszem Jankó*. For most, the events of Tiszaeszlár appeared as a sensational crime story and murder mystery, rather than the site of an unprecedented political threat. The major illustrated family magazine, *Vasárnapi Újság* (Sunday magazine), for instance, regularly reported on the Tiszaeszlár trial in an objectivist spirit without the hint of didacticism. These reports suspended judgment on the political implications of the affair, which was presented as part of a broader cultural world of likely interest to the average reader. Reports of the ritual murder trial were included with society gossip, vignettes about the doings of Europe's royal families, information about world's fairs, and insights into the lives of cultural celebrities like Victor Hugo.[79]

Salamon Seiffensteiner's hypothetical tale of ritual murder in Palestine would hardly have made much of an impact on this larger public that it hoped to reach. This is hardly surprising, since moral and political suasion were never an integral part of the original project of *Borsszem Jankó*. Its true purpose was cultural and symbolic, rather than practical and political. As Freud pointed out, humor stands outside the reality principle; its true function is to express human desire and libido, rather than change the empirical world. Yet in the very act of helping deflate the pressures of the social and political worlds, humor did in the end create alternate cultural conditions that made possible the relatively harmonious coexistence of a multi-ethnic and multicultural society. For Jews, increasingly besieged by the aggressive forces of ethnic nationalism, *Judenwitz* provided not only a form of cultural inclusion but also a model for personal behavior in an inhospitable world.

5

The Scandal of the
Budapest Orpheum

Budapest and the Orpheum

In 1873 modern Budapest was born out of the unification of three ancient municipalities—Pest, Buda, and Óbuda—into a single metropolis spanning both sides of the Danube. The humor magazine *Borsszem Jankó* marked the occasion with an appropriately celebratory caricature. It presented the newly born Hungarian capital in the guise of a beautiful young woman surrounded by a bevy of admirers, with Vienna appearing in the background as an ill-tempered dowager forced to witness the triumph of her youthful rival. The image was more complex than it seemed. Far from being an innocent expression of urban pride, it was also a witty reformulation of official visions of identity that could have been pleasing neither to the Hungarians nor to the Austrians. On the one hand, it transformed the heroic narrative of Hungarian nationalism into a feminized melodrama of urban rivalry; on the other, it challenged the image of Habsburg power by symbolically inverting the relationship of center and periphery and ranking upstart Budapest above imperial Vienna.

The dialectically linked figures of the flirtatious cocotte and the dour matron had cultural rather than political implications and enjoyed a long, subterraneous history in European popular literature. They were tropes of urban parody reaching back to the Paris of the 1830s when the mass-circulation newspaper and the rise of commercial publishing first challenged established cultural norms and traditions.[1] The contrast between sexual appeal and boring respectability became rhetorical tools in the culture wars between commercial and canonical art, popular and elite culture,

"Niece and aunt." Allegory of Budapest and Vienna in 1873. Published in *Borsszem Jankó* (August 3, 1873). Petőfi Literary Museum.

modernity and tradition, in which the former was automatically presumed to triumph over the latter. *Borsszem Jankó's* use of this highly charged symbol to celebrate the unification of Budapest was more than coincidental. It was an implicit challenge to the preeminence of Vienna in the name of a more youthful, more dynamic, more truly modern urban culture that had the power to captivate contemporaries.

No one could have predicted in 1873 how successful the challenge would be. In the course of the final quarter of the nineteenth century, Budapest rapidly developed into a vibrant metropolis that found itself in implicit competition with both the imperial culture of Vienna and the political traditions of the Hungarian nobility. The modernity of fin-de-siècle Budapest found expression not so much in its innovative art scene as in its dynamic commercial life and its exuberant embrace of popular culture.[2] It had a brash entrepreneurial spirit that caused contemporary observers to remark—not necessarily in a complimentary spirit—that the city resembled an American rather than a Central European metropolis. By 1892, when Budapest was formally declared the co-capital of the Dual Monarchy, its identity as the cultural other of Vienna had become firmly established.

The phenomenon found light-hearted commentary on the pages of popular urban texts, feuilletons, caricatures, and music hall skits. As an 1896 guidebook to the city ironically proclaimed, Budapest had triumphed over Vienna, if not in the beauty of its historic squares and palaces, then certainly in the liveliness and modernity of its nightlife. The article contrasted the youthful energy of Budapest with the stuffy conservatism of Vienna and alerted prospective tourists to very different types of urban pleasures that awaited them in the two cities. Vienna, it pointed out, closed down at nightfall and provided the delights of peaceful sleep, uninterrupted from 10:00 in the evening till 8:00 in the morning. Budapest, by contrast, presented a frenetic scene of urban revelry and subversive entertainment that continued unabated from midnight until dawn. "Even we Budapestians," the author confided, "have to go to Vienna if we want to get an honest-to-good night's sleep. We are the virtual slaves of our nightlife. We maintain without the slightest irony that we go to Vienna to sleep, and the Viennese come to us to have fun."[3]

These claims, though slightly exaggerated, were not without substance. In the decades between 1880 and 1914, Budapest became famous for its edgy music halls, opulent Orpheums, and titillating all-night coffee houses, which were widely admired and emulated throughout Central Europe. According to the tongue-in-cheek remark of Adolf Ágai, the editor of *Borsszem Jankó*, the Orpheum was fast becoming Hungary's national symbol abroad, displacing such historical icons as "Petőfi, Tokai wine, and Hungarian horses."[4] Nighttime entertainment was more than a tourist attraction or a source of urban distraction. It came to define the very meaning of modern experience and identity in Budapest. The music hall stage was the public forum where the transformative energies of metropolitan life were crystallized, performed, and made visible to a newly constituted urban public. Writing in the 1920s, by which time the golden age of music hall was over, one of its comic stars confirmed the centrality of music hall for the age. The city itself, he reminisced, had become "an enormous Orpheum, with beautiful women, third-rate popular dives, and café chantants featuring sparkling talents. The streets resounded with the sound of Orpheum hits and Viennese waltzes. In those days, our magnificent Pest was truly one gigantic Orpheum."[5]

Official Hostility to the Orpheum

One of the many paradoxes of the world of Budapest commercial entertainment is its disappearance from collective historical memory. No legends survive about its larger-than-life stars and comic personalities. No museum exhibitions celebrate its colorful and innovative programming. No commemorative planks remind urban strollers of where the sites of music halls had been. The very existence of music hall culture seems to have been erased from canonical narratives of the city. If discussed at all, music hall is treated as a minor subfield of theater history or as a curious episode of Jewish lower-middle-class life. In either case, it remains divorced from the larger story of Budapest itself.[6] The once vibrant world of Budapest music hall survives only in the hundreds of boxes of playbills, advertisements, photographs, and sheet music preserved in the archives of the National Széchényi Library on Castle Hill.

The lack of public recognition of what had been one of Central Europe's most innovative entertainment industries cries out for explanation. Part of the answer undoubtedly lies in the orientation of Hungarian historiography, which remains hostile, or at best indifferent, to the manifestations of popular culture, especially when they appeared in such problematic form as music hall.[7] Ultimately, however, the erasure of music hall as a legitimate form of cultural activity was not the work of historians but of contemporaries themselves, whose relationship to the phenomenon was characterized by profound and unresolved ambivalence.

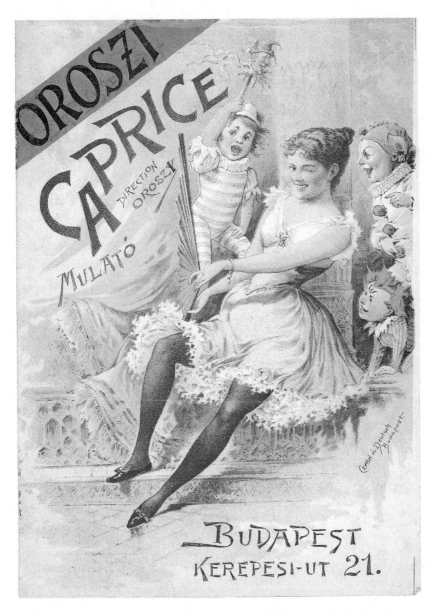

Playbill for the Folies Caprice music hall. Courtesy of Collection of Theater History at Hungarian National Széchényi Library.

Playbill for the Somossy Orpheum. Courtesy of Collection of Theater History at Hungarian National Széchényi Library.

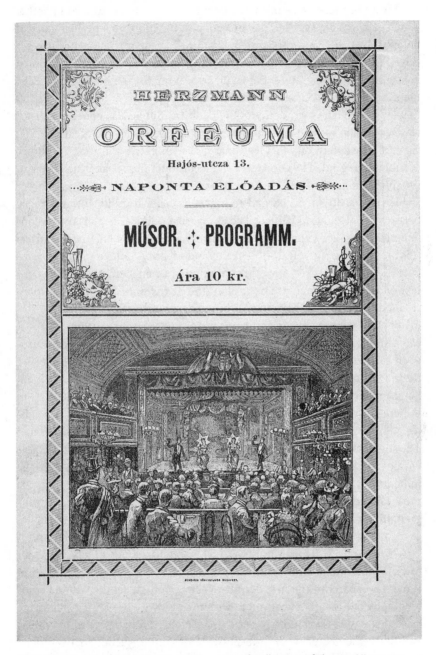

Playbill for the Herzmann Orpheum. Courtesy of Collection of Theater History at Hungarian National Széchényi Library.

This ambivalence was in marked contrast to attitudes toward operetta, which first made its appearance in Budapest in 1860 with a performance of Offenbach at the Nemzeti Szinház (National Theater).[8] The genre was received with immediate enthusiasm by the general public and with qualified approval by official culture. Pál Gyulai, speaking for the literary establishment, acknowledged that operetta was a popular form of the dramatic arts that lay outside the boundaries of high culture. But he also conceded that it was acceptable so long as it did not try to compete with the great national classics. The condition of its legitimacy, he elaborated, was that "its choice of subjects be guided by good taste and its productions speak in accord with the spirit and taste of general Hungarian culture."[9]

In contrast to such guarded tolerance, official hostility toward music hall was vocal and unqualified. The Hungarian political establishment condemned the capital's entertainment industry as alien to Hungarian historical traditions and dangerous to the health and identity of the nation. So compromised was the very topic of music hall that when it emerged in the context of a parliamentary debate in 1891, the prime minister, Gyula Szapári, rejected the subject as beyond the "bounds of good taste."[10] The pariah status of the Budapest music hall appeared unprecedented to entertainment professionals, who were in a position to compare the situation to other European cities. As an editorial of the European entertainment journal *Internationale Artisten-Revue* declared in 1891, "In no metropolis on the continent do authorities put such pressure on music halls and variety theaters as in Budapest. We can state without any exaggeration that the industry is subjected here to more draconian taxation measures than any other business."[11] The stigma of writing for music hall was so great that it prevented reputable writers and journalists from even acknowledging their affiliation with the industry. "It is well known," wrote a Budapest music hall journal, "that the most talented members of the younger literary generation write the programming of the Orpheum. And yet, when they take their place at the tables of the newspaper editorial offices, their pens turn against the Orpheum."[12]

A surprising voice in the litany of complaints about official attitudes toward commercial entertainment was that of Endre Nagy, the inventor of Budapest cabaret in the first decade of the twentieth century. In his autobiography of his early engagement with the avant-garde genre, Nagy made clear that cabaret was not spared the social ostracism reserved for music hall. He remembered with bitterness the deafening silence that the daily press maintained toward his enterprise, which night after night drew full houses and enthusiastic audiences. Cabaret, he observed, "with its innovative programming and satirical reviews," may have been the talk of the town, but "not a word was published about it in the newspapers." There were some papers where "preliminary diplomatic negotiations" were necessary even for the privilege of placing paid advertisements. No amount of success, he concluded, could change official distrust of cabaret, which "always carried on its forehead the badge of shame associated with its origins."[13]

Nagy was tantalizingly vague about the nature of the "badge of shame" that branded cabaret, but for contemporaries the reference would have been transparent. The problem with cabaret was its close association with music hall and with the Jewish lower middle classes whose ranks supplied most of the audiences, proprietors, managers, writers, and performers of these venues.[14] The physical location of the entertainment industry was itself sufficient to identify its ethnic and religious origins. As a contemporary entertainment journal helpfully hinted, Budapest music halls were situated in an identifiable urban space bounded by "the Andrássy Avenue, the Erzsébet Boulevard, and the Kerepesi Avenue, whose streets were almost as lively by night as by day."[15] It was common knowledge, of course, that these streets formed the heart of the Terézváros, whose population was three-quarter Jewish and amounted to roughly 150,000 inhabitants by the turn of the century. The major thoroughfare of the neighborhood, Király Street, was the center of the industry, with innumerable music halls lining its narrow sidewalks and adjourning streets.

Anti-Semites were less oblique in spelling out the Jewish character of commercial entertainment. Right-wing students regularly demonstrated against music halls in the Terézváros, in order, as they put it, "to safeguard the honor and reputation of the fatherland."[16] Their moral, aesthetic, and patriotic objections invariably centered on the language of performance in these places, since Budapest music hall was still exclusively German at the fin de siècle. "The Folies Caprice," wrote a typical critique in 1904, "is a hornet's nest of disgusting German jokes. . . . This place of spiritual corruption daily spews forth the poison that is eagerly absorbed by the deluded masses in their search for amusement. Despite the patriotic efforts of a few admirable artists, Hungarian entertainment is overwhelmed by the mass production of German indecencies. The regrettable result is that the tourists who flock to the Folies leave Budapest with the impression that they had witnessed the production of genuine Hungarian culture in the dens of the Révay Street."[17]

So serious was the language issue in popular entertainment that in 1895, the minister of the interior issued an ordinance requiring all commercial venues to perform at least 50 percent of their programming in Hungarian.

Music halls complied with the formal language requirement by beginning their programming two hours earlier with a special Hungarian performance, and continuing at 8:00 p.m. in German, which was the everyday language of Budapest Jews.[18] Only by the first decade of the twentieth century, with the emergence of a new generation of urban Jews equally at home in Hungarian and German, did the language of Budapest nighttime entertainment finally change to Hungarian. Whether performed in German or Hungarian, however, the fact remained unchanged that popular entertainment was considered beyond the bounds of national culture.

The Jewish-identified entertainment industry presented a problem not only for Hungarian officialdom but also for the city's upwardly mobile Jewish middle classes. On one level, the often crude, sexually explicit, invariably lower-class world of music hall threatened Jewish aspirations to respectability and social legitimacy. More disturbing still were the explicitly Jewish themes and jargon performances of music hall, which clashed with assimilated Jewry's desire to erase all signs of ethnic or religious difference. On another level, however, music hall, with its irreverent gestures and spirit of parody, was a source of irresistible attraction to middle-class Jews. It reflected the conflicts of the Jewish social experience, offering a safe place for articulating, amplifying, and laughing at the paradoxes of assimilation. The comic characters of music hall, often drawn from familiar Jewish social types, offered a source of temporary community and secret identification for middle-class audiences struggling to live up to external cultural expectations. Jewish difference, when stylized and performed on stage, was not only safe but often exhilarating. Under the circumstances, Budapest Jews responded to music hall culture with unacknowledged inconsistency: they privately patronized it and publicly condemned it. Their unresolved attitudes were reflected in the official Jewish press, which remained mostly silent on the entire subject. One of the rare articles to comment on the topic singled out music hall's jargon performances for criticism. Such performances, it commented, typically appealed to anti-Semites, who saw their own negative stereotypes reinforced, or to unassimilated Jews, who recognized their own early experiences in the shows. In either case, these spectacles were harmful or, at best, lacking any redeeming cultural value. They were the simple-minded amusements of "cultural neophytes, who sought only games and distraction, rather than genuine cultural experience."[19]

Entertainment professionals, recruited almost exclusively from the Jewish lower-middle classes, responded to the hostile environment with caution and discretion. Shrewd businessmen, they implicitly acknowledged the climate of disapproval surrounding their enterprise, but they attempted to present it in as favorable light as possible. Their first publication, the *Mulatók Lapja* (Journal of carousers), came out in 1890 with identical Hungarian and German texts printed side by side on the same page. A decade later, the journal was succeeded by the more ambitious *Mulató Budapest* (Carousing Budapest), which was written entirely in Hungarian. The immediate objective of these publications was the practical task of providing useful information about the times and places of music hall programming in the city. Inevitably, however, they also acted as mediators between the entertainment industry and its public. They avoided all claims to serious aesthetic merit or cultural value in explaining their enterprise to their readers. The goal of commercial entertainment, the founder of *Mulatók Lapja* explained in his opening editorial, was nothing more serious than to "banish people's troubles, to drive away their gloom, to entertain the audience and amuse the reader."[20] The same minimalist program characterized the public position of Károly Somossy, possibly the most flamboyant Orpheum proprietor of the age. Linking music hall to the challenges of urban life, Somossy proposed that his sole mission was to provide "nighttime entertainment to a mass audience, physically and mentally fatigued by the daily work of the modern metropolis." While amusement was the primary function of music hall, Somossy did point to its possible benefits. He suggested that the acrobatic performances and artistic spectacles presented on the stage of the Orpheum had the potential to awaken in the audience an interest in the perfection of the body and the refinement of their taste.[21]

Such normalizing discourses successfully sidestepped the social and ideological stigma surrounding music hall, but they failed to shed light on the true complexity and actual function of the phenomenon. One needs to turn to the informal reminiscences of contemporaries in order to understand the centrality of music hall for the life of the city. The following charming anecdote evokes the spontaneous, everyday relationship of the Jewish lower-middle classes to the music halls in their neighborhood. "After supper," the writer recounts, "the typical citizen of Pest [code name for the urban Jew] takes his wife by the arm, possibly brings along the children as well, and they all head toward the Mandel music hall. They stand and stroll in front of the restaurant, listening to the songs streaming through the open windows. In this way, they are able to enjoy the show for free without being obliged to shell out the twenty pennies for the entrance fee."[22]

By all accounts, the appeal of music hall extended well beyond the narrow streets of the Terézváros. Fans converged on the neighborhood from Prague, Vienna, and Graz, often heading to their favorite music hall directly from the train station.[23] The Hungarian provincial nobility also made regular trips to Budapest to sample the offerings of the capital's notorious nightlife. Such excursions included, we are told, an obligatory visit "to the Folies Caprice in order to laugh at the greatest comic of the age, the 'little Rott.' They also involved the enjoyment of the most up-to-date crop of German and Jewish jokes, to be recounted at the county casino at home; and the mastering of the latest dance step, the shimmy . . . which was performed at the local ball of the ladies' auxiliary."[24]

Aristocratic patronage of music hall was also a common practice and famously illustrated by the example of the Blaue Katze, a notorious establishment on Király Street, which counted among its clients not only the local inhabitants of the neighborhood but also an assortment of aristocrats and members of the nobility. "The guests arrived in innumerable elegant carriages," remembered a contemporary. "The Prince of Wales (later Edward VII) came in strict incognito, along with the Archduke Rudolf, Count Pista Károlyi, Miklós Szemere, and a whole company of aristocrats who were all in love with the two famous songstresses, Fraulein Frici Edelweiss and Jeanette Waldau. These ladies caroused with their illustrious guests from dusk to dawn. The owner of this famous night spot was a man called Katzer, hence the name, 'Blaue Katze.'"[25]

These random examples of music hall lore do not, of course, provide a coherent image or convincing analysis of nighttime entertainment in Budapest. The frugal Jewish couple that identified music hall with the catchy tunes overheard on street corners was one kind of music hall consumer. The county gentry that approached music hall as an object of urban pleasure and conspicuous consumption was yet another type. And the eccentric aristocrat, who patronized music hall in the spirit of upper class slumming, was still another. None of these examples are definitive. They do, however, illustrate the diversity of audiences and the variety of cultural meanings associated with the phenomenon. They suggest that there is no single overarching narrative to explain the simultaneous attraction and uneasiness provoked by music hall.

Unlike the coffee house, which appeared to contemporaries as an unproblematic source of urban sociability, the resonances of music hall seemed more ambiguous and troubling. Critiques invariably pointed to the vulgarity

Playbill for the Blaue Katze music hall. Courtesy of Collection of Theater History at Hungarian National Széchényi Library.

and immorality of music hall, whose programming was sexually explicit and whose premises were not infrequently sites of formal and informal prostitution. The scandal of music hall, however, went deeper than its associations with urban low life. The institution implicitly challenged both national ideals and bourgeois norms by reconstituting the very nature of modern experience and identity in the metropolitan setting. The fact that this challenge was invariably associated with the Jewish presence in the city only helped deepen and exacerbate the conflict, lending it a distinctly political and ideological charge it did not have in other European capitals.

Indeed, Budapest music hall needs to be understood as simultaneously playing a cultural, as well as a political, role in the life of the fin-de-siècle city. It became, first and foremost, the source and symbol of a distinct kind of cosmopolitan modernity that transformed the very fabric of metropolitan life and affected all layers of the population. It was also, however, a specific instrument of Jewish self-fashioning that ultimately provided alternative paths to assimilation and collective identity for Budapest secular Jews. These two strands of the story were obviously inseparable and experienced as part of the same reality. Nevertheless, they have different implications and outcomes and are best told separate from each other. For this reason, the following attempt to recuperate the erased history of Budapest music hall will be of necessity fragmented and mosaic-like. It will start with an external, institutional approach to the commercial features of music hall; move on to an internal, theoretically based analysis of the music hall experience itself; and conclude with the specifically cultural-ideological exploration of the issues that music hall raised for fin-de-siècle Budapest Jewry.

The Commercial and Public Functions of Music Hall

Music hall lacked a general cultural theory or a coherent articulation of its complex relationship to metropolitan life. The institution enacted its transgressive project through the seemingly trivial gestures of popular culture and everyday life, whose deeper meanings were often hidden from the participants themselves. At its most general level, music hall was an early manifestation of commercial mass entertainment, which created socially and culturally new forms of amusement for urban populations. Nineteenth-century critics of music hall like the Goncourt brothers already realized its revolutionary social implications for the future. Writing in 1860 about the Eldorado, one of the grand *café-chantants* that sprang up in Haussmann's Paris, they remarked: "Social life is going through a great evolution, which is just beginning. I see women, children, household, families, in this café. The interior is passing away. Life turns back to become public. The club for those on high, the café for those below, that is what society and people are come to."[26] Though the Goncourts were hesitant to specify the implications of the transformations they were witnessing, their intuitive sense was that the new trends posed an equal challenge to the conventions of bourgeois domesticity as well as to high culture as exemplified in the traditions of the concert hall and the theater. They were not wrong in these assumptions.

Music hall programming was unabashedly popular, consisting of musical, acrobatic, and humorous numbers meant to provide amusement and entertainment to even uneducated people. Equally striking was the heterogeneity of music hall audiences, which were drawn from all layers of the population. In places like the Mandel music hall, for instance, it appears that members of the nobility could easily find themselves seated next to market women, shop assistants, and office clerks.[27] The Folies Caprice was also notorious for its mixed audiences, attracting "members of the National Casino along with rag-pickers from the Dob Street."[28] The social promiscuity of music hall was reflected in its ideology, which was self-consciously democratic and inclusive. Entertainment journals like *Mulatók Lapja* and *Mulató Budapest* expressly appealed to people of modest means, who were promised access to the journal and the music hall experience for the modest price of a subscription or an entrance ticket.

Perhaps just as important was the frankly commercial nature of these venues, which were run as business enterprises and were literally extensions of the bustling commercial life of the streets outside their premises. This fact was graphically illustrated in the physical layout of the music hall playbills, whose pages were saturated with advertisements for consumer goods. Ads for gloves, underwear, furniture, home remedies, even birth control devices, competed for attention on the title pages of music hall playlists, appearing at times to jostle the featured performances off the page. Music hall proprietors made no pretense of distinguishing between their cultural offerings and ordinary commercial consumption.

The interchangeability of culture and consumption was symbolized by the universal practice of serving food and drink during music hall performances. The tradition was a reminder that music hall had its roots in the humble neighborhood restaurant or coffee house, where itinerant singers and entertainers were hired by the owner to entertain guests and presumably increase the consumption of food and alcohol in particular.[29] The potential conflict between these two aspects of music hall was always a problem and was to increase exponentially as the entertainment portion grew in complexity and sophistication. The 1910 playbill of the Friedman Orpheum explicitly acknowledged the conflict by requesting that the audience pay for its food and drink during the intermission in order to minimize the disturbance of the performance on stage. For the same reason, the playbill further recommended that doctors and other professionals who might be called away during the performance should leave the number of their table or lodge with the ticket office so that they might be contacted with the least amount of disruption.[30]

In the case of cabaret, the symbolic tensions between food consumption and artistic respectability reached a breaking point. Endre Nagy recounts in his autobiography his outrage when his cabaret was forced to perform in the restaurants of provincial hotels during a humiliating summer tour on the countryside. On returning to Budapest, he took the unprecedented step of removing from his theater all the small tables around which audiences were accustomed to have food and drinks served during the performances. The attempt to transform cabaret into an avant-garde theater proved a failure, however, and cabaret remained in popular imagination an integral part of the popular entertainment scene of the capital.[31]

The commercial imperatives of music hall ownership also explain the tremendous variety of its venues, which ranged from the simple neighborhood *zengeri* or *chantant*, through the sophisticated variété theater, all the way to the opulent Orpheum and the avant-garde cabaret. A characteristic example of the low end of music hall was the Wekerle, a small, family-run establishment where the owner-director was responsible for the musical and acrobatic numbers while the wife supervised the kitchen. The place was not only intimate but could also become raucous, especially if the performance on stage did not meet the approval of the audience. On one such occasion, an acrobatic team called the Goldstein Brothers displeased the audience, which initially responded with icy silence, then with boos, and finally with the hurling of sausage casings, onions, and beer bottles at the unfortunate performers. The conclusion was a disaster: "The Goldsteins fled, the curtain fell, and an embarrassed silence ensued."[32]

Perhaps even more typical of such modest establishments was the Imperial, one of the oldest *chantants*, "where wandering singers and other veterans of the stage" presented Jewish jargon performances. Characteristic of the Imperial, wrote one contemporary account, was the performance of Jewish jokes and humorous religious references, which were not always fully comprehensible to the audience. That is why, it seems, Saturday nights were the most interesting times to attend, "because then experts in religious lore are out in full force and are able to understand and interpret the intricacies of this kind of humor, which often leave the amateur mystified."[33] As this revealing aside suggests, the Imperial's mainly Jewish audiences were no longer familiar with the technical details of religious writing and practice and needed the help of "experts" to translate their meaning.

For this reason, Yiddish performances by professional traveling troops were always considered a separate genre and were judged by distinct criteria of their own. Such performances were highly popular among audiences and particularly valued by intellectuals, who regarded them as unalloyed forms of Jewish folklore, artistically superior to the typical commercial programming of music halls. Adolf Ágai considered the Yiddish theater as "genuine works of art," characterized by "trained and pleasant musical numbers, accurate performance style, and farces that even in their exaggeration are made appealing by their wit, humor, and grace."[34] Pepi Littman, the charismatic Yiddish singer who performed in drag as a Hasidic man, was one of the most popular stars of prewar music hall, appreciatively reviewed by modernist critics such as Ignotus.[35]

The true vernacular of Budapest music hall was not Yiddish but the characteristic *Juden-Deutsch* of everyday life, which found humorous exaggeration and parodic distortion in music hall performances. The acknowledged innovator of the genre of Jewish humor was the Folies Caprice, which was unquestionably the most artistically ambitious and respected Jewish satirical review in Budapest. The brainchild of Antal Oroszi, a former bookkeeper who had become enamored of the creative possibilities of music hall parody, the Folies Caprice featured such spoofs of classical theatrical pieces as "Jokel Gerger," "Cyrano de Berger Jakab," and "Romeo Kohn and Julia Lewy." Oroszi was not only a talented author of Jewish burlesque but also a brilliant talent scout who was able to recruit to his company some of the outstanding actors and comics of the age.

The Folies Caprice's most important asset was unquestionably Sándor Rott, who was generally recognized as the greatest comic artist of his age. The avant-garde Viennese critic Karl Kraus referred to him with respect, but he was equally appealing to popular audiences, who flocked to see his famous interpretations of the "the figure of the little Jewish proletarian."[36] Though frequently compared to Charlie Chaplin, Rott's stage persona had a distinct quality that unmistakably reflected a Central European Jewish stereotype. He performed the role of the archetypal outsider "who scandalizes his environment with his amazing and conscious turpitudes, but also projects the joy and pleasure of having managed to outwit the world."[37] Rott's reputation transcended the world of Jewish music hall. Prestigious drama instructors from the national theater sent their students to the Folies in order to observe and learn from the technique of the great comic. Given the scandalous reputation of the place, however, this professional advice could only be made unofficially and in strict confidence. Both students and teachers made the trip to the Folies "with their collars symbolically turned up, incognito."[38]

The most opulent example of commercial entertainment in Budapest was the Somossy Orpheum, which first opened its doors in 1894. The Somossy did its best to emulate the upscale review theaters of London and Paris and transplant their features to Budapest. Like its models, the Somossy combined "material luxury, sexual license, and cultural hybridity" in a dazzling array of experimental programming directed mostly at wealthy male patrons.[39]

Sándor Rott. Courtesy of Collection of Theater History at Hungarian National Széchényi Library.

In the words of the contemporary urban chronicler Gyula Krúdy, "this was the one place where one felt for the first time the genuinely metropolitan character of Budapest. . . . The establishment had a virtually transformative impact on the old city, whose nightlife was still stuck in the debaucheries of the old 'Blaue-Katze'"[40]

The Etablissement Somossy, as it was called, actually consisted of two interconnected public spaces: the coffee house and the theater, which fulfilled different functions in the increasingly elaborate rituals of nighttime entertainment. The theater, with its attached winter garden on the second floor, was the place where the Orpheum reviews were performed before an audience of 1,400 people. It brought to Budapest an international cast of entertainers, including stars such as Yvette Guilbert, Paulus, La Belle Otero, Armond Ary, and the famous Barrison sisters, as well as local attractions, such as Carola Cecilia.[41] After midnight, following the Orpheum show, guests could continue their nighttime revelry in the coffee house facing the street, where they were entertained by the famous gypsy band of Lajos Munczy and served champagne, cognac, and caviar by glamorous hostesses in evening gowns.[42]

The owner-direct of this entertainment palace was Károly Somossy, who had started his career as Carl Singer in a shabby coffee house on the outskirts of town. The establishment was immortalized in József Kiss's *Mysteries of Budapest* as a notorious gathering place for criminals and prostitutes.[43] By the time of the creation of the Somossy Orpheum, its owner had changed not only his name but also his outward appearance. Somossy become an arbiter of taste and elegance in Budapest, famous for the cut of his suits and the extravagance of his champagne suppers. Krúdy, ever sensitive to the nuances of the urban scene, provided possibly the most enduring encapsulation of Somossy's contribution to Budapest culture. In his view, Somossy was "the man who taught Budapest the art of carousing."[44] The true significance of Somossy's career, as Krúdy seemed to instinctively realize, lay not in his rise from rags to riches but in his ability to invent a personal style that epitomized urban worldliness. Somossy's story was ultimately about the power of aesthetic self-invention in a modern world where inherited status was no longer the sole arbiter of personal worth. He died a penniless man in 1903, but his colorful life remained a source of urban legend. The following anecdote, published in his obituary, provides a striking illustration of Somossy's famously extravagant style, as well as his subversive individualism. "It happened in the good old times," the article recounts, when Somossy had just opened his Orpheum and the young, fun-loving Jenő Zichy decided to initiate the place with a large-scale bash.[45] His bill came to 400 forints, which he handed over with an off-the-cuff remark: "This is how a Hungarian lord carouses!" A few days later, Somossy invited Zichy back for a friendly little revelry in his nightclub. The event cost Somossy the round sum of 4,000 forints. Among the many exotic dishes served up by the waiters were young girls presented on silver platters. At the end of the merry-making, Somossy addressed Zichy with the following words: "This is how Somossy carouses!"[46]

The challenge implied in Somossy's witty rebuttal was clear: in the realm of commercial entertainment, an individual with wealth and imagination could not only compete with an aristocrat but also surpass him.

The story of Somossy's challenge to Zichy may well be apocryphal, but it serves to illustrate the complex codes of engagement fostered by music hall culture. The institution was both integrative and yet subversive; it brought together individuals of different social classes and cultural affiliations in a common experience of urban spectatorship and entertainment. At the same time, it challenged existing social codes and inherited identities in a process of radical individuation. This double-edged process was spelled out in a revealing article published in *Mulatók Lapja* in 1890, which for the first time explicitly linked music hall with the creative possibilities of metropolitan life and identity. "Uprooted by the tornado of modern times," the account begins, "Hungarians generally do not know how to enjoy themselves in public places. The tavern and traditional carousing need to be replaced by new kinds of amusements, which meet the demands of an urban population of even modest means." The conveyors of modern public leisure were, of course, music halls, which ideally fostered attitudes such as "originality, spirit, cleverness, tact, good instincts, and many other characteristics; in other words, genuine talent and art." Implicit in the concept of the exemplary music hall patron was the more general idea of the discriminating consumer, whose individual creativity allowed him to choose between competing options offered by the city and thus engage in an act of aesthetic self-fashioning.[47]

The ideal of urban sophistication depicted in this article was often associated with the music hall comics (*dal komikosok*) who enjoyed celebrity status in fin-de-siècle Budapest. They provided models of personal style for a mass public eager for novelty and glamour. They inspired a whole generation of

Jewish shop assistants, office clerks, and apprentices to break from tradi-tional styles of dress and behavior and to imagine a specifically modern, urban identity. Indeed, so enticing was the music hall world that cautionary articles were published in entertainment journals, warning lower-middle-class youth of the dangers of abandoning their steady jobs for the uncertain lures of the stage.[48] In spite of such warnings, many attempted the chal-lenges of the "artistic life," and even if they did not, most tried to emulate its gestures and create themselves in the image of their idols.

The Music Hall Experience

While the broad appeal of music hall is beyond question, the nature of the music hall experience itself remains elusive and difficult to decipher. Simple

Music hall comic.
Courtesy of Collection
of Theater History at
Hungarian National
Széchényi Library.

questions such as what took place in music halls and how audiences incorporated the music hall spectacle into their daily lives prove surprisingly difficult to answer. There are a number of reasons for the challenges of interpreting the music hall experience. Unlike traditional theater, music hall programming was generally unscripted and improvised and has left few traces behind. In the absence of stable texts and sustained reviews, historians of music hall can only make conjectures about the nature of the phenomenon. They are forced to base their analyses on fragmentary sources such as the occasional music hall lyrics published in cheap editions, informal reminiscences preserved as music hall lore, and subjective autobiographical accounts recounted by performers and audiences.

Even in cases where the actual music hall texts have been preserved, however, their meanings are hardly self-evident. They resist attempts at a literal reading and provide few clues as to how audiences might have understood them. Viewed as historical sources, music hall songs and skits appear unstable, tied to the passing moment, difficult to interpret from the outside. The opacity of the music hall text is strikingly confirmed by one of the key contemporary writers of Budapest music hall, Jenő Heltai, who, from the distance of sixty years, attempted to reread the songs, poems, and plays that had made his reputation as a young man. To his consternation, he found these writings incomprehensible. "With the best of intentions," he ruefully concluded, "I was unable to see what was funny about them."[49]

Recent historians of music hall have suggested several reasons for the gap between text and meaning that Heltai encountered in his attempt to recuperate his early music hall writings. The problem with such texts is not necessarily their quality, as has often been implied by critics. The real issue is that music hall songs and sketches do not conform to the aesthetics of realism as developed by traditional theater. Music hall performances used a mode of signification that was fundamentally distinct from high culture. According to Shane Vogel, who has written about Harlem cabaret in the 1920s, the genre "does not represent the world, but addresses it in its local environment, incorporates the audience into its fold, and organizes social arrangements."[50] Peter Bailey made essentially the same point in his work on British music hall, where he argued that text and performance were inseparable from each other. Considered as text, he admitted, "the music hall song was intellectually banal, but as performance style, its levels of engagement are complex and various, at once idealized and realistic, normative and satirical."[51]

Music hall songs were by definition oblique and indirect, only hinting at truths that existed behind appearances. The elliptical style of the performer was a self-conscious device to draw the audience into the action taking place on stage. Audiences were invited to supply the missing links of the texts and thus share with the singer the authority to interpret them. The implicit identification between performer and audience was confirmed by the refrain at the end of each verse, in which the audience often joined in, thus enacting their collusion with the message being performed in the song. The choreography behind the music hall song, writes Bailey, was a kind of "transaction and coproduction," in which the audience shared in the worldliness of the performer. The audience's ability to decode the implied meanings and subtexts of the performance created "a flattering sense of membership," which was all the more intense, because "such privileged status was not so much conferred as *earned* by the audience's well-tested cultural and social competence."[52]

As these observations suggest, music hall and cabaret were more than new forms of popular entertainment. They were also alternate social spaces where audiences were enabled to define themselves as active participants in, and interpreters of, modern life. On the most obvious level, music hall gave cultural expression and legitimization to the kinds of everyday experiences and perceptions that ordinary people were likely to encounter in the city. According to one performer in the cabaret of Endre Nagy, the songs that made him famous invariably focused on the tribulations of metropolitan life that were considered too fleeting and trivial to be taken seriously by established artists and social critics. "I sang of bedbugs," he illustrated, "which even then rendered the lives of the city dweller hellish; of the unwelcome houseguest who tyrannized his hosts; of the vanity of the Budapest woman, of the miseries of subletting; and of the soothing pleasures of the steam bath."[53]

More than simply facilitating the recuperation of the everyday, music hall songs helped define a distinctly metropolitan style and sensibility. They gave expression to qualities of knowingness and worldliness that conveyed skepticism about the conventions of respectable society and official culture. Music hall lyrics were invariably risqué and titillating, light-heartedly exposing the hidden underside of modern urban life that everyone knew about but no one talked about in public. They told elliptical tales about working-class girls who end up in fancy brothels; unemployed lawyers who pray for the indefinite prolongation of their court cases; female coffee house patrons who haggle over their bills; amorous couples who sing the praises of unavailable birth-control devices; and cuckolded husbands who celebrate the birth of their newborn sons with their ever-helpful shop assistants, whose contributions to the family business extended beyond his official functions.[54]

Music hall's challenge to the respectable façade of Victorian society was made in a spirit of collusion and joviality that contained no hint of serious social or political critique. For all its light-heartedness, however, its goals and impact were both serious and far-reaching. Music hall was, in the final analysis, a revolt against moral absolutes of all kinds, including the sanctity of domestic life. The subject found characteristic expression in comic one-act plays such as one originally performed at the Folies Caprice and later published as a short story. The play is an account of marital infidelity with a happy ending. It tells the story of the beautiful twenty-year-old daughter of a textile merchant who marries a wealthy older man but continues to see her young lover, who is employed by her new husband. On giving birth to a son, she asks her happy husband to provide a raise for her lover, who is thus allowed to marry and set up a family of his own. Not only does this tale amiably repudiate the conventions of traditional family life but it also seems to flaunt its own transgression by including the seemingly gratuitous detail that the rabbi granted absolution to the actions of the adulterous couple.[55]

Music hall's challenge to the protocols of bourgeois society found possibly its most explicit formulation in a musical number performed at the Folies Caprice sometime in the first decade of the twentieth century. Titled "Without Clothes All People Appear Equal," the piece was written by Szőke Szakáll, a practiced songwriter and performer who combined caustic self-irony with acute insight into the cultural implications of his enterprise.[56] The explicit theme of the song was the essential equality of naked bodies, whose social status, sexual behavior, and cultural identity were inseparable from their clothing. The song, however, was also a sly allegory about the audiences, performers, and writers of music hall, who become interchangeable in the radical environment music hall. The first stanza establishes a metaphorical identification between the music hall with the steam bath, whose clients are equally divested of their clothes and social selves once they enter their premises:

No matter how widely I have looked,
There only exists one place in Pest,

Nowhere else have I observed it
Where rich and the poor sit side by side.
No velvet pillow will you find here, only vulgar stone.
The steam bath makes no exceptions for anyone.
Attendants deal the same with everyone
They address even beggars as a lord.
How could they dare pronounce judgment on anyone
For without clothes, all people appear the same.

The second stanza evaluates the scandalous performances of music hall stage, presented through the voyeuristic eyes of the author's little sister:

My little sister Fancsi,
Is a terribly curious child.
She peeps into the neighbor couple's window
To observe them making love.
I asked her the other day
To describe what she saw inside,
Whether it was a man or woman that she spied.
To which she only answered that she did not recognize them,
Since neither of them had their clothes on.
How could I pronounce judgment on them,
For without their clothes, all people appear the same.

The final stanza turns its wit on the author himself, exposing the anonymity and mass production of the music hall song. It is the number of his dressing room, rather than the unique qualities of his art, that ultimately identifies the writer of music hall:

The number of my dressing room is "seven,"
Whoever comes to visit,
Will find me here.
If a writer calls, he will see the number.
Without a number he will seek me in vain,
For many are the dressing rooms down here.
Useless to look into each one in a row,
No one will recognize me there, to this I can attest,
For without their clothes, all people appear the same.[57]

Szőke Szakáll's ironic celebration of the steam bath was ultimately a self-referential allegory of music hall as a distinct social institution as well as art form. This was a place, he suggested, where the conventions of the theater and high art were not only challenged but also redefined in radically unconventional ways. Here, notions of privacy were replaced by the experience of public intimacy, the habit of moral censure was suspended in the name of sexual tolerance, and the ideal of aesthetic originality was replaced by the practice of cultural mass production. Music hall's resemblances to the steam bath lay in its capacity to erase individualism and to create a temporary community of anonymous selves.

The definition of music hall in terms of the steam bath experience was hardly a new idea by the early twentieth century. In 1913 Endre Nagy used the same image to describe what he termed as the "mysterious alchemy" by which individuals were transformed into the organic mass of cabaret

Szőke Szakáll.
Courtesy of Collection of
Theater History at
Hungarian National
Széchényi Library.

or music hall audiences. "Honored ladies and gentleman!" he proclaimed in an article that was a transcription of one of his performances. "When you occupy your seats in the house in exchange for an entrance ticket, I wonder if you realize that you have entered into a kind of spiritual steam bath. The worldly clothing of your inner life has remained outside in the vestibule, and, in the thick, steamy atmosphere, you have all individually melted together into a new, unrecognizable community."[58]

The analogy between music hall and the steam bath suggests an alternate form of social experience and aesthetic practice that the contemporary cultural theorist Lauren Berlant has associated with the concept of publicly mediated intimacy. Public intimacy, she writes, was radically incompatible with traditional forms of bourgeois life, which typically divided the intimate, controllable, expressive spaces of private life from the impersonal, commercial, instrumental spaces of public action. The new symbolic style of music hall reconstituted modern experience, abolishing the stabilizing public/private taxonomy of bourgeois ideology. It challenged traditional narratives of middle-class life and opened up possibilities for new stories about self and other that were no longer defined by bourgeois family life or liberal ideology.[59]

While there seems little doubt about the subversive nature of the music hall experience itself, there is considerable disagreement among historians about the broader social and political implications of the phenomenon. Did the challenge of music hall extend beyond the world of commercial entertainment, or was it restricted to its nonserious spaces? Was music hall nothing more than a commercial enterprise, or could it be seen as an agent of deeper social and cultural change? Perhaps the most common perspective has been to associate music hall with class identity and to see it as the distinct voice of the lower-middle classes in the context of a destabilized urban culture. According to this argument, the development of late nineteenth-century capitalism brought into existence new social layers that could no longer fit the category of the bourgeois or the working class and found collective self-expression through the music hall. The art historian T. J. Clark famously articulated this position in his categorical assertion that music hall was an "instrument of class formation, and the class so constructed was the petite bourgeoisie."[60]

Yet the aesthetic and conceptual instabilities of music hall could not fully be accommodated by the logic of class analysis. "Music hall was both more and less than a class mode of expression," Peter Bailey writes, "and has

yet to be fully understood in terms of its participants' measures of significance and what its meaning was to them."[61] Viewed from the perspective of
its audiences, it appears that music hall was about not just class but also a
new kind of urban self that transcended social status. "Music hall regulars,"
Barry Faulk illustrates, "consistently prided themselves on knowing more
about the city than did novices. Music hall habitués, then, might well feel
that they alone had the real scoop on modernity; that is, they had an authen-
tic experience of vernacular culture unsullied by bourgeois conventions."[62]

Other historians have gone even further in stressing the urban character
of music hall, explicitly linking it with the project of bohemia. According to
Charles Rearick, the Montmartre music hall represented "an antidote to the
pomposity and stiff class rules that reigned elsewhere. In its dance halls and
cabarets Parisians could temporarily free themselves from the inhibitions
of everyday respectability."[63] Peter Bailey also saw an overlap between the
gestures of bohemia and music hall. Both, he points out, managed to offend
bourgeois taste by setting "play against work, heroic consumption, against
exemplary abstinence." Music hall resembled bohemia even in its final fate,
which was absorption and appropriation by mainstream culture. "By the
turn of the century," Bailey concludes, "music hall's knowingness was fast
becoming a second language for *all* classes, as music hall itself became an
agreeable national alter-ego, a manageable low other."[64]

More recently, the interpretation of music hall has been still further extended to include the redefinition of race, sexuality, and ethnicity, whose
normative narratives were frequently parodied, reversed, and destabilized
in music hall performances. As Shane Vogel writes, the intimate spaces of
cabaret and music hall offered new horizons "to imagine and enact alternative possibilities for racial, sexual, and socioeconomic subjectivities" that
resisted the normalizing pressures of mainstream culture.[65] Marline Otte
made similar claims in her study of Jewish jargon theaters and popular culture in imperial Germany. These were places, she suggests, where conflicted
identities could be negotiated and new ways of belonging to the nation explored. Indeed, it was mostly in the context of popular entertainment that
Jewish ethnic particularity could be presented and enacted without bringing into question their political loyalty to the state.[66]

The empirical examples of music hall largely confirm these interpretive
models, which simply amplify and elaborate different facets of the same phenomenon. As the case of Budapest commercial entertainment vividly illustrates, music hall was simultaneously an expression of lower-middle-class

life, metropolitan consciousness, bohemian innovation, and Jewish self-expression, without one strand separating off from the other. The exclusively Jewish identification of Budapest music hall, however, had consequences that exaggerated and politicized these functions, ultimately distinguishing it from other European urban cultures. Here, music hall could never become the "manageable low other" of dominant culture, as it did in Britain or in France, precisely because of its perceived foreign origins.

The hostility of the Hungarian political establishment to the institution of Budapest music hall has already been mentioned, and this hostility was not entirely unfounded. For despite its deliberately apolitical posture, music hall did pose a genuine threat to official articulations of national identity, especially as they found expression in the Jewish question. What made music hall particularly dangerous was the fact that it did not simply repudiate the ideological formulae of Hungarian nationalism but also offered a radical alternative to them. It helped create a new vision of self and identity no longer structured along the binaries of public and private, insider and outsider, Hungarian and Jewish. It eliminated the need to choose between these identifications for the simple reason that such choices appeared increasingly divorced from the empirical experiences of urban populations. The generation of Hungarian Jews who came of age in the 1880s and 1890s did not perceive their Jewish and Hungarian identities as in conflict with each other or in need of being harmonized. They felt rooted in Hungarian life simply as a consequence of speaking Hungarian and participating in an urban world they helped create. This new metropolitan Jewish self, however, did not come into existence by itself but was pioneered in the context of the popular music hall.

The Creation of "Eine Klabriaspartie"

A celebrated music hall skit, first produced on the stage of the Folies Caprice in 1889, provides a convenient entry point into our analysis of the cultural and political work performed by music hall. "Eine Klabriaspartie" (The card game) was the brainchild of Antal Oroszi, who had made his reputation as a producer of Jewish music hall parodies at the Folies Caprice.[67] "Eine Klabriaspartie" was, in many respects, a continuation of the tradition Oroszi helped establish. It was a satirical sketch with musical interludes that depicted the comic interactions and off-color banter of four Jewish card players in a fictional Budapest coffee house called the Café Abeles.[68] All of Oroszi's plays were successful, but this particular conception of Jewish lower-middle-class urban life created an instant sensation. Adaptations and offshoots of the play spread like wild fire, first among Budapest music halls, and then throughout Central European capitals with large Jewish populations. In Vienna, "Eine Klabriaspartie" became the signature piece of the Jewish-inflected cabaret, the Budapester Orpheum Gesellschaft, where it was performed uninterrupted for more than a quarter century.[69] In Berlin, the play became part of the repertoire of the famous Herrnfeld Theater, which specialized in jargon performances depicting humorous episodes from contemporary Jewish life.[70]

What was the seductive appeal of this seemingly trivial example of music hall buffoonery? Why did it captivate the imagination of such wide and diverse audiences? The answer is neither simple nor self-evident. As is the case with most music hall productions, it is impossible to re-create the comic impact of the actual performance. We can only speculate about the original performance at the Folies Caprice, which featured an exceptional cast of actors, including the "little Rott" in the title role of the kibitzer among the card players.[71] However, two published versions of "Eine Klabriaspartie" have fortuitously survived and provide some idea of the cultural formulae that were activated in the innumerable productions and adaptations of the skit. The first example is a Viennese transcription by Adolf Bermann, which was presumably the basis for the performances of the Budapester Orpheum Gesellschaft. The second is a revised and abridged version of the play, written by Oroszi himself, and published in 1902 in a transient humor magazine he edited.[72]

Both versions of "Eine Klabriaspartie" present emphatically Jewish characters defined by their inventive and hilarious vulgarity. In Bermann's incarnation of the skit, the card players are loud and contentious; they endlessly interrupt and contradict one another; they cheat at cards and lie about it; they secretly drink from one another's coffee cups; and when opportunity presents itself, they demonstrate their lack of respect by insulting the wife of one of the card players. In Oroszi's version, they are also associated with sexual irregularity and petty dishonesty that is ironically smoothed over at the end in a gesture of camaraderie and complicity. On the most obvious level, the clownish characters of "Eine Klabriaspartie" were reenactments of negative Jewish stereotypes whose jargon dialect and uncouth behavior immediately identified them as cultural pariahs.

The comic message of the play was inscribed into the insistently and emphatically Jewish names of the characters. At a time when the vast majority of Budapest's Jewish population was assuming Hungarian names in order to erase all signs of ethnic or religious difference, the protagonists of "Eine Klabriaspartie" flaunted their Jewish-sounding names. In fact, their names became the defining feature of their comic personae, encoding and in a sense dramatizing their Jewish identities. The play was not about individual characters but rather the quality of Jewishness itself, as perceived and defined by society at large. This explains why the names of the protagonists were freely interchanged in the various productions of "Eine Klabriaspartie." In the original Folies Caprice version, for instance, the card players were called Kohn, Lewi, Brill, and Grün; in the Viennese production, they became Dalles, Reis, Janicsek, and Dawidl; and in Oroszi's 1902 transcription they were Lewi, Maier, Stiglitz, and Grün. "Eine Klabriaspartie" was a deliberate spoof, presenting Jews through the eyes and cultural imagination of mainstream society. It ironically mirrored the cultural stereotypes of the age, which saw Jews collectively as vulgar, dishonest, and irredeemably foreign.

The transgressive implications of "Eine Klabriaspartie" lay precisely in its ability to exploit and reverse these conventional stereotypes. Through comic exaggeration, the play exposed the abstract, ideological nature of these collective images and forced both Jewish and non-Jewish audiences to confront their own complicity in perpetuating them. The satirical performance of Jewish difference on stage lifted the taboos surrounding the subject in empirical social life, creating a carnivalesque celebration of the very ambiguities associated with Jewish identity. What was ultimately at stake behind the comic conception of "Eine Klabriaspartie" was its repudiation of the very possibility of defining Jewish identity as a coherent and recognizable phenomenon. According to the logic of the play, Jewishness had no empirical content and thus the so-called Jewish question had no solution. The Jewish question could not be solved, for the simple reason that no such question existed.

This satiric attack on the Jewish question was inseparably linked to the coffee house where the card game took place. The coffee house was not simply a casual backdrop for the skit but a central organizing principle of the action itself. It was the incarnation of an alternative social and cultural space where modern Jewish experience could unfold in public without external or internal constraint. Both the Budapest and Viennese versions of the play closed with a ritualized musical number celebrating the pleasures of the card game and the coffee house, which were associated with personal freedom and camaraderie, as well as escape from the constraints of family life and politics. The message of the closing number could not have been clearer. The true context for modern Jewish identity lay not in the interior spaces of bourgeois domesticity nor in the official public realm of political life but in institutions of urban culture such as the coffee house, the boulevard, and the music hall, where a new world of personal significance and make-believe could be constructed.

For Jewish audiences who first encountered performances of "Eine Klabriaspartie," the skit appeared as a revelation but also as a potentially dangerous break from inherited constructions of Jewish identity. In his autobiographical account *From Berlin to Jerusalem*, Gershom Scholem offers insight into different ways that the play was received and interpreted by Jewish audiences. It seems that Scholem and his father had attended a performance of "Eine Klabriaspartie" at the Herrnfeld Theater in Berlin sometime in the years before World War I. Scholem's liberal father was deeply disturbed by the implications of the play, fearing that it would promote anti-Semitism. Scholem responded to these fears with the laconic comment: "as though anti-Semitism had been waiting for the Herrnfeld brothers."[73]

The conversation between father and son is revealing on many levels. It presents not just a difference of interpretation about the meaning of "Eine Klabriaspartie" but also an illustration of the gulf separating the political and cultural readings of Central European Jewish life. Gershom Scholem was right, of course, to express skepticism about the ability of any cultural production to directly influence politics. Hence his ironic comment that anti-Semites did not need scandalous Jewish self-parodies to help define their negative stereotypes of Jews. But his father was equally correct in perceiving a radical innovation in the play. What made him uneasy about the performance was not so much its subject matter—after all, self-parody was the stock-in-trade of Jewish humor—but the fact that it was performed in a public forum in front of an audience that included Jews and non-Jews. By transforming the intimate realm of social interaction into public spectacle, he intuitively understood that the play had crossed an invisible yet clearly delimited boundary. It had challenged fundamental notions of bourgeois propriety and the separation of private/public identities, on which the very project of German Jewish assimilation was founded. On its deepest level, "Eine Klabriaspartie" represented a repudiation and renegotiation of the complex notion of *Bildung* or rational self-fashioning, which, as David Sorkin and George Mosse have shown, formed the bedrock of German Jewish identity throughout the nineteenth century.[74]

For Hungarian Jews in particular, the play marked a turning point in cultural perceptions and strategies. It signaled the waning of the political hopes of the 1860s, which had sustained the project of Jewish emancipation and assimilation for almost a quarter century. The so-called emancipation contract between Jews and Hungarians had been seriously compromised by the perpetuation of social exclusion and the emergence of political anti-Semitism in the 1880s. Consciously or unconsciously, many Hungarian Jews came to the conclusion that, if there had ever been such a contract, it had effectively been broken by Hungarian society, which could never consider a Jew, no matter how assimilated and patriotic, sufficiently Hungarian to be socially acceptable. The profound disjunctions between Jewish and Hungarian cultural experiences failed to be bridged by even such positive political achievements as the Reception Law of 1895 that declared Judaism equal with the other religions of the state. Such political measures proved incapable of overcoming an incommensurability of social and political experience that divided Jews from Hungarians. The two sides were defined by paradoxical perceptions and expectations of each other that could not be resolved by mere good intentions. On the Jewish side, the paradox was that the more enthusiastically they embraced the Hungarian language and culture, the more excluded and marginalized they felt within the national community. On the Hungarian side, the paradox was that the more fully Jews accomplished the task of acculturation that constituted the condition of emancipation, the more threatening they appeared to the traditional values of Hungarian life.

For Hungarian Jewish artists and intellectuals coming of age at the fin de siècle, the never-ending ideological debates about Jewish assimilation and the Jewish question were losing relevance. They did not so much repudiate the project of assimilation as rewrite its script according to their own cultural experiences. The younger generation had internalized and been transformed by the paradoxical logic of music hall and commercial entertainment, which had destabilized essentialist notions about identity and social belonging. It had successfully appropriated the ironic discourse of difference pioneered by Jewish humorists and music hall entrepreneurs, who challenged anti-Jewish stereotypes through exaggeration and satire. In the context of metropolitan culture, a new kind of modernist, urban identity had come into existence that was no longer defined by the experience of marginality and the stigma of the outsider.

The well-heeled Jewish audiences that flocked to performances of "Eine Klabriaspartie" seemed increasingly receptive to the new perspective pioneered by commercial entertainers and radical intellectuals. In the course of the 1890s, the scandalous music hall skit became a respected cultural icon consumed by broad segments of polite society. At the same time, however, the original play underwent some transformations to fit the tastes and imaginations of the Jewish bourgeoisie that was appropriating it. A new version of the play that opened in May 1894 suggests the nature of these changes. The venue for the performance was no longer the notorious and slightly disreputable Folies Caprice but the elegant Somossy, which had traditionally kept clear of explicitly Jewish music hall numbers. The style of the play was also altered from its original form. The new version of "Eine Klabriaspartie" was performed in Hungarian rather than in German, unmistakably signaling its shift from the margins to the center of cultural life. Perhaps the most telling feature of the new performance was the identity of the actors, who had been recruited from the established stars of the National Theater rather than from the rank of the music hall comedians who had originally interpreted the play. To leave no doubt about the newfound respectability of the piece, the management self-consciously announced that the proceeds from the performance would be donated to charity. Music hall was becoming both respectable and Hungarian by the end of the century.[75]

Budapest humorists registered their mixed feelings about the phenomenon in a manner worthy of the original spirit of music hall comedy. Simultaneously with the elegant production of "Eine Klabriaspartie" at the Somossy, there appeared in the modernist literary journal *A Hét* a satirical reenactment of the play. The piece was provocatively titled "A klasszikus orfeum" (The classic Orpheum) and was an ironic commentary on the process that was transforming Jewish music hall from subversive entertainment into a midcult art form. The parody re-created the well-known scenario of the coffee house with the four card players, but this time the roles of the card players were assumed by Oroszi, the inventor of the skit, and the three original actors, including the "little Rott" who had interpreted the figures in the kibitz. The protagonists of the spoof spoke in German-Hungarian jargon, reflecting their abiding loyalty to the humble origins of music hall. The content of the play consisted of their reactions to a series of devastating news, brought by different cast members of the Folies Caprice, about the appropriation of their signature hit by more and more of the established theaters of the capital. Oroszi's initial reaction to the crisis was to respond in kind by instructing his flurried troop to steal back a characteristic production from the offending theaters. However, as news of further appropriations kept pouring in, it finally became obvious that theirs was merely a rearguard action with no chance of a successful outcome. Oroszi's final gesture was to order the waiter to prevent any more visitors from entering the coffee house and resuming the game of Kalábrias that had been interrupted by the unwelcome intrusion of the outside world.[76]

Jenő Heltai and the Creation of Metropolitan Identity

Perhaps no figure gave more nuanced expression to the new metropolitan style and persona than Jenő Heltai, one of the most beloved and prolific writers of Budapest popular entertainment. Heltai belonged to a second generation of entertainment professionals, fully at home in Hungarian and whose cultural sensibilities were already shaped by the modernist currents of the early twentieth century. He saw the trends of the new century in a new, more sophisticated, more abrasive intellectual and performance style exemplified by the avant-garde cabaret of Endre Nagy and the artistry of Yvette Guilbert. It was Guilbert's performance at the Somossy that brought Heltai to the conclusion that the music hall of the 1880s was "artistically trivial and morally unjustifiable." As he later confessed, Guilbert's electrifying performance reminded him of an invigorating northern gale that swept away all the dusty claptrap of music hall conventions, along with the "Viennese comics in white cotton gloves and cylinders, the actresses disguised as washer women, the twittering French *gameuse*, the lace-trimmed female underwear, and the gigantic fans and dazzling jewelry."[77]

Heltai's modernist commitments went hand-in-hand with the urgent desire to transform the language of Budapest popular entertainment from German to Hungarian. Indeed, Heltai was one of the leaders who spearheaded the campaign for language reform in the capital, which was accomplished in the course of the first decade of the new century. The shift from German to Hungarian has often been seen as a sign of successful Jewish assimilation and full identification with the Hungarian nation. While the interpretation correctly identifies the significance of the phenomenon, it misconstrues its causes. The underlying motivations of the language reform movement were not about national politics but rather cultural politics. For Heltai and his generation, German was the compromised idiom of the Jewish music hall and the intellectual style of the ghetto. Hungarian, by contrast, was the language of the social and intellectual elite, invariably associated with a larger and more complex world beyond the Jewish community.

Ironically, the drive to assume Hungarian as the language of modernist production in Budapest took place in the context of an increasingly xenophobic political environment that saw the language issue in narrowly nationalistic and essentialist terms. For Hungarian conservatives, the adoption of the Hungarian language by Jewish cultural innovators was suspect by definition, representing a dangerous and illegitimate appropriation of the national idiom. Indeed, the Hungarian-speaking Jewish modernists of the early twentieth century seemed to pose an even greater threat to the integrity of Hungarian culture than their German-speaking predecessors, whose lack of national credentials was at least readily identifiable. By the early twentieth century the fundamental ideological schisms of Hungarian political life had not disappeared but were actually intensified.

Jenő Heltai. Courtesy of Collection of Theater History at Hungarian National Széchényi Library.

The ominous and exclusionary implications of the language debates were not immediately obvious to Heltai and the Hungarian Jewish artists and intellectuals who came of age after 1900. Their semibohemian artistic and journalistic world seemed securely embedded in the familiar spaces of the city, which gave rise to a new kind of urban self and experience indelibly associated with Budapest. Heltai articulated the possibilities of this world in a trilogy about artistic-journalistic life in Budapest, which he published between 1897 and 1914.[78] Using the well-known conventions of bohemia, Heltai chronicled the lives and escapades of young artists and carefree journalists who spent their nights and days in coffee houses, pursued hair-brained schemes for making money, and fell in love with actresses, music hall queens, and sometimes even respectable middle-class girls, whom they occasionally even ended up marrying. Heltai's appealing portraits of Budapest bohemia were not meant to be realistic. These stories no more resembled the ordinary lives of Budapest Jews than the jargon performances of music hall. What they did show, however, was a change in cultural imagination reflecting new circumstances and experiences. Heltai's implicitly Jewish heroes no longer spoke in a comic German-Jewish dialect and they were no longer conceived in terms of the stereotypes of Jewish difference. Neither pariahs nor parvenus, they were indistinguishable from the majority of urban types one was likely to encounter on the streets of Budapest.

This new, implicitly Jewish urban culture found characteristic expression in the glossy humor magazine *Fidibusz*, which Heltai edited between 1905 and 1910. The new magazine repudiated the sharp satirical style and adversarial political gestures of *Borsszem Jankó* and gave voice to an apolitical world of urban enjoyment and personal fulfillment. The depiction of Jewish stereotypes that had been central to the cultural project of *Borsszem Jankó* seemed almost entirely absent from the light-hearted short stories and sophisticated illustrations of *Fidibusz*. At the same time, however, the urban characters that made their appearance on its pages were defined by subtle cultural codes that identified them as Jewish to a knowing reading public. In a revealing caricature, which was the only time an explicitly Jewish theme appeared in the entire history of the magazine, the hidden codes of Jewishness were unexpectedly spelled out. The cartoon depicted a husband and wife in a middle-class setting; their features clearly identified them as Jewish, but they spoke correct Hungarian and were no longer presented as grotesque stereotypes. The conversation between husband and wife revolved around the topic of converting to Christianity, a move advocated by the wife and resisted by the husband. "Convert? Why?" the husband asked. "I beg of you, people will forget and god will forgive," the wife pleaded. "But the nose will remain!" the husband countered.[79] The exchange provides an extraordinary condensation of the nature of Jewish identity in pre–World War I Budapest. Jews were no longer a stigmatized minority and Jewishness was no longer presented through negative stereotypes. Yet the sense of difference continued undiminished and, under pressure, was resurrected as a salutary reminder of the futility of all attempts to erase Jewish difference.

The caricature gave voice to the fundamental instability lurking beneath the self-confident façade of the new urban Jewish identity that came into existence in Budapest after 1900. It had not resolved the Jewish question but simply banished it from its intellectual horizons and cultural imagination. The continuing anomalies of Hungarian Jewish identity found expression in Heltai's own self-definition, which revealed an extraordinarily complex sensibility beneath the light-hearted sociability and playfulness of his official literary persona. In an autobiographical account, he provided the following contradictory portrait of his development as an artist. By background, he revealed, he was a "petty bourgeois revolutionary," who was "born to be in eternal opposition." By culture, he was an "incurable lover and loyal and adoring son" of Budapest, whose "sacred mission" had been to advance its transformation from a "German small town into a Hungarian metropolis." Finally, by vocation, he was an artist whose livelihood was defined by his immersion in the commerce of entertainment. Perhaps the striking feature of this self-portrait was its heterogeneous quality, which was composed of conflicting elements held together in provisional and dynamic synthesis. The binaries of bourgeois and revolutionary, city and nation, art and commerce, were equally important in defining Heltai's public self and creative drive.

The central binary in this confession, however, was the pairing of Heltai's Jewish and Hungarian selves, which had become so much part of everyday life and unconscious habit that it did not even need to be specified. Yet there was nothing inevitable about this bifurcated identity that defined Heltai's persona. It was, as he confessed in an interview shortly before his death, the result of choice and circumstances rather than inevitable destiny. In this interview, Heltai reminisced that he grew up completely bilingual, equally at home in German and Hungarian, and he came within "a hair's breadth of becoming a German writer." His uncle, who in the 1880s was feuilleton editor at the Viennese daily the *Neue Freie Presse*, urged him to join him on the paper. "I angrily rejected the offer," Heltai recalled, "considering it a despicable assault on Hungarian literature." The uncle, Heltai added as an afterthought, was "the great Zionist, Dr. Theodore Herzl."[80]

Very little is known about the details of Heltai's relationship with his uncle, but it seems to have been a close one. At any rate, the few anecdotes that exist about their interactions suggest that Herzl remained determined to draw his nephew into his orbit even after the journalistic offer. Heltai recalled a later conversation with Herzl that apparently took place in the Leopoldstadt in Vienna around the time of the publication of Herzl's *Judenstat*. Herzl's dramatic announcement that he had huge plans to share with his nephew took the younger man by surprise and made him surmise that it must have been about "some ambitious literary or theatrical project, since by then several of his plays were being performed at the Burgtheater." The plans that Herzl had in mind, however, were not about literature but rather politics. He asked his nephew to represent the Zionist idea in Hungary. "You have to be my deputy and representative," he continued. "I will make sure that you have available every means to advance the cause, including financial resources. Accept the job!" Heltai's response to these urgings was identical to his earlier rejection of the position at the *Neue Freie Presse*. "I cannot accept it," Heltai responded. "I can discover no impulse in my heart and mind that would induce me to do it. I will tell you in all honesty: I am not a Jew. I am a Hungarian."[81]

Superficially, Heltai's adamant refusal of his uncle's offer seemed to be a recapitulation of what has generally been interpreted as the fanatical patriotism of Hungarian Jews, who seemed unable to break free from their illusions of national affiliation. In fact, however, the exchange contained a more complex subtext that Heltai seemed unable or unwilling to spell out more fully. Heltai's position was not a naïve recapitulation of Hungarian nationalism but a more amorphous vision that affirmed a particular way of being in the world. The seemingly straightforward choice between Hungarian and Jewish identification was not so straightforward for Heltai, who rejected the very notion of a unitary political identity. Heltai's reference to being Hungarian rather than Jewish gestured to a cultural space beyond politics, defined by creative marginality and critical opposition to the status quo. It meant in the final analysis being a citizen of Budapest, where ambiguity and a fractured sense of self were not only possible but also the norm. The choice of modernist alienation over political rootedness was in the final analysis a profoundly modern option. Heltai's position was not so much a repudiation of Herzl's Zionism as a parallel response to it in the light of the failure of assimilation and the cultural collapse of liberalism.

6

Critical Cross-Dressing and
Jewish Bourgeois Identity

The Historical Problem of the Hungarian Bourgeoisie

Hungarian liberal dreams of a national middle class, combining the progressive values of the West with the historical traditions of Hungary, did not come to fruition under Dualism. The vision was no doubt a utopia that could never be realized in the form imagined by the Hungarian liberal elite. The concept itself, however, was not inconsequential or unproductive. It provided the symbolic frame for a distinctly Hungarian liberal myth that linked nationalism and modernity in a progressive historical vision that commanded formal allegiance among large segments of the population till the end of Dualism. The premises of this vision were violently repudiated after the political collapse of World War I, but its inner crisis was already apparent by the fin de siècle. At the center of this crisis was the conflicted identity of the Jewish bourgeoisie, which failed to evolve according to the abstract precepts and expectations of Hungarian liberals. It is true that the embryonic Jewish bourgeoisie displayed remarkable aptitude for economic modernization and social mobility.[1] Yet it proved less successful in generating cultural and civic transformation. The imperatives of becoming bourgeois, while remaining both Hungarian and Jewish, proved to be an elusive, and ultimately impossible, undertaking. Jewry's collective identity crisis became a mirror of the larger crisis of Hungarian liberalism and modernity itself.

Gusztáv Beksics, a prominent liberal journalist-politician and one of the best-known advocates of the Hungarian middle class ideal, already expressed pessimism about the enterprise by 1885.[2] "It is a commonplace to disdainfully dismiss even the existence of a bourgeoisie in Hungary," he claimed before the predominantly Jewish civic association of the sixth and seventh districts of Budapest. "The very mention of a Hungarian bourgeoisie or a Hungarian democracy," he continued, "provokes predictable gales of laughter or vociferous denials." The explanation Beksics offered for this state of affairs was deeply ambiguous. He faulted the Jewish middle class for its continuing attachment to retrograde aristocratic values and its failure to create a truly modern bourgeois culture. In contrast to more advanced European societies, he claimed, which had been transformed by bourgeois values, leaving only a few ornamental remnants from the aristocratic past, just the opposite was the case in Hungary. Here, the existing bourgeoisie denied its own class identity and aped the values, manners, and traditions of the nobility. Beksics assigned particular culpability in this development on bourgeois women, who failed to embrace the characteristic bourgeois virtues of modesty, moderation, equality, and civic-mindedness but were seduced by the excesses and extravagances of aristocratic fashion.[3]

Beksics's critique was not only paradoxical but also divorced from Hungarian realities. It ignored the extremely limited opportunities for collective Jewish self-fashioning and class definition in the Hungarian context. Hungarian Jewry was assigned the contradictory task of developing a model for bourgeois life while assimilating to a nonexistent national middle class. The contrast with the project of German Jewish assimilation is notable. As Marion Kaplan has pointed out, in Germany, there existed a national bourgeoisie that provided, if not paths to social integration, then at least a viable model for middle-class identity for Jews. German Jews found in the concept of *Bildung* a common cultural standard for imagining a secular Jewish identity that was both bourgeois and German. As a consequence, Kaplan concluded, Germany Jewry "not only internalized the economic and cultural standards of the bourgeoisie, but also became ardent admirers and promoters of many of its values."[4]

Hungarian liberalism could offer no comparable model for integrating its Jewish middle classes. In the absence of a collective cultural ethic, Hungarian discourses about the middle class tended to focus on the realms of private life and domestic style. As Beksics make clear in his 1885 speech, the solution for bourgeois culture ultimately devolved on the shoulders of women. "Without women," he proclaimed, "it is impossible to realize any kind of social change. Their presence is felt at all the points where society springs into activity. Success is only possible with the cooperation of their gentle hands." Significantly, he included only bourgeois women in his call to action. "In the name of democracy," he concluded, "they are asked to foster the bourgeois virtues. And the starting point of this process is that they proudly acknowledge the qualities that make them bourgeois."[5]

The Lesson of Etiquette Books

Beksics's conviction that the solution for the crisis of Hungarian Jewish middle-class identity was to be found in the cultivation of private life was reflected in the avalanche of etiquette books, conduct guides, and advice manuals that were published in the course of the 1880s. These publications offered models for everyday conduct, genteel behavior, and appropriate social interaction that were implicitly directed at the city's assimilating Jewish population. Probably the most successful producers of the genre were Janka and Stephanie Wohl, the daughters of a converted Jewish doctor who made their living as writers, translators, and editors of women's magazines. Despite their relatively undistinguished social origins, the Wohl sisters acquired considerable cultural capital in the course of their literary careers. As hostesses of one of the most successful salons in fin-de-siècle Budapest, they intermingled with the aristocratic, artistic, and intellectual elite of their age. Their lives were living proof of the efficacy of their advice manuals, which held that good manners and social refinement could triumph over the barriers of class and religion. Their most successful style manual, *Illem: A jó tarsaság szabályai—Útmutató a művelt társaséletben* (Politeness: The rules of good society—Guide to cultivated social life) came out in 1880 and went through no fewer than four editions by 1891. It was followed in 1885 by an equally popular opus devoted to the task of tasteful interior decoration, which attempted to extend their normative vision of bourgeois life to the more tangible realm of home furnishing. The goal of these enterprises was not simply to set an example for individual social behavior but also to bring about the integration of the newly assimilated Jewish middle classes into polite society.[6]

As the Wohl sisters made clear in the introduction to *Illem*, the basis of middle-class culture was "correct behavior, pleasant manners and true politeness."[7] The book's more than two hundred pages were dedicated to the task of helping readers negotiate the pitfalls and challenges of polite society, especially as it might appear to the neophyte. No detail was too small or too trivial to escape the attention of the authors, who confidently pronounced on a bewildering number of topics that might emerge in the course of ordinary social interactions. Individual chapters contained information about the formalities of introduction among men and women, equals and superiors, young and old; about the conventions of paying and not paying social visits; about the rules of appropriate dress for different social occasions; about the intricacies of staging dinner parties, *jours fixes*, and balls; and about the etiquette for visits to the countryside, sport events, watering spas, and even the royal court.

These rules of civilized behavior were, however, only the formal aspects of a general strategy of self-cultivation that defined, in the view of the Wohl sisters, the ideals of bourgeois life. Not surprisingly, the rituals of marriage and the protocols of engagement and sexuality played an important role in this larger project. Young men were enjoined to show an interest in an eligible young lady only if their intentions were serious and only once they had received reliable information on whether "the girl's economic circumstances and family connections corresponded to his expectations." The establishment of a family was presented as not only a serious but also a pragmatic undertaking in which poetry and love were subordinated to considerations of social and economic advantage. "The man must be clear," the authors cautioned, "about how much he needs to maintain, not only his wife, but also his entire family, in the style appropriate to his social standing. If this is not achievable on his own salary, he should either not marry, or make every effort to marry a young woman, whose dowry can compensate for the deficiencies of his income." Women, for their part, were advised against displaying too much physical affection, lest they lose their feminine allure. "The young girl," they suggested, "should discourage the kind of physical freedom and unconstrained and immodest expression of emotion that is not only bad form, but also destructive of the shiny halo of innocence that surrounds the woman of refined character and cultivated nature, not only till her marriage, but beyond it as well."[8]

Practical calculation in marriage went hand-in-hand with a broader strategy of self-discipline that was presented as the essential characteristics of the refined life. Whether in the intimate circle of one's family or in the larger social world of friends and acquaintances, it was suggested that the true mark of good manners was moderation, self-restraint, and the avoidance of excessive or conspicuous behavior. Perhaps nowhere were the laws of good breeding considered more essential than in the home, where people tend to "indulge in changing moods, irritation, careless behavior, or sometimes even in vulgarity." It is precisely in the intimate spaces of family life, the authors enjoined, that people needed to present their natures "in ceremonial garb," making sure that mutual courtesy, mildness, and refinement define their interactions.[9]

At the root of the Wohl sisters' vision of respectability was an ideal conception of self and personality that was based on repression. They concluded that the highest form of politeness, without which no cultivated social exchange was possible, lay in the suppression of one's true thoughts, "especially if our thoughts might offend others' self-esteem or vanity." True politeness, they warned, was acquired "at the price of constant self-observation. We have to watch every act and sentence, but we have to scrutinize even our thoughts, until everything that initially involved great difficulty is internalized through habit and becomes a part of our second nature." The logic of politeness ultimately involved a dual process, creating not only networks of sociability but also walls of exclusion: "Calculated politeness is always a good barrier that keeps anyone away with whom we do not wish to become more closely acquainted; moreover, it does so without hurting the self-esteem of that person."[10]

As even a brief survey of their etiquette book makes apparent, the Wohl sisters' cultural prescriptions were disconnected from the daily realities of its target audience, the Jewish middle and lower-middle classes of Budapest. Their vision of genteel life and personal behavior inadvertently reflected the habits of the nobility and aristocracy rather than of an empirical middle class. The protocols of polite behavior they conjured up presented an imaginary bourgeois culture meant to address the ideological issues of Jewish assimilation rather than the actual social questions of middle-class life. Without explicitly mentioning the problem of Jewish assimilation, *Illem* was, in fact, dedicated to the task of easing Jewish integration into the larger society by making Jews externally more acceptable. The point was made rather circumspectly in the following passage: "A person may be principled, talented, and honest and still appear unbearable if he lacks good manners. Such a person, who often neglects good manners, considering them unimportant and mere external trivialities, often finds himself misunderstood and the object of hostility. If, on the other hand, he attempted to acquire a courteous and pleasant demeanor, his noble qualities would be appropriately recognized."[11]

This sensitive political agenda, only tentatively raised in *Illem*, could find cruder and more direct articulation in other style manuals of the time. One of the most curious examples of the genre was a pamphlet of 1886 titled *Nem illik: Útmutató a társadalmi érintkezésben többé kevésbé elterjedt visszásságok, nyelvi hibák s egyébb botlások elkerülésére* (It is not polite: Guide to the avoidance of obstacles to social interaction associated with more or less frequently committed faults, linguistic mistakes and other missteps). The author of the manual assumed the pseudonym of Censor but was unrelated to Beksics, who also used the same name in his discussion of Jewish cultural matters in the liberal press. *Nem illik* was neither a theoretical discussion of bourgeois culture nor an etiquette book in the usual sense of the term. It was rather a catalogue of negative stereotypes about Jewish behavior that presumably prevented well-bred Hungarians from being able to interact with them as equals.

Censor's booklet was explicitly directed toward Jewish men, whose "missteps" were presented in exhaustive and unusually heavy-handed manner. They included uncouth table manners, slovenly personal habits, loud clothes, less than spotless underwear, and inappropriate behavior in company. Such failures of good breeding were further exacerbated by an addiction to humorous wordplay, punning, and joking, considered annoying by polite company. Perhaps the most fundamental infraction by Jews against the rules of politeness, however, was the fact that they were outsiders, a condition betrayed by their common grammatical mistakes and improper usage of Hungarian words and idioms. An entire chapter was devoted to this problem.

The final and much briefer section of the book was devoted to the less weighty matter of women's clothing, manners, and behavior, which made even less effort to imitate the format of an etiquette manual. Reverting to a list of commonplaces that circulated in society about the habits of Jewish women, the book warned that it was not polite to be overdressed and excessively preoccupied with fashion; that it was incorrect to wear flashy jewelry, especially during the day; and that it was vulgar to eat too many sweets, speak in a shrill voice, read an excessive number of novels (especially ones borrowed from a lending library), haggle with merchants about the price of goods, or boast about the cleverness of one's children.

An anomaly of this inherently paradoxical book was its introduction, which was written by none other than Adolf Ágai, the distinguished Jewish editor of *Borsszem Jankó*. Ágai's willingness to throw his prestige behind Censor's dubious enterprise may be explained by the fact that he belonged to an older generation that remained stubbornly committed to the liberal project of a national middle class that Censor represented even if in a problematic form. Ágai's introduction, which waxed lyrical about his memories of

Paris, where he had observed the social achievements of true good breeding, was strikingly out of sync with the general tenor of the book. Indeed, it suggested a certain degree of defensiveness in the face of what must have been a less than enthusiastic reception of the manual among Jewish audiences. "While the well-bred individual, familiar with the rules of refined society," Ágai tentatively argued, "approaches this volume with satisfaction, perhaps even finding in it something new that could lead to his self-improvement, the superficially cultivated cavalierly reject it, arguing that the messages of *Nem illik* are 'all outdated issues!'"[12] As Ágai anticipated, Censor's clumsy efforts to reform the manners of Hungarian Jewry provoked widespread skepticism and ridicule. The enterprise was almost immediately satirized on the pages of *Borsszem Jankó* through the voice of the Orthodox rabbi Menachen Cziczeszbeiser, who characterized the pamphlet as a well-deserved punishment for the apostasy of secular Jewry.

The Aesthetic Formulation of Hungarian Jewish Bourgeois Culture

The discourse on bourgeois identity, whether insinuated through crude style manuals like Censor's or articulated in more sophisticated etiquette books like that of the Wohl sisters, had little practical impact on its target audience. Hungarian Jewry had only limited interest in the normative precepts of the bourgeois ideology, associated with the ideals of gender, domesticity, and the work ethic. Its collective values found expression in an aesthetic culture that idolized the writer, the poet, and the musician and lifted artistic achievement above practical activities. The iconic Jewish poet József Kiss tellingly summarized this ethos when he categorically defined individual talent as the supreme good of human life. "For talent is a rare gift of fate," he reminded his mostly Jewish readership in 1900. "Money can buy everything: rank, love, health, even long life; but not talent!"[13] It is noteworthy that Kiss's celebration of the superiority of talent over material success was addressed not to artists or other nonconformists but primarily to businessmen, middle-class professionals, and industrialists, who might have been expected to hold different attitudes. Kiss was, in fact, articulating what might be considered the consensus views of his culture. Jewish Budapest was characterized not so much by ambivalence toward bourgeois culture as a selective appropriation of its different components. In the realm of everyday life, it was distinctly bourgeois, but in its cultural style and literary imagination, it was unmistakably bohemian.

This hybrid culture found its characteristic voice in a literary publication that came into existence in 1890 in the ornate interior of the Central Café, one of the new cultural institutions of the inner city. *A Hét* (The week) was the first explicitly modern and truly urban literary periodical in Budapest, reflecting the outlook, and catering to the tastes, of the city's emerging Jewish middle classes. As József Kiss, the founder and editor of the enterprise, pointed out in its opening number, the goal of the magazine was to "combine the timeliness of the daily newspaper with the elevated style of the literary review." Its mission, he elaborated, was to become "an interesting, modern, lively review, whose lightness of touch was never at the expense of the seriousness of its content."[14]

The characteristically midcult literary agenda of the publication was accompanied by a self-consciously respectable social façade. The covers of the magazine, which regularly featured the portraits of luminaries from the political, literary, and theatrical worlds, gave direct expression to its aspiration for respectability and social acceptance. Kiss was remarkably frank in acknowledging the motivation behind these covers. "The infant," he explained not without irony, "needs distinguished godparents in order to prove

József Kiss, 1907.
Courtesy of Budapest
History Museum,
Museum Kiscell.

to the world that it comes from a good family."[15] The advertisements at the back of each number were in perfect congruence with the image of social respectability projected by the frontispieces. Ads for expensive ladies' tailors and hat makers, furniture and rug salons, department stores and photographic studios reflected the tastes and budgets of an obviously affluent readership. Even more striking was the list of powerful industrial and commercial concerns, such as the Gresham Life Insurance Company, the Ganz Iron and Machine Foundry, the Hungarian Electric Joint Stock Company, the Mutual Insurance Company and the United States Life Insurance Company, which appeared as sponsors of the journal.

Kiss was relentless in mobilizing the support of the Jewish business and professional class, whose subscriptions were essential for the survival of his magazine. He was not above using his enormous personal prestige to pressure individuals to subscribe or to prod them to recruit supporters among their own circle of acquaintances.[16] Despite such methods, *A Hét* never became an illustrated family magazine resembling the German *Die Gartenlaube* (The garden arbor) or the Hungarian *Vasárnapi Újság* (The Sunday paper). There was a radical edge and modernist spirit to the articles published in *A Hét* that sometimes made even its most loyal supporters uneasy. In 1897 a female reader complained to Kiss about some of the French translations in the magazine, which forced her "to hide certain numbers from various members of my family." She hastened to add, however, that in spite of this, she intended to continue subscribing to the magazine and had even persuaded two of her girlfriends to become readers.[17]

Kiss was never able to satisfactorily define the nature of the relationship between his modernist literary journal and its overwhelmingly Jewish bourgeois audience. He humorously referred to the problem in his official remarks on the tenth anniversary of the founding of *A Hét*. "A strange journal!" he mused. "It is read in the coffee house and it is also written in the coffee house. Do we write in the coffee house because this is where people read it? Or is it the other way around, do people read it in the coffee house, because this is where it is written? I could never figure out this question."[18] These were obviously rhetorical questions. On some level, Kiss was perfectly aware of the solution to the conundrum he pretended to be puzzled by. The unique character of *A Hét* lay not in the apparent circularity of influence between its readers and writers but in the prior reality of the coffee house itself, which imperceptibly shaped and defined the cultural and personal horizons of both its readers and writers. The coffee house abolished the

Frontispiece of *A Hét*, 1890. Petőfi Literary Museum.

dichotomies between private and public life and created a new public space receptive to the protean, destabilizing energies of modern life. The coffee house was not simply a physical place where people gathered for conversation and sociable exchange. It became the symbol of the modern experience itself, which was no longer characterized by foundational truths and normative values but by fleeting impressions and subjective states of mind.

Aesthetics, rather than science or politics, provided the defining feature of the new modernist sensibility that found expression on the pages of *A Hét*. By all accounts, Kiss was an aesthete and a fanatical perfectionist when it came to literary style. "It was permitted to write about anything and everything on the pages of *A Hét*," remembered Tamás Kóbor, the assistant editor of the journal. "There was no external control over subject matter or ideological direction. Only one thing was forbidden: to write inartistically."[19] The pervasive aestheticism of the journal suggests a superficial affinity with Carl Schorske's characterization of the Viennese avant-garde of the fin de siècle.[20] On closer view, however, the two modernist projects were not analogous, though they were certainly related. The modernity articulated by *A Hét* tended to prioritize a particular kind of personal experience rather

Café Central, ca. 1910. Courtesy of Historical Photography Collection of National Museum.

than a specific form of artistic activity. Its characteristic product was the aestheticized self rather than the aesthetic text. To expand on Schorske's familiar metaphor, the Budapest modernists resembled actors in a street performance rather than recluses in an aesthetic garden.[21]

The tendency to conceive of personal identity in aesthetic and performative terms found idiosyncratic expressions among the talented troupe of young writers and journalists who crystallized around *A Hét*. They had an inveterate habit of literary masquerade through which they gave expression to multiple, sometimes conflicting, social roles and cultural agendas. Kiss himself was famous for his aesthetic poses and addiction to literary disguises. In 1872 he authored the popular urban potboiler *Mysteries of Budapest* under the appropriately romantic pseudonym Rudolf Szentesi. Tamás Kóbor also reverted to fictive names to distinguish his diverse literary activities as naturalist novelist, feuilleton writer, and urban ethnographer. He eventually abandoned his original name, Adolf Berman, for the more elusive Tamás Kóbor, which better evoked his overlapping roles of wanderer, flâneur, and urban explorer, as Kóbor means "wanderer" in Hungarian. Perhaps no one on the staff of *A Hét* used the possibilities of literary masquerade more inventively than Hugó Veigelsberg, who became permanently associated with one of his pen names, Ignotus. Before becoming Ignotus, however, he also wrote under the names of Globtrotter, Tannhauser, Homunculus, Dixi, Fakir, Piktor, and, most provocatively of all, Emma. It was his persona as Emma that was to have had the greatest impact on his long and productive association with *A Hét*.

The Letters of Mrs. Emma

Between 1893 and 1906, Ignotus appeared on the pages of the magazine in the guise of Emma, the witty, opinionated, and rebellious Jewish housewife whose letters to the editor denounced male domination in the name of a radical feminist agenda. The figure of Emma was originally conceived as a concession to the "woman's point of view" in the magazine. Given the overwhelmingly female readership of *A Hét*, this was a strategic decision entirely in keeping with Kiss's shrewd business sense. With time, however, Emma's letters gained a life of their own and a far more complex ideological agenda than her original light-hearted conception implied. So popular did Emma become among her readers that in 1901 *A Hét* actually published a cookbook edited by the fictional Emma, which was based on genuine recipes submitted to the journal by women from all over the country.[22]

Ignotus on frontispiece of *A Hét*, 1890. Petőfi Literary Museum.

Ignotus's Emma letters were a brilliant example of what the feminist scholar Elaine Showalter has called "critical cross-dressing."[23] The practice involved men assuming feminine identities in order to dramatize and amplify their own sense of marginalization in society. Male cross-dressing was, in fact, a common practice on the stage of music halls, Orpheums, and cabarets in fin-de-siècle Budapest. It undoubtedly served to satirize and humorously reframe the common anti-Semitic stereotype that feminized Jewish men and even attributed female physiological traits to their bodies.[24] Ignotus was no doubt familiar with these stereotypes, as well as with the more sophisticated philosophical formulations that created cultural analogies between Jewish and feminine characteristics.[25] He was also thoroughly acquainted with contemporary psychoanalytic theories of gender difference, bisexuality, and transference. As a close friend of the psychiatrist Sándor Fereczi and the translator and propagator of Freud's work in Hungary, Ignotus was an unambiguous supporter of these avant-garde trends. Significantly, however, his intellectual commitments to psychoanalysis played no visible role in his conceptualization of Emma.

Emma was not only indifferent to theories of sexual difference but she also actively repudiated them in her acerbic letters to the editor. She had nothing but skepticism, she wrote, about the work of those "fashionable young writers" who were determined "to descend into the depth of the feminine soul, where they imagine they will discover rooms furnished according to an entirely different design from their own." In her view, the "mysterious feminine soul" was nothing but a hoax, invented by men who refused to regard women as fully developed human beings, "equipped with the same impulses, emotions and capacities—and last but not least, the same aspirations—as their own exemplary souls."[26] Emma's perspective was fundamentally defined by political rather than psychological concerns, and her vision of gender was inextricably linked to the external social world rather than the internal emotional one.

In her rebellion against male domination in particular, and social conventions in general, Emma superficially resembled stereotypes of the Jewish woman widely circulating in contemporary popular culture. The nondomestic Jewish housewife, unwilling or unable to assume her appropriate role in private life, was a common feature of Orpheum acts, music hall skits, popular plays, and caricatures.[27] These were fundamentally misogynistic images with an implicitly conservative message about how family life and gender relations should function. The genre found characteristic incarnation in a

KÁVÉHÁZI ÉLET BUDAPESTEN.

"Life in a Budapest coffee house." Published in *Borsszem Jankó* (July 20, 1890). Petőfi Literary Museum.

full-page caricature of *Borsszem Jankó*, depicting card-playing and gossiping women in a coffee house, who were obviously neglecting their children and domestic duties in order to occupy a public space implicitly reserved for men. The same preoccupation found expression in one of the all-time hits of Budapest cabaret, which, according to its inventor, Endre Nagy, consisted of a ten-minute skit about the archetypal Jewish housewife in the coffee house, as she "gossips, preens, plots, throws hysterics, tortures her husband, and flirts with her admirers."[28]

Despite her superficial resemblance to such popular representations, the cultural codes mobilized by Emma's figure were fundamentally different from these critical images. Emma was not a parodic incarnation of the non-domestic woman but rather a caustic critic of the very institutions of bourgeois domesticity that were supposed to define her true place in life. Indeed, as the creation of a man, her gender identity was by definition unstable, characterized by traits that were partly male, partly female. Emma's androgyny was never flaunted but was nevertheless an integral part of her public persona. Readers were repeatedly reminded of her indeterminate gender through a number of subtle devices that served to both define and also destabilize her persona. As early as 1894 Ignotus decided to "out" Emma by spreading rumors about her "true" identity as a man and a Jew. Emma responded with a declaration of hurt feelings but no explicit denial. Being considered a Jew, she quipped, was bad enough, but to have questions raised about her "womanly identity" and the authorship of her letters was particularly painful. Sometimes, however, it was Emma herself who expressed doubts about her feminine qualities. "I reread my lines," she confided in one letter, "and was horrified by their lack of what is commonly called feminine charm." Even Emma's enthusiastic fans were presented as uncertain about her true identity. Emma ironically complained that she received letters from young girls who were enchanted by her feminism but wondered whether perhaps "I was not even a woman, but a man writing under the name of a woman, for I seem to know such a frightful amount."[29]

Emma's androgyny was not merely a comic device used to distinguish her from misogynistic representations of the nondomestic Jewish woman in popular culture. It was also a symbol of a utopian self that had transcended the limitations and partial truths of gender. In her capacity as both male and female, Emma was invested with the cultural authority to speak about general issues that went well beyond the woman question and feminism. For Emma, women were the universal subjects of exploitation that symbolically incorporated all other oppressed groups, including the working classes. "All those predominantly concerned with the social question," Emma declared, "should never forget that, first and foremost, this is a woman's question. For it is not just the working-class man that lives in slavery, but half of humanity. . . . The elite woman in her spoiled privilege is just as much oppressed as the poor working class woman thrown on the mercies of the marketplace."[30]

Only rarely did Emma refer specifically to the problem uppermost in the minds of her readers: the Jewish question. Yet it would be wrong to assume that the dilemmas of Jewish life were absent from her universal discourse on social equality and justice. The Jewish question was, in fact, a central preoccupation in these letters, though it remained an invisible subplot within her broader narrative of exploitation in modern societies. Through direct and indirect references, Emma's letters suggested an unmistakable analogy between the stigmatization of Jews and the oppression of women and the working classes. Indeed, Emma's letters attributed a central role to the Jewish story without ever actually making it a centerpiece of her narrative. Jewish marginalization was lifted to a privileged symbolic status precisely through its integration within a universal narrative of human freedom and emancipation. In this sense, Emma performed a double act of critical cross-dressing in her remarkable letters. Not only was she a man masquerading as a woman but she was also an advocate of Jewish equality masquerading in the role of a feminist and a socialist.

The Identity Crisis of the Jewish Bourgeoisie

Emma performed this dual task through an ironic masquerade of the characteristic habits and preoccupations of the typical upper-middle-class Jewish housewife of Budapest. She was a representative member of her class, with a boring husband, two school-aged children, and a large household in an affluent section of town. To make the impression even more convincing, the drama of Emma's social and personal life played out against the iconic backdrop of the Wohl sisters' domestic manual, no doubt familiar to most of the readers of *A Hét*. The sisters actually made a cameo appearance in one of Emma's letters in the guise of "the so-called lady of high society" (the Wohl sisters' pen name), who, Emma quipped, "no doubt would smile condescendingly at the size of my household budget." The version of middle-class life presented in Emma's letters was not only more modest but also more prosaic than the imaginary bourgeois household presented in the manual of the Wohl sisters. Emma took malicious delight in pointing out the actual as opposed to the imaginary tasks of the middle-class housewife. "Do you have any conception," she asked, what it means to deal on a daily basis with "the butcher, the upholsterer, the egg merchant, the green grocer, the house cleaner, the cook, the parlor maid, the French governess, the piano teacher, the porter and the assistant porter?" For Emma, household duties hardly constituted the natural realm of female activity and self-expression. On the contrary, they were presented as obstacles to individual fulfillment and intellectual creativity. The typical bourgeois housewife, she lamented, was condemned to an "endless train of laughably petty obligations and constraints, and her social world consisted of a preset stage, whose faded scenery has lost all inherent meaning and originality."[31]

Emma's discontent with the monotony of housekeeping was partially compensated for by the world of fashion, which held considerable practical and theoretical interest for her. Characteristically, however, her expert knowledge of the minutiae of women's toilettes served to undermine, rather than consolidate, the ability of fashion to legitimate social hierarchy. It is true, she admitted, that bourgeois women could never aspire to the "famously expensive simplicity" of aristocratic women's costumes." Their achievements "related to our pathetic exertions the way the frosty heights of the Alps compare to the Sváb hegy [one of the hills of Buda]." Nevertheless, Emma reasoned, the seemingly insurmountable barriers between bourgeois and aristocratic women were erased by their essential similarity beneath the superficial veneer of their toilettes. "Their stays are as uncomfortable as mine," Emma consoled herself. "Their husbands cheat on them and vice versa, just as my old man cheats on me and I on him. They are as irritated by the admiring glances their lovers cast in my direction as the most ordinary bourgeois woman who peels her own potatoes for dinner."[32]

Emma's vision of the institution of marriage was as subversive as her views about domestic duties and women's fashion. Marriage may have been as much of an economic necessity for Emma as it was in the Wohl sisters, but its very foundation in economic considerations rendered it coercive and illegitimate in her eyes. Bourgeois marriage, based on inherently unequal relations between men and women, failed to live up to expectations of emotional fulfillment and intellectual communion that Emma unquestionably subscribed to. She illustrated the boredom of modern marriage through her own life, which quickly transformed her husband from "an amorous lion" into a "yoke-bearing ox." The results were a disappointing familiarity that yielded no intimacy or novelty. "We know each other so well, so well," she sighed: "alas only too well to retain even a spark of interest in each other. I know what he is thinking of, which is primarily about eating as well as possible, and sleeping as much as possible. And he knows which of my teeth are false, the number of my gray hairs, when I have migraines, and that I cost him too much money, a great deal of money."[33]

The failure of domestic life to live up to its promised ideal found brilliant illustration in the incompatible views of men and women on the very meaning of the bourgeois household. In what was clearly meant to be a domestic farce, Emma provided parallel versions of the woman and man's version of the duties of running a middle-class home. "No one," Emma declared, "hates more than I the infinitely lowly, soulless, petty, stupid, and exhausting tasks associated with housework. And it is not enough that I am forced to spend my entire life performing meaningless labor that is contrary to my human dignity and aspirations for higher things. I am forced to fight a separate battle with my husband about it." Her husband, for his part, fired back with a salvo of ammunition that was meant not only for his wife but also for the entire tribe of bourgeois womanhood. "Your aspirations," he accused them, "are not to run reasonable households, but to maintain princely courts. In the little time you have left after taking care of your housework, you behave not as housewives but as countesses. It is true that this comes at a price; when you are not playing at countesses, you are exhausted domestic drudges, incapable of assuming the genuine roles of mothers, wives, and women."[34]

Emma was obviously capable of playing the roles of both husband and wife in her humorous unmasking of the idealizations of bourgeois marriage. Her witty performances of the follies of bourgeois life were not only highly amusing but also secretly appealing to both female and male audiences. She created a sense of collusion between herself and her public, in part by setting herself apart from her male colleagues, who became surrogates for the folly of male society in general. "Your secret machinations against me are all futile," she charged in a characteristic fit of pseudo-anger, "for the audience loves me and they do not love you. The reason is that I use my tongue to lash out against you, but never against them."[35] Emma's voice resonated with Jewish audiences not because she presented an objective or representative view of bourgeois culture but because she succeeded in articulating its fundamental dualities and unresolved ambiguities in a way that compelled general recognition.

At her most successful, she both represented and undermined the rituals of Budapest bourgeois life. She was simultaneously the social insider as well as the critical outsider, the conformist and the hyper-individualist, the passive consumer and the active creator of modernist culture. Not surprisingly, the precarious equilibrium between these antithetical impulses proved impossible to maintain in the long run. The artful incorporation of Emma's female and male qualities within an androgynous persona began to break down with time. Increasingly, Emma's chatty letters and gossipy free-associations gave way to conventional polemics and formal expositions about the pressing social issues of the day.

The growing crisis in Emma's public persona found revealing expression in a letter of 1900 that was a curious attempt to create a new, explicitly radical, alter-ego for the Budapest housewife through identification with the figure of Rosa Luxemburg. Rosa Luxemburg, of course, exemplified all three of Emma's increasingly conflicted identities as a Jew, a woman, and a socialist. In Emma's eyes, however, Luxemburg's true credentials as a suitable model for personal conduct lay not in her fame as a socialist activist but in her remarkable ability to cause irritation among her respectable male colleagues. Indeed, the task for which Emma summoned Luxembourg's symbolic alliance required precisely this kind of talent. The project involved a polemical and satirical exposé of the liberal and philosemitic Viennese physician Dr. Nothnagel,[36] who had recently come out against the admission of women to the university on the grounds that the feminine soul would lose its poetry and idealism if exposed to the rigors of higher education. Speaking collectively in the name of "Rosa and I," Emma proceeded to unmask the hypocrisy of Nothnagel, whose condescending vision of female capacities contained the seeds of all other forms of prejudice and stereotyping. She reminded the progressive professor that his remarks about women's inaptitude for scholarship and artistic creativity sounded suspiciously familiar: "Rosa and I have already heard these pleasantries before, except that they concerned not women, but Jews. Yes, dear Professor, they attempted to deny the human rights of your favorite minority [the Jews] on exactly the same grounds as women: that they were capable only of producing jokes, mimicries and popularizations, not genuine acts of creativity. . . . The commonplace, Herr Professor, that the woman should just remain in the roles of mother and wife, sounds exactly the same as saying that the Jew is only acceptable and poetic, only ideal and natural, if he remains in the role of the petty merchant and the usurer."[37]

Emma's impassioned polemics against Dr. Nothnagel no longer resembled the ironic intimacy of the early Emma letters. Her readers and her editor in *A Hét* did not fail to notice the change, and Emma was forced to offer a characteristically flamboyant defense of her new, more clearly polemical concerns. "You have hurt my feelings so deeply that you can never undo the damage," she wrote in response to what must have been a rebuke from Kiss. "I put my soul into my letters and suddenly you send me a missive that you need frivolous chit-chat rather than serious treatises. Thank goodness I am not a talented young raconteur that can be made to chatter on demand. . . . I will speak about whatever I want to and will say whatever is on my mind; whoever loves me will listen and whoever does not love me is of no concern to me. Do you understand? Good!"[38]

Despite her public bravado, Emma was beginning to find it increasingly difficult to maintain the dynamic balance between the different facets of her persona that had allowed her to become a cultural icon of fin-de-siècle Budapest. In 1904 she publicly announced the desire to "quit this profession, which I undertook in any case purely by chance." Her decision was apparently provoked by her public's dissatisfaction with the increasingly acerbic style of her letters. As one of her female readers suggested, Emma's social critiques "should not be written in the form of an Emma letter, but should be sent from behind a man's visor." The criticism was astute, highlighting Emma's growing inability to maintain her ironically conceived androgynous self in an aesthetic synthesis that was believable. She ended her role as critical cross-dresser with the following self-critical admission: "I find that men write entirely too much about the woman question, and we women, entirely too little."[39]

Ignotus wrote his final Emma letters in 1906, using an appropriately comic note on which to end his thirteen-year masquerade as a woman. The final letter depicted Emma and her husband in the midst of a domestic crisis that also seemed to herald the disintegration of their orderly universe. The immediate cause of the crisis was the disappearance of the domestic staff that had maintained Emma's bourgeois household in impeccable order. Abandoned to her own devices, Emma found herself "in the midst of the most unspeakable chaos," affecting both her moral and physical wellbeing.[40] Her world had been turned topsy-turvy, with the very gender roles she had opposed suddenly overturned. In a self-conscious echo of contemporary misogynistic caricatures, Emma depicted her husband clumsily clearing the table and washing the dishes while she sat in a corner of her dining room at a movable tea table, writing her final letter.

The causes for this farcical situation were never fully disclosed or satisfactorily explained in Emma's letter, which was characteristically impressionistic in its narrative strategies. It ranged from a presentation of her futile efforts to hire a cook and a maid, to a discussion of the rise of the cost of living and the wages of domestic employees, to a concluding vision of social revolution that would destroy the privileged bourgeois lives that Emma and her husband had been living. Reverting to her role as social critic, Emma characterized her entire culture as engaged in a hopeless struggle against "the tide of history, which will most certainly sweep us from the lush island of social privilege onto the sandy shores of proletariat existence." In her final projection of her doomed culture, Emma tried to imagine a socialist future, hastened and made inevitable by her domestic failures: "My cooks have already become socialists, but this is nothing compared to how socialist I will become in a few years, when cooks become completely unavailable and I am forced to do my own cooking."[41]

It is tempting to read Ignotus's final Emma letter as a tragic premonition of political disasters and revolutions just around the corner. The coming of world war and the collapse of the Dual Monarchy, did, indeed, radically transform the world of the Budapest Jewish bourgeoisie that Emma conjured up in her complex masquerade. Ignotus, however, could not have had foreknowledge of these events in 1906, and even if he had, his audiences would not have responded to it. His Emma letters were not prognostications of the future but witty reflections on the state of contemporary Jewish bourgeois life as perceived from a distinctly modernist perspective.

Ignotus's Emma letters were, in some respect, a cultural response to liberal critics like Gusztáv Beksics, who reproached Budapest Jewry for its failure to create a viable bourgeois culture of its own. Emma, the radical feminist and inveterate social activist, was obviously not the domestic woman that Beksics had hopefully conjured up in his speech of 1885. She was, in fact, not a woman at all, but an androgyne that gave voice to the unique situation of the Hungarian Jewish bourgeoisie. The fact that this bourgeoisie could only be depicted in drag was the central point of Ignotus's prolonged masquerade. It signaled the distinct conditions under which a Hungarian Jewish bourgeoisie could come into existence in the first place. The peculiarity of Hungarian liberal political culture was its prohibition of even limited expressions of Jewish collective identity within the nation-state. Indeed, anxiety about the persistence of Jewish solidarity was among the recurring questions of Hungarian political life. The idea of Jewish group loyalty provoked anxieties and apprehensions that no counterarguments or empirical proof could dispel. Under the circumstances, the formation of a distinctive Jewish bourgeoisie in Hungary was not only impolitic but also virtually unthinkable. Lacking the possibility of collective social or ideological definition of its own, the Jewish bourgeoisie assumed the voices of subaltern subjects such as women, workers, or other disadvantaged groups, who became symbolic displacements for Jewish social marginalization that could not be directly articulated.

This complicated form of cultural masquerade or critical cross-dressing, however, had profoundly ambiguous implications that were already apparent in Ignotus's Emma letters. On the one hand, the implicit identification between Jews and exploited groups such as women and the working classes provided a substitute public identity for a Jewish bourgeoisie forced into invisibility by Hungarian political culture. Its identity crisis found partial resolution through the appropriation of the universal cause of human emancipation. Yet the solution invariably undermined the very identity it was supposed to give voice to. The acknowledgment of the superior ethical and historical claims of women and workers also, of necessity, implied the denial of the social legitimacy and historical viability of the bourgeoisie. Emma's letters proved to be a tortuous and ultimately unsuccessful experiment at reconciling these irreconcilable options. They are for this reason one of the most illuminating windows into the cultural dilemmas of Hungarian Jewry at the fin de siècle. They offer simultaneously a mirror and a critique of Hungarian Jewish bourgeois life, ultimately exposing its profound vulnerabilities and instabilities as a cultural identity.

Epilogue

The Waning of Jewish Budapest after World War I

The historical culture of Jewish Budapest came to an abrupt end with World War I. The collapse of the Austro-Hungarian Empire in October 1918 irrevocably destroyed the complex social fabric and political institutions that had allowed this cultural world to flourish for more than a half century. From being members of a sprawling Central European empire with multiple ethnicities and nationalities, Hungarian Jews found themselves transformed into citizens of a truncated ethnically homogeneous state, where their status as a religious and cultural minority was increasingly contested.

The reconstituted Kingdom of Hungary of 1920 had lost 72 percent of its territory to neighboring states and 64 percent of its former population, including millions of ethnic Hungarians. The historic trauma of 1918–1919 proved devastating for Hungary, provoking a ferocious nationalist reaction that had a direct impact on its Jewish citizens. Jews became the focus of national frustrations and were designated as the culprits for Hungary's disastrous losses.[1] The diminution of Jewish influence in the affairs of the state became part of official policy in the conservative nationalist government of Admiral Horthy that took power in 1919. One of the earliest signs of official retrenchment of Jewish rights came with the passage of the notorious Numerus Clausus Law of 1920. The law restricted the enrollment of Jewish students at universities to 5.9 percent of the student body, which represented the proportion of Jews within the general population.[2] The overt purpose of the law was to remedy the overrepresentation of Jewish students at institutions of higher learning, a problem that had aroused controversy even before the war. Further reaching than its pragmatic considerations, however, were the underlying legal and symbolic implications of the new law. These were spelled out even before the passage of the measure in parliament. The minister of religion and education issued an ordinance at the beginning of the fall semester of 1920, pointing out "that in student admissions for the 1920–21 academic year, the Israelites would be considered a 'separate nationality.'"[3] For the first time since their emancipation in 1867, the Jews of Hungary were declared to be an ethnically foreign group with curtailed legal rights within the state.

Jewish responses to the gradual erosion of their civic status in the new Hungary were not unified and did not happen overnight. Long-held political identities and cultural reflexes died hard, and in many cases not at all. Hungarian Jews had been accustomed to think of themselves as integral parts of the nation and found it difficult to abandon their habits of national identification and patriotism. The painful stages of the transformation found self-conscious documentation in the correspondence between the psychoanalysts Sándor Ferenczi and Sigmund Freud, who were in almost daily contact with each other during these critical years. Ferenczi sent detailed accounts to Freud of the changing political landscape of Budapest, invariably including analyses of his own state of mind and emotional reactions to the events. The letters provide one of the most revealing accounts of the close interaction between the political and psychic worlds during the political cataclysm of 1918–1919.

In early October 1918, shortly before the political abolition of Austria-Hungary, Ferenczi still saw himself as an organic member of the Hungarian nation, whose fate was closely intertwined with his emotional life. "The beginning of the breakdown of our old political world, among other things also of the *Globus Hungaricus*, is deeply injuring our narcissism," he wrote Freud on October 4, 1918. Yet he was not entirely at the mercy of the new political world unfolding around him. As he made clear in the same letter, his private and professional lives remained intact, providing a measure of continuity and normalcy in the midst of the political crisis: "It is a good thing that one has a Jewish and a psychoanalytic ego along with the Hungarian, which remains untouched by these events."[4] A few weeks later, Ferenczi returned to his increasingly beleaguered Hungarian identity after the vote by Romanian, Slovak, and Croat delegates to officially end their associations with historic Hungary. "These days," he wrote Freud on October 22, 1918, "I am going through the sad farewell to the former Hungary. The feeling that comes over me in the process is similar to mourning. It means dissociating myself from a part of the country with which I have identified."[5]

Despite Ferenczi's personal distress at the disintegration of the Hungarian political world in 1918, he was not yet fully absorbed by its cataclysmic force. It was still possible for him to maintain his prewar analytic distance between his national, religious, and professional affiliations. In less than a year, no such distinctions were possible, and his Jewish identity became the determining factor that overrode all other forms of identifications. Writing to Freud on August 28, 1919, in the aftermath of a failed Bolshevik Revolution and a counterrevolutionary insurgence, Ferenczi described a new political landscape that left little room for personal ambiguity or complexity. He was forced to confront the implications of a new social order in which anti-Semitism had become a permanent social reality and an officially sanctioned policy:

> If everything does not deceive, we Hungarian Jews are now facing a period of brutal persecution of Jews. They will, I think, have cured us in a very short time of the illusion with which we were brought up, namely, that we are "Hungarians of Jewish faith." I picture Hungarian anti-Semitism—commensurate with the national character—to be more brutal than the petty-hateful type of the Austrians. It will very soon become evident how one can live and work here. It is naturally the best thing for psychoanalysis to continue working in complete withdrawal and without noise. Personally, one will have to take this trauma as an occasion to abandon prejudices brought along from the nursery and to come to terms with the bitter truth of being, as a Jew, really without a country. One must distribute the libido which became free in that way between the few friends whom one has rescued from this debacle, the only true soul that accompanies one through thick and thin, and science.[6]

Ferenczi's choice of internal emigration was only one of the options available to Hungarian Jews in the 1920s and 1930s. Many of the most creative members of this generation, including some non-Jews as well, decided to emigrate from Hungary, choosing to settle in Vienna, Prague, or Berlin, where the intellectual and political atmosphere was less stifling and professional opportunities more abundant than in Budapest. Berlin was by far the most attractive of these destinations, since the Hungarian émigrés spoke fluent German and often had personal relations and professional contacts in German universities and avant-garde intellectual and artistic circles. Germany, however, did not turn out to be the final destination of the group. With the rise of Hitler in 1933, most of the émigrés moved on to the United

States, where they found renewed opportunities to establish their lives and exercise their talents.

Tibor Frank has described the trajectory of this massive intellectual migration in the interwar years as a "double exile," which involved a triangulation between the cultural worlds of Budapest, Berlin, and New York.[7] As his nuanced study makes clear, the emigrant experience varied considerably for individuals and groups. Some, especially the scientists, were spectacularly successful in finding opportunities and recognition in their new environments. Others, especially the writers, artists, and musicians, were often less so. Notable among the success stories were Budapest filmmakers and actors, who often established flourishing careers in Hollywood. For some of these transplants, emigration was only a superficial episode that did not significantly interrupt their ongoing engagement with Hungarian culture. Ignotus, for instance, who moved to Vienna in 1919, and then to the United States in the 1940s, always maintained close intellectual and cultural ties with Hungary, returning to Budapest in the final year of his life, in 1949. For others, emigration was a permanent condition that involved a deliberate obliteration of their former identities as Hungarians. This latter type of emigration characterized the star of Budapest music hall Szőke Szakáll, who established a successful acting career in Hollywood under the name of S. Z. Sakall and chose never to return to his country of origin. He signaled his disaffiliation from Hungary by intentionally identifying his official birthplace as "Austria-Hungary."[8]

Those who chose to remain in Hungary after 1919 faced different but equally complex tasks of readjustment and redefinition. The most urgent need was to formulate a collective response to anti-Semitism by refashioning the public image of Jews in the radicalized world of right-wing Hungary. The second, less obvious task was to come to terms with the cultural inheritance of the fin de siècle, whose subversive modernism was increasingly irrelevant within the politicized environment of the interwar years. One of the earliest attempts to clarify these issues was undertaken by Tamás Kóbor, the former editor of *A Hét*. In a pamphlet from 1920 titled *Mi az igazság? A zsidókérdésről* (What is the truth? The Jewish question), Kóbor set out to publicly articulate a coherent defense of the Jewish position in the face of growing political exclusion and cultural marginalization.[9]

Anticipating by two years the Viennese journalist Hugo Bettauer's satirical account *The City without Jews*,[10] Kóbor attempted to visualize the drastic consequences of a symbolic expulsion of Jews from Hungarian life. Would the nation survive such an operation? he asked rhetorically. What would be the consequences of measures that led to the extirpation of Jews "from the national body where they have served the functions of vital organs? Is it imaginable that this perilous operation could succeed, when all else has failed?"[11] In order to make such a procedure unthinkable, Kóbor proceeded to refute clause-by-clause the common anti-Semitic accusations made against Jews in the contemporary mass media. These included the charge that Jews had played a disproportionate role in the Hungarian Bolshevik Revolution of 1919; that they exercised undue and illegitimate domination over the economy; and finally, that they repaid political emancipation by contributing to the destructive forces undermining the nation.

Kóbor's negation of these claims required a subtle but important transformation of previous strategies for conceptualizing Jewish life and identity in Hungary. In marked contrast to the practices of prewar Jewish politicians like Mór Wahrmann, who refused to engage intellectually with anti-Semites, Kóbor had no choice in the matter. Faced with a political environment where anti-Semitism had become a legitimate political discourse, he was forced to take their ideas seriously if he wanted to remain a relevant participant in the national conversation. The very act of engagement with anti-Semitism, however, required serious intellectual concessions and a loss of cultural complexity.

In making his claims for a Jewish public identity in Hungary, Kóbor appropriated the same essentialist and collectivist models used by his antagonists. He countered anti-Semitic claims against Jewish individualism and subversion with the discourse of identity and nationalism. This strategy involved a categorical affirmation of the Hungarian roots of Jewish identity, which had already been sounded in less absolutist terms in the prewar narratives of the Jewish elite. Kóbor's essentialist argument, however, led to startling and contradictory conclusions. Pursuing his ideas to their logical end, he claimed that Jews needed to be considered not only as irreducibly Hungarian but also as irreducibly Jewish. Within the absolutist nationalist universe of the 1920s, there was no room for the hybrid identities performed in Jewish music hall, or even for the hyphenated identity developed by prewar ideologists of assimilation. For Kóbor, as for his environment, Jews could only be considered a racial group. Over the centuries, Kóbor illustrated, Jews had acquired the characteristics of a race whose "distinct racial features were visible and perceptible in both its physical and spiritual qualities."[12] In his attempt to counter the claims of anti-Semitism, Kóbor had paradoxically reaffirmed the very position he had set out to confront.

Kóbor's contradictory article reflected the tragic choices faced by Hungarian Jewry after the war. Under conditions of unprecedented political pressure, they had no choice but to dismantle the theoretical underpinnings, if not the superficial achievements, of prewar modernism. Kóbor, the former modernist, whose nuanced portraits of fin-de-siècle Budapest had given voice to the complexity of the metropolitan experience, became a cultural essentialist, disowning the urban project he himself had helped create. His break from the past was perhaps more categorical than that of other contemporaries, but it contained a cultural logic that would be more and more explicitly played out during the coming decades. A political world that considered Jews as suspect outsiders whose very existence needed to be justified in national terms could not be mollified by the ironic discourse of difference and self-parody developed by Jewish popular culture in the prewar years. In the same article that Kóbor refuted anti-Semitic accusations, he made one significant concession to his opponents: Jewish culpability for the creation of the modern mass media in Budapest. "I acknowledge unconditionally," he wrote, "the role of the modern media in spreading immorality, cynicism, triviality, and frivolity in family relations. But here, an optical illusion is self-evident. For those are the decadent symbols of Western culture, not those of the Hungarian Jew. The cult of scandal, the screaming headlines, the curiosity-mongering advertisements, these are all copied by Hungarians from the foreign press. They cannot exactly be described as Jewish traits."[13]

Symbolically, if not empirically, Jewish Budapest ended in 1918, bringing to a close the activities of two generations of cultural innovators that had helped create the urban world of late nineteenth-century Budapest. The first generation, which had come of age in the progressive decade of the 1840s and had lived through the hopes of the dualistic compromise and Jewish emancipation of 1867, was mostly gone by the early 1920s. Wahrmann had died in 1892, Somossy in 1902, and Ágai in 1916. The only member of this founding generation to survive the war was József Kiss. In 1922 he tellingly distanced himself from his celebrated role as the iconic national poet who had brought the Hungarian and Jewish traditions into aesthetic synthesis with each other. In an amendment to his final testament shortly before his death, Kiss dramatically renounced his dual identity as a Jewish

Hungarian poet and declared his allegiance to Judaism as the primary source of his identity: "I was born a Jew and that is how I want to remain. When I lay down my head in eternal sleep, place my body in a rough-hewn wooden coffin according to Jewish traditions. I forbid all elaborate mourning rituals. I don't need a memorial. There are so many memorials in this country that a revision of the custom will not do any harm. Among my writings, there are one or two rhymes that cannot be banished out of existence. I don't fear for them."[14]

Despite the disenchantment with the modernist experiment, expressed by many of the founding members and participants of Jewish Budapest, the project never really came to a close. The genie that had been allowed to escape from the bottle could not be forced back, and Budapest retained its metropolitan character, renowned for its spirit of irreverence, subversion, and irony. Insofar as Jewish Budapest was a state of mind and not just an identifiable community, it could not be eradicated from the collective consciousness and experience of the general population. Budapest remained the "sinful city," despite the concerted efforts of right-wing nationalists to extirpate its modernist spirit. In 1935, almost a quarter century after Adolf Ágai published his celebration of metropolitan life in Budapest, another lover of the city, Béla Bevilaqua, attempted to give his own definition to the city. His version proved remarkably similar to Ágai's. Bevilaqua, too, painted a city of restless mobility and constant change that was torn between the noisy cosmopolitanism of Pest and the eternal romanticism of Buda. With or without Jews, Budapest had become an emblematic symbol of the modern condition that challenged foundational definitions of culture and identity.[15]

NOTES

Introduction

1. See Károly Vörös, *Egy világváros születése* [The birth of a metropolis] (Budapest: Kossuth Kiadó, 1973); Péter Hanák, *The Garden and the Workshop: Essays on the Cultural History of Vienna and Budapest* (Princeton: Princeton University Press, 1988); Gábor Gyáni, *Parlor and Kitchen: Housing and Domestic Culture in Budapest, 1870–1940* (Budapest: Central European University Press, 2002); Gábor Gyáni, *Identity and Urban Experience: Fin-de-Siècle Budapest* (New York: East European Monographs, 2004); Gábor Gyáni, *Budapest—Túl jón és rosszon: A nagyvárosi múlt mint tapasztalat* [Budapest—Beyond good and evil: The history of the metropolis as experience] (Budapest: Napvilág Kiadó, 2008); Vera Bácskai, Gábor Gyáni, and András Kubinyi, *Budapest törénete a kezdetektől 1945-ig* [The history of Budapest from its origins till 1945] (Budapest: A Nemzeti Kultúrális Örökség Minisztériuma, 2000); John Lukacs, *Budapest 1900: A Historical Portrait of a City and Its Culture* (New York: Weidenfeld & Nicolson, 1988); Robert Nemes, *The Once and Future Budapest* (De Kalb: Northern Illinois University Press, 2005).

2. The concept of a Jewish-identified modernism has a fairly extensive literature. See, in particular, Ezra Mendelsohn, ed., *People of the City: Jews and the Urban Challenge*, Studies in Contemporary Jewry 15 (New York: Oxford University Press, 1999); Steven Beller, *Vienna and the Jews, 1867–1938: A Cultural History* (Cambridge: Cambridge University Press, 1989); Scott Spector, *Prague Territories: National Conflict and Cultural Innovation in Franz Kafka's Fin de Siècle* (Berkeley: University of California Press, 2000); Emily D. Bilski, *Berlin Metropolis: Jews and the New Culture, 1890–1918* (Berkeley: University of California Press, 1999)

3. For the classic formulation of this position, see Zoltán Bosnyák, *Fővárosunk elzsidósodása* [The Judaicization of our capital] (Budapest: Held János, 1935).

4. Endre Ady, "Korrobori," *Nyugat* 17, no. 1 (1924): 4.

5. Géza Komoróczy, ed., *Jewish Budapest: Monuments, Rites, History* (Budapest: Central European University Press, 1999), 468.

6. A controversial example of this debate is the work of Yuri Slezkine, *The Jewish Century* (Princeton: Princeton University Press, 2004).

7. Scott Spector, "Modernism without Jews: A Counter-Historical Argument," *Modernism/Modernity* 14, no. 4 (November 2006): 616.

8. Ibid., 617.

9. American Jewish historians have noted the strong connections between Jewish self-formation and popular culture. See Harley Erdman, *Staging the Jew: The Performance of an American Ethnicity 1860–1920* (New Brunswick: Rutgers University Press, 1997); Michael Alexander, *Jazz Age Jews* (Princeton: Princeton University Press, 2001); Ted Merwin, *In Their Own Image: New York Jews in Jazz Age Popular Culture* (New Brunswick: Rutgers University Press, 2006); Andrea Most, *Making Americans: Jews and the Broadway Musical* (Cambridge, MA: Harvard University Press, 2004); Neal Gabler, *An Empire of Their Own: How the Jews Invented Hollywood* (New York: Crown, 1988); Michael Rogin, *Blackface, White Noise: Jewish Immigrants in the Hollywood Melting Pot* (Berkeley: University of California Press, 1996); Matthew Frye Jacobson, *Whiteness of a Different Color: European Immigrants and the Alchemy of Race* (Cambridge, MA: Harvard University Press, 1998).

10. Much of this activity found crystallization in the periodical *Budapesti Negyed* [The districts of Budapest], whose thematic numbers, published between 1993 and 2010, provided a forum for creative research and debate for a diversity of subjects about the emergence of Budapest metropolitan culture in the late nineteenth century.

11. Julia Richers, *Jüdisches Budapest: Kulturelle Topographien einer Stadtgemeinde im 19. Jahrhundert* [Jewish Budapest: Cultural topography of an urban community at the turn of the century] (Cologne: Bohler Verlag, 2009); Anikó Prepuk, *A zsidóság Közép-és Kelet-Európában* [The Jews of Central and Eastern Europe] (Debrecen: Csokonai Kiadó, 1997); Viktor Karády, *Zsidóság, polgárosodás, asszimiláció: Tanulmányok* (Jewry, modernization, assimilation: Studies] (Budapest: Cserepfalvi, 1997); Michael Silber, ed., *Jews in the Hungarian Economy, 1760–1945* (Jerusalem: Magnes Press, 1992); Vera Ranki, *The Politics of Inclusion and Exclusion: Jews and Nationalism in Hungary* (New York: Homes & Meier, 1999); Raphael Patai, *The Jews of Hungary* (Detroit: Wayne State University Press, 1996); Katalin Fenyves, *Képzelt asszimiláció? Négy zsidó értelmiségi nemzedék önképe* [Imagined assimilation? The self-presentations of four Jewish intellectual generations] (Budapest: Corvina, 2010).

12. Eli Lederhendler, "New York City, the Jews, and 'The Urban Experience,'" in Mendelsohn, *People of the City*, 49–67.

13. Ibid., 54.

14. Dan Miron, "The Literary Image of the Shtetl," in *The Image of the Shtetl and Other Studies of Modern Jewish Literary Imagination* (Syracuse: Syracuse University Press, 2000), 1–48.

15. László Varga, "Szerkesztői előszó" [Editor's foreword], in *Zsidóság a dualizmus kori Magyaroszágon: Siker és válság* [Jewry in Hungary of the age of Dualism: Success and crisis], ed. László Varga (Budapest: Pannonica Kiadó, Habsburg Történeti Intézet, 2005), 8. Unless otherwise noted, all translations are mine.

Chapter 1. Cultural Visions of the Emerging City

An earlier version of this chapter was translated into Hungarian and appeared as "A budapesti zsidó flâneur" [The Budapest Jewish flâneur], *Múlt és Jövő* [Past and future], no. 4 (2012): 60–81.

1. The hymn is known as "Mah Tovu" and comes from Numbers 24:5. The speaker is Balaam, a seer from Northern Syria, who is hired by Balak, king of Moab, to curse Israel. Instead, he blesses them, and this is the most famous line from the blessing.

2. Ignotus, "Kronika, Reczepczio" [Chronicle, reception], *A Hét* [The week] 5, no. 39 (September 30, 1894): 609.

3. For a summary of the history of Budapest Jewry in the late nineteenth century, see Károly Vörös, "A budapesti zsióság két forradalom között, 1849–1918" [Budapest Jewry between two revolutions, 1849–1918], in *Zsidóság a dualizmus kori Magyarországon: Siker és váalság* [Jewry in dualistic Hungary: Success and crisis], ed. László Varga (Budapest: Pannónia Kiadó, Habsburg Történteti Intézet, 2005), 40–57.

4. Borsody Béla Bevilaqua and Béla Mazsáry, *Pest-Budai kávéházak: Kávé és kavémesterség, 1535–1935* [The coffee houses of Pest-Buda: Coffee and the profession of coffee making, 1535–1935] (Budapest: Athenaeum, 1935), 1:102.

5. For an account of the urban renewal of Budapest in the 1870s, see Nemes, *The Once and Future Budapest*, 166–180.

6. László Siklossy, *Hogyan épült Budapest? 1870–1930* [How was Budapest built? 1870–1930], (Budapest: Fővárosi Közmunkák Tanácsa, 1931), 80.

7. A similar process was taking place throughout Europe in the late-nineteenth century. See Eric Hobsbawm and Terence Ranger, eds., *The Invention of Tradition* (Cambridge: Cambridge University Press, 1983).

8. Zsolt Beöthy, *Magyar irodalom kis-tükre* [A small mirror of Hungarian literature] (Budapest: Athenaeum, 1900), 1.

9. Dr. Jenő Lechner, *A régi Pest és Buda* [The former Pest and Buda] (Budapest: Németh József Technikai Könyvkiadóvállalata, 1922), 3.

10. The history of the religious fragmentation of Hungarian Jewry into orthodox, Neolog, and status quo ante factions goes back to the Hungarian Jewish Congress of 1868–1869, which failed to create a unified administrative structure for the newly emancipated Jewish community of Hungary. The Neolog faction corresponded to a reform tendency that remained the more numerous and most publicly visible face of the Hungarian Jewish community.

11. Editorial, "A hitoktatás ujjászervezése a fővárosban" [The reorganization of religious education in the capital], *Magyar Zsidó Szemle* [Hungarian Jewish review] 1, no. 8 (1884): 537.

12. N. Weiszman, "A hitközségek és a hitoktatás" [The congregations and religious instruction], *Magyar Zsidó Szemle* 2, no. 3 (1885): 182.

13. Márton Schreiner, "Az újkori zsidóság vallásos életéről" [The religious life of modern Jewry], *Magyar Zsidó Szemle* 5, no. 1 (1888): 20.

14. Eleazár Szántó, "Tanügy" [Educational matters], *Magyar Zsidó Szemle* 8, no. 1 (1890): 54.

15. Lujza Freyhan, "A nőnevelésről" [The education of women], *Magyar Zsidó Szemle* 2, no. 4 (1885): 396–398.

16. Péter Újvári, ed., "Előszó" [Introduction], in *Zsidó lexikon* [Jewish encyclopedia] (Budapest: A Zsidó Lexikon Kiadása, 1929), n.p.

17. Levél a szerkesztőhöz [Letter to the editor], *Magyar Zsidó Szemle* 1, no. 2 (1884): 160.

18. There is a very large literature on the flâneur, whose history is inseparable from the cultural analysis of modernity. See, for example, Keith Tester, ed., *The Flaneur* (London: Routledge, 1994); and Mary Gluck, "The Flaneur and the Aesthetic Appropriation of Urban Culture," *Culture, Theory and Society* 20, no. 5 (October 2003): 53–80. See also Walter Benjamin, *Charles Baudelaire: A Lyric Poet in the Era of High Capitalism*, trans. Harry Zohn (London: Verso, 1973); and Walter Benjamin, *The Arcades Project*, trans. Howard Eiland and Kevin McLaughlin (Cambridge, MA: Belknap Press of Harvard University Press, 1999).

19. Priscilla Parkhurst Ferguson, *Paris as Revolution: Writing the Nineteenth-Century City* (Berkeley: University of California Press, 1994), 37.

20. John Jervis, "Street People: The City as Experience, Dream and Nightmare," in *Exploring the Modern: Patterns of Western Culture and Civilization* (Oxford: Blackwell, 1998), 65.

21. Imre Vahot, *Budapesti kalauz* [Budapest guidebook] (Pest: Nyomtatott Vodianer F.-nél, 1864).

22. See Gelléri Mór, ed., *Budapest a kiállitás alatt* [Budapest during the National Exhibition] (Budapest: Kiadja Dobrowsky és Franke, 1885); *Budapest fővárosi kalauz* [Guide to the capital city of Budapest] (Budapest: Lampel R., Wodianer F. Konyvkiadóhivatala, 1885); Dr. Zsiklay János, *Budapest összes látnivalóinak kimeritő kalauza: Az 1885-iki Országos Kiállitás utmutatója* [A comprehensive guide to all the sights of Budapest: A guide to the National Exhibition of 1885] (Budapest: Légrády Testvérek, 1885).

23. Lajos Hevesi, *Budapest és környéke* [Budapest and its suburbs] (Budapest: Kiadja Ráth Mór, 1873), 45–47.

24. Ibid., vi.

25. See Benjamin, *The Arcades Project*; Jervis, *Exploring the Modern*; Raymond Williams, *The Country and the City* (New York: Oxford University Press); Richard Sennett, *The Fall of Public Man* (London: Penguin Books, 2002).

26. József Kiss (Rudolf Szentessi), *Budapesti rejtelmek* [The mysteries of Budapest] (Budapest: Argumentum, 2007), 427. Petőfi and Arany wrote Hungarian classics in the mid-nineteenth century.

27. Ibid.

28. Ibid., 427, 428.

29. Ibid., 430–431.

30. Ibid., 432.

31. Ibid., 429.

32. Ibid., 434.

33. Ibid., 428.

34. See Peter Brooks, *The Melodramatic Imagination: Balzac, Henry James, Melodrama and the Mode of Excess* (New Haven: Yale University Press, 1972).

35. The type first appeared in Lesage's *Le Diable boiteux* [The lame devil] (1706) and was adapted by later writers of urban text. See Ferguson, *Paris as Revolution*, 47–48.

36. Ödön Salamon, "Budapest a nyugat városa" [Budapest, a western city], in *A mulató Budapest* [Budapest, the city of entertainment], ed. Henrik Lenkei (Budapest: Singer és Wolfner, 1896), 15.

37. Ödön Gerő, "Budapest fiziognomiája" [The physiognomy of Budapest], in Lenkei, *A mulató Budapest*, 44.

38. Ibid., 45.

39. Viharos [Ödön Gerő], *Az én fővárosom* [My capital city] (Budapest: Révai Testvérek, 1891), 81.

40. Sándor Bródy, quoted in Gábor Sánta, "'Vigasztal, ápol és eltakar': A budapesti kávéházak szociológiai es pszichológiai természetrajza a század fordulón" ["'Consolation, therapy, and refuge": The sociological and psychological portrait of the coffee houses of Budapest at the turn of the twentieth century], *Budapesti Negyed* 12–13, nos. 2–3 (1996): 49.

41. Bódog Holmi, *Kóbor Tamás, az iró és az ember* [Tamás Kóbor, the writer and the man] (Budapest: A Szerző Kiadása, 1935), 16–17.

42. See Kóbor's autobiography, *Ki a ghettóból* [Out of the ghetto] (Budapest: Franklin-Társulat, 1911).

43. Tamás Kóbor, "Budapest a kávéházban, Part I" [Budapest in the coffee house, Part I], *A Hét* 3, no. 52/56 (December 25, 1892): 829.

44. Tamás Kóbor, "Budapest a kávéházban, Part II," *A Hét* 7, no. 1/57 (January 1, 1893): 7.

45. Ibid., 6.

46. Ibid., 7.

47. Kóbor, "Budapest a kávéházban, Part III," *A Hét* 4, no. 7/163 (February 12, 1893): 199.

48. Kóbor, "Budapest a kávéházban, Part V," *A Hét* 4, no. 16/172 (April 16, 1893): 247.

49. Porzó (Adolf Ágai), *Utazás Pestről–Budapestre 1843–1907: Rajzok és emlékek a magyar főváros utolsó 65 esztendejéből* [Travels from Pest to Budapest 1843–1907: Sketches and memories about the last 65 years of the Hungarian capital] (Budapest: Fekete Sas Kiadó, 1998), 5.

50. Ibid., 7.

51. Ibid., 106, 133.

52. Ibid., 212, 189.

53. Ibid., 225.

54. Ibid., 238.

55. Ibid., 440.

56. Hannah Arendt, "The Jew as Pariah: A Hidden Tradition," in *The Jewish Writings*, ed. Jerome Kohn and Ron H. Feldman (New York: Schocken Books, 2007), 275.

57. Aladár Schöpflin, "A város" [The city], *Nyugat* (April 1, 1908): 354.

58. Ibid., 360–361.

Chapter 2. The Jewish Question and the Paradox of Hungarian Liberalism

1. Porzó, *Utazás Pestről–Budapestre*, 161–162.

2. For an analysis of this central contradiction within the modern nation state, see Zygmunt Bauman, "Allosemitism: Premodern, Modern, Postmodern," in *Modernity, Culture and "the Jew,"* ed. Bryan Cheyette and Laura Marcus (Stanford: Stanford University Press, 1998), 143–156; and Zygmunt Bauman, *Modernity and Ambivalence* (Cambridge: Polity Press, 1991).

3. For contemporary historical discussion of this question, see Tamás Ungvári, *Ahasvérus és Shylock: A "Zsidókérdés" Magyarországon* [Ahaseurus and Shylock: The "Jewish Question" in Hungary] (Budapest: Adadémiai Kiadó, 1999); János Gyurgyák, *A zsidókérdés Magyarországon: Politikai eszmetörténet* [The Jewish question in Hungary: The history of a political theory] (Budapest: Osiris Kiado, 2001); Gábor Gyáni, *Nép, Nemzet, Zsidó* [Volk, Nation, Jew] (Pozsony: Kalligram, 2013).

4. There is an enormous scholarly and popular literature in Hungarian about the Tiszaeszlár affair. See, for example, Andrew Handler, *Blood Libel at Tiszaeszlár* (New York: Columbia University Press, 1980). See also György Kövér, *A tiszaeszlári dráma: Társadalomtörténeti látószögek* [The drama at Tiszaeszlar: Social scientific perspectives] (Budapest: Osiris, 2011).

5. Károly Eötvös, *A nagy per, mely ezer éve folyik s még since vége* [The great trial, which has been going on for a thousand years and is still not over], 3 vols. (Budapest: Révai Testvérek, 1904), 1:5.

6. Hillel J. Kievel, "The Importance of Place: Comparative Aspects of the Ritual Murder Trial in Modern Central Europe," in *Comparative Jewish Societies*, ed. Todd M. Endelman (Ann Arbor: University of Michigan Press, 1997), 135–166.

7. Helmut Walser Smith, *The Butcher's Tale: Murder and Anti-Semitism in a German Town* (New York: W. W. Norton, 2002), 123.

8. *A tiszaeszlári vértanú leány és az óhitű zsidók* [The maiden who became a sacrificial victim at Tiszaeszlár and the Old Testament Jews] (Eger, 1882).

9. "Az antiszemita izgató röpiratok ellen" [Against provocative anti-Semitic pamphlets], *Függetlenség* (July 6, 1882). The outpouring of pamphlets and articles published in the daily press during the Tiszaeszlár and the Russian immigration crisis was collected by a contemporary observer and compiled in a collage of press clippings that constitutes 73 volumes. The collection is available as "'Jüdische Delikatessen': Öregebb Bonyhády Perczel István tulajdona [Zsidókra vonatkozó hirlapkivágatok és apró nyomtatvány gyüjtemény] (1880–1885)," 73 vols., Archive of the Országos Széchény Könyvtár, Oct. Hung. 730. Henceforth, references to the collection will be OSZK, Oct. Hung. 730.

10. Eötvös, *A nagy per*, 230.

11. See Walter Pietsch, "A zsidók bevándorlása Galiciából és a magyarországi zsidóság" [Galician Jewish immigration and Hungarian Jewry], *Valóság* 2 (1988): 46–59.

12. "Az orosz-zsidó menekültek" [The Russian Jewish refugees], *Egyetértés* [Agreement] (May 13, 1882), OSZK, Oct. Hung. 730.

13. *Egyetértés* (June 6, 1882), OSZK, Hung. 730.

14. *Egyetértés* (May 11, 1882), OSZK, Hung. 730.

15. *Egyetértés* (May 15, 1882), OSZK, Hung. 730.

16. "Törvényhatóságok a zsidó bevándorlás ellen—Pestmegye közgyűlése" [Municipalities against Jewish immigration—Public deliberation of county Pest], *Függetlenség* [Independence], (June 7, 1882), OSZK, Hung. 730.

17. *Egyetértés* (April 21, 1882), OSZK, Hung. 730.

18. "Veszprém," *Egyetértés* (June 6, 1882), OSZK, Hung. 730.

19. "Szatmármegye kérvénye a képviselőház előtt" [The petition of county Szatmár in front of parliament], *Egyetértés* (June 8, 1882), OSZK, Hung. 730.

20. Ibid.

21. Ibid.

22. Ibid.

23. *Függetlenség* (July 12, 1882), OSZK, Hung. 730.

24. "Minisztertanács a zsidókérdésben" [Cabinet meeting about the Jewish question], *Függetlenség* (June 29, 1882), OSZK, Hung. 730.

25. Gyula Verhovay, "A zsidók és a közvélemény" [Jews and public opinion], *Függetlenség* (June 23, 1881), OSZK, Hung. 730.

26. Ibid.

27. Gyula Verhovay, "A tisza-eszlári rejtély" [The mystery of Tiszaeszlár], *Függetlenség* (June 28, 1882), OSZK, Hung. 730.

28. These were details associated with the investigation of the crime scene.

29. "A tisza-eszlári gyilkosság" [The murder at Tiszaeszlár], *Függetlenség* (June 29, 1882), OSZK, Hung. 730.

30. Quoted in Judit Kubinszky, *Politikai antszemitizmus Magyarországon* [Political anti-Semitism in Hungary] (Budapest: Kossuth Könyvkiadó, 1976), 171.

31. Ibid., 168.

32. Gyurgyák, *A zsidókérdés Magyarországon*, 14.

33. Ödön Farkas, *A zsidó kérdés Magyarországon* [The Jewish question in Hungary] (Budapest: Aigner Lajos, n.d.), 5.

34. Ibid.

35. Lajos Csernátory, "Zsidóinkhoz, II" [To our Jews, II], *Nemzet* [Nation] 1, no. 19 (September 19, 1882), OSZK, Hung. 730.

36. Pál Hoffmann, *A Zsidókérdés* [The Jewish question] (Budapest: Schlesinger és Wohlauer, 1882), 8.

37. Farkas, *A zsidó kérdés Magyarorszagon*, 15.

38. Ibid., 6.

39. Pál Hoffmann, *A Zsidókérdés*, n.p.

40. Lajos Csernátory, "Zsidóinkhoz, II," *Nemzet* (September 19, 1882).

41. Péter Ágoston, *A zsidók útja* [The path of the Jews] (Nagyvárad: Nagyváradi Társadalomtudományi Társaság Kiadása, 1917), 40.

42. Censor (Gusztáv Beksics), *Társadalmunk és nemzeti hivatásunk* [Our society and our national mission] (Budapest: Zilahy Sanuel, 1884), 27.

43. Censor, *Társadalmunk és nemzeti hivatásunk*, 71.

44. Ibid., 131.

45. Endre Ady, "Korribori," *Nyugat* (1924): 4.

46. Count Hermán Zichy and Gy. M. Derestye, eds., *Magyar zsidók a millenniumon* [Hungarian Jews during the millennium] (Budapest: Miljkovic Dragutin, 1896), 5.

47. Ágoston, *A zsidók útja*, 294.

48. Ibid., 308.

49. For an analysis of this Jewish public sphere, see Aniko Prepuk's unpublished manuscript, "Befogadás mint öndefinició: A neológ zsidó identitás sajátosságai az emancipáció után az izraelita sajtó tükrében" [Assimilation as self-definition: The characteristic features of postemancipation Jewish Neolog identity in the mirror of the Jewish press] (Habilitációs értekezlet, Kézirat, Debrecen 2013).

50. Introduction to *Magyar Zsidó Szemle* [Hungarian Jewish review] 1 (1884): 1.

51. Ignácz Acsády, *Zsidó és nemzsidó magyarok az emánczipáczió után* [Jewish and non-Jewish Hungarians after emancipation] (Budapest: Weiszmann testvérek, 1883), 4.

52. Ibid., 5.

53. Ibid.

54. Ibid., 35–36.

55. Ibid., 14.

56. Ibid., 7.

57. Eric Hobsbawm and Terence Ranger, eds., *The Invention of Tradition* (Cambridge: Cambridge University Press, 1992).

58. Raphael Patai, *The Jews of Hungary: History, Culture, Psychology* (Detroit: Wayne State University Press, 1996), 345.

59. József Bánóczi, "Bécsi kollégáink" [Our Viennese colleagues], *Magyar Zsidó Szemle* [Hungarian Jewish review] 4, no. 8 (1887): 495–496.

60. *Egyenlőség* [Equality] 8, no. 6 (February 10, 1889): 2.

61. Ibid.

62. Ibid.

63. "A Magyar-Zsidó Irodalmi Társaság alapszabályainak tervezete" [Plans for the Hungarian Jewish Literary Society], *Magyar Zsidó Szemle* [Hungarian Jewish review] 10, no. 2 (1893): 236.

64. Ferenc Mezey, "Az Izraelita Magyar Irodalmi Társulat megalakulása" [The founding of the Jewish Hungarian Literary Society], *Magyar Zsidó Szemle* 11, no. 2 (1894): 74–75.

65. Gábor Schwartz, "Epilógus a reczeptióhoz" [Epilogue to the Reception Law], *Magyar Zsidó Szemle* 12, nos. 10–11 (1895): 469.

66. Vilmos Vázsonyi, "A diadalmas reakció" [The triumph of reaction], *Egyenlőség* [Equality] 9, no. 40 (October 3, 1890): 2.

67. See Péter Bihari, *Lövészárkok a hátországban: Középosztály, zsidókérdés, antiszemitizmus és az első világháború Magyarországon* [Trenches in the hinterland: The middle class, the Jewish question, anti-Semitism and the First World War in Hungary] (Budapest: Napvilág Kiadó, 2008).

68. Ágoston, *A zsidók útja*, 8.

69. Géza Supka, "A zsidókérdéshez" [Contribution to the Jewish question], *Huszadik Század* [Twentieth century] 35, no. 6 (June 1917): 523.

70. This project has received considerable scholarly attention in recent years. See Ferenc Laczó, "Das Problem nationaler Heterogenität: Die Diskussion über die Judenfrage in der Zeitschrift *Huszadik Század* im Jahr 1917," in *Die "Judenfrage"-ein europäisches Phänomen?*, ed. Manfred Hettling and Michael G. Müller (Berlin: Metropol Verlag, 2013), 123–158.

71. "A zsidókérdés Magyarországon: A *Huszadik Század* körkérdése" [The Jewish question in Hungary: The questionnaire of the *Huszadik Század*], *Huszadik Század* 19 (1917): 1. The next nine sources are from this issue.

72. Sándor Fleissig, director of the Hungarian National Bank, *Huszadik Század*, 10.

73. Lajos Blau, director of the Franz Joseph National Rabbinical Institute, *Huszadik Század*, 3.

74. Zoltán Bosnyák, writer, *Huszadik Század*, 59.

75. Benő Haypál, Protestant minister, *Huszadik Század*, 11.

76. Pál Liebermann, university professor, *Huszadik Század*, 19.

77. Anna Lesznai, writer, *Huszadik Század*, 108.

78. Jenő Cholnoky, university professor, *Huszadik Század*, 72–73.

79. Oszkár Jászi, *Huszadik Század*, 96.

80. "Summary of the Questionnaire," *Huszadik Század*, 155.

Chapter 3. A Jewish Politician in a Divided Public Space

An earlier version of this chapter first appeared as "'The Jewish Ambassador to Budapest': Mór Wahrmann and the Politics of 'Tactfulness,'" *Hungarian Historical Review* 3, no. 4 (2014): 787–817.

1. See Vilmos Tóth, "Wahrmann Mór temetése és a Wahrmann-mauzoleum" [The funeral of Mór Wahrmann and the Wahrmann mausoleum], in *Honszeretet és felekezeti hűség: Wahrmann Mór, 1831–1892* [Love of nation and loyalty to religion: Mór Wahrmann, 1831–1892], ed. Tibor Frank (Budapest: Argumentum, 2006), 205–211.

2. For a comprehensive analysis of Wahrmann's life, see Tibor Frank, "Magyar és zsidó: A Wahrmann-életrajz kérdései" [Hungarian and Jewish: The problematic of Wahrmann's biography], in Frank, *Honszeretet és felekezeti hűség*, 11–35.

3. *Pesti Hirlap* [Budapest daily] 14, no. 328 (November 27, 1892). Wahrmann's obituaries were collected in "Néhai Wahrmnn Mór országgyűlési képviselő, a Pesti Izraelita Hitközség elnöke stb. stb. emlékezete" [Remembrances of the deceased

Mór Wahrmann, Member of Parliament and President of the Budapest Jewish Congregation], in Magyar Zsidó Múzeum és Levéltár, Budapest. Henceforth all quotations from the collection will be referred to as "Magyar Zsidó Múzeum és Levéltár."

4. *Nemzet*, Esti Kiadás [The nation, evening edition] 11, no. 330 (November 29, 1892), in Magyar Zsidó Múzeum és Levéltár.

5. *Vasárnapi Újság* [Sunday paper] 39, no. 49 (December 4, 1892), in Magyar Zsidó Múzeum és Levéltár.

6. *Pesti Napló Esti Lapja* [The evening edition of the Budapest news], no. 329 (November 28, 1892), in Magyar Zsidó Múzeum és Levéltár.

7. *Egyetértés* [Agreement], no. 328 (November 27, 1892), in Magyar Zsidó Múuzeum és Levéltár.

8. Sándor Bűcher, "Wahrmann Mór életrajza," *Magyar Zsidó Szemle* [Hungarian Jewish review] 10, no. 3 (1893): 9, in Magyar Zsidó Múzeum és Levéltár.

9. Haber Samu, "Wahrmann Mórról" [About Mór Wahrmann], *Egyenlőség* [Equality] 11, no. 49 (December 2, 1892), in Magyar Zsidó Múzeum és Levéltár.

10. Andrew Handler, *Blood Libel at Tiszaeszlár* (Boulder, CO: East European Monographs, 1980), 10.

11. *Magyar Állam* [Hungarian state] 3, no. 274 (November 30, 1892), in Magyar Zsidó Múzeum és Levéltár.

12. *Neue Freie Presse*, no. 10153 (November 28, 1892), in Magyar Zsidó Múzeum és Levéltár.

13. For a discussion of the prohibition on the public articulation of Jewish identity, see András Kovács, "A magyar zsidók és a politika" [Hungarian Jews and politics], *Világosság* 39, no. 2 (January 1998): 78–85.

14. "Börzeviczy W. M. élczei" [The witticisms of W. M. Börzeviczy], *Borsszem Jankó* (December 4, 1892): 4.

15. The joke still had enough traction as late as 1972 to find its way into Georg Lukács's autobiography *Gelebtes Denken*, where he characterized his father's conformism and patriotism with the dismissive phrase "Jewish ambassador to Budapest."

16. A version of the episode found inclusion in one of Wahrmann's obituaries, which recounted that "many of [Wahrmann's] former colleagues in parliament still remember the following witty saying of his. It took place during the outbreak of anti-Semitism, when Istóczy suggested that the Jews of Hungary should be deported to Jerusalem. Wahrmann humorously commented on this idea to his friends: 'The plan is not a bad one and I have no objections to it. But I reserve the right to stay among you as ambassador from Jerusalem.'" "Wahrmann Mór," *Egyetértés* [Agreement], no. 328 (November 27, 1892), in Magyar Zsidó Múzeum és Levéltár.

17. For a full version of the incident, including its sources, see Frank, *Honszeretet és felekezeti hűség*, 36–37.

18. Kenneth Burke, *A Grammar of Motives* (Berkeley: University of California Press, 1969), 324.

19. Lajos Nagy, "Este van" [It is evening], *Nyugat* 1, no. 10 (May 16, 1908): 554–558.

20. The circumstances of the publication of the short story were recounted in the autobiography of the author. Lajos Nagy, *Lázadó ember, 1883–1914* [The rebel, 1883–1914] (Budapest: Szépirodalmi Könyvkiadó, 1956).

21. "Polgári házasság" [Civil marriage], *Borsszem Jankó* (April 3, 1881): 10.

22. Porzó, *Utazás Pestről,* 408.

23. "Az országházból" [The annals of parliament], *Magyar Zsidó Szemle* [Hungarian Jewish review] 1, no. 9 (1884): 580.

24. The Law of Reception proposed to grant Judaism equal status with other religions in the state.

25. Béla Vajda, "A zsidóság és a prozelita-csinálás" [Jewry and the making of proselytes], *Magyar Zsidó Szemle* [Hungarian Jewish review] 12, no. 3 (1895): 260.

26. *Budapesti Hirlap* 12, no. 331(November 30, 1892), in Magyar Zsidó Múzeum és Levéltár.

27. "A Tisza-eszlári gyilkosság" [The murder at Tiszaeszlár], *Függetlenség* [Independence] (July 1, 1882), in Országos Széchényi Könyvtár [National Széchényi Library], Oregebb Bonyhády Perczel István, "Jüdische Delikatessen," Oct. Hung. 730. (Henceforth all references to this collection will be OSK, Oct. Hung. 730).

28. Lajos Palágyi, "Zsidók a társaságban" [Jews in society], *Egyenlőség* [Equality] 8, no. 42 (November 17, 1890): 7–8.

29. See Kálmán Mikszáth, "Karcolatok Wahrmann Mórról" [Sketches about Mór Wahrmann], in Frank, *Honszeretet és felekezeti hűség,* 557–587.

30. *Magyar Hirlap* [Hungarian daily] 2, no. 329 (November 28, 1892), in Magyar Zsidó Múzeum és Levéltár.

31. *Pesti Hirlap* [Budapest news] 14, no. 328 (November 27, 1892), in Magyar Zsidó Múzeum és Levéltár.

32. *Budapesti Hirlap* [Budapest daily] 12, no. 331 (November 30, 1892), in Magyar Zsidó Múzeum és Levéltár.

33. For an analysis of Wahrmann's economic activities, see György Kövér, "Wahrmann és fia" [Wahrmann and son], in Frank, *Honszeretet és felekezeti hűség,* 77–90.

34. *Képviselőházi Napló* [Parliamentary records], 1884–1887, vol. 15, session 320 (February 12, 1887): 159, quoted in Ferenc Pölöskei, *A magyar parlamentarizus a századfordulón: Politikusok és intézmények* [Hungarian parliamentary politics at the fin de siècle: Politicians and institutions] (Budapest: História—MTA Történettudományi Intézet, 2001), 33–38. Quoted in Frank, *Honszeretet és felekezeti hűség,* 19.

35. Sándor Hegedűs, "Wahrmannról" [About Wahrmann], *Vasárnapi Ujság* [Sunday paper] 39, no. 49 (December 4, 1892), in Magyar Zsidó Múzeum és Levéltár.

36. Mór Wahrmann, *A lipótvárosi választó kerület polgáriahoz: Elmondott 1884. május 27. a lipótvárosi válsztók előtt* [To the electorate of the Lipótváros: Delivered on May 27, 1884, to the electorate of the Lipótváros] (Budapest: Az Athenaeum R. Társulat Könyvnyomdája, 1884), quoted in Frank, *Honszeretet és felekezeti hűség,* 539.

37. Ibid., 542.

38. *Nemzet* [Nation] (November 27, 1892), in Magyar Zsidó Múzeum és Levéltár.

39. *Budapesti Hirlap* [Budapest daily] 12, no. 329 (November 28, 1892), in Magyar Zsidó Múzeum és Levéltár.

220 Notes to pages 93-104

40. *Borsszem Jankó* (November 4, 1884).
41. *Borsszem Jankó* (October 5, 1879).
42. *Borsszem Jankó* (December 4, 1881).
43. "Szatmármegye kérvénye a képviselőház előtt" [The petition of county Szatmár before the house of representatives], *Egyetértés* (June 8, 1882), OSZK, Hung. 730
44. "Az Istóczy-Wahrmann botrány a képviselőházban" [The Istóczy-Wahrmann scandal in the parliament], *Függetlenség* (June 10, 1882), OSZK, Oct. Hung. 730.
45. "Az Istóczy-Wahrmann-féle ügy" [The Istóczy-Wahrmann affair], *Függetlenség* (June 11, 1882), OSZK, Hung. 730.
46. "A fővárosi V-ik kerület választópolgárainak felirata Wahrmann Mór képviselőjükhöz" [The petition of the voters of the Vth district of Budapest to their representative, Mór Wahrmann], in Frank, *Honszeretet és felekezeti hűség*, 527.
47. Victor Turner, "Social Dramas in Brazilian Umbanda: The Dialectics of Meaning," in *The Anthropology of Performance* (New York: PAJ Publications, 1986), 3.
48. Ibid.
49. Victor Turner, "Social Dramas and Stories about Them," in *From Ritual to Theater: The Human Seriousness of Play* (New York: PAJ Publications, 1982), 71.
50. "Az Istóczy-Wahrmann botrány a kéviselőházban" [The Istóczy-Wahrmann scandal in the parliament], *Függetlenség* (June 10, 1882), OSZK, Oct. Hung. 730.
51. "Az Istóczy-Wahrmann féle ügy" [The Istóczy-Wahrmann affair], *Függetlenség* (June 11, 1882), OSZK, Oct. Hung. 730.
52. Ibid.
53. "A Wahrmann-Istóczy ügy" [The Wahrmann-Istoczy affair], *Egyetértés* (June 11, 1882), OSZK, Oct. Hung. 730.
54. "Istóczy és Wahrmann párbaja: A párbaj meghiúsitása a lóverseny téren" [The duel of Istóczy and Wahrmann: The prevention of the duel on the racing track], *Függetlenség* (June 12, 1882), OZK, Oct. Hung. 730.
55. "Budától Ercsiig" [From Buda to Ercsi], *Függetlenség* (June12, 1882), OSZK, Oct. Hung. 730.
56. Ibid.
57. "A zsidó papság és a zsidóság" [The Jewish clergy and Jewry], *Függetlenség* (June 14, 1882), OSZK, Oct. Hung. 730.
58. Turner, "Social Dramas and Stories about Them," 71.
59. Frontispiece, *Borsszem Jankó* (June 15, 1882).
60. Kálmán Mikszáth, "A hősök sorsa: Karcolat" [The fate of heroes: A sketch], *Pesti Hirlap* [Budapest daily] (March 29, 1883), in Frank, *Honszeretet és felekezeti hűség*, 568.
61. Ron H. Feldman, "Introduction: The Jew as Pariah: The Case of Hannah Arendt," in Hannah Arendt, *The Jewish Writings*, li.
62. Arendt, "The Jew as Pariah," 280.

Chapter 4. The Jewish Humor Magazine and Collective Self-Parody

1. Csicseri Bors (Adolf Ágai), "A 'Borsszem Jankó' története" [The history of *Borsszem Jankó*], *Borsszem Jankó* (April 10, 1887): 3-4.

2. See Tamás Dersi, *Századvégi üzenet—Sajtótörténeti tanulmányok* [Message from the fin de siècle—Studies in the history of the press] (Budapest: Szépirodalmi Könyvkiadó, 1973); and Géza Buzinkay, *Borsszem Jankó és társai: Magyar élclapok és karikatúrák a XIX. század második felében* [Borsszem Jankó and companions: Hungarian humor magazines and caricatures in the second half of the nineteenth century] (Budapest: Corvina, 1983).

3. Csicseri Bors, "A 'Borsszem Janko' története," 11.

4. Ibid., 10–11.

5. For a reformulation of the positive, integrative role of humor, see F. H. Buckley, *The Morality of Laughter* (Ann Arbor: University of Michigan Press, 2005).

6. Jefferson S. Chase, *Inciting Laughter: The Development of "Jewish Humor" in Nineteenth-Century German Culture* (Berlin: Walter de Gruyter, 2000).

7. See Paul Reitter, *The Anti-Journalist: Karl Kraus and Jewish Self-Fashioning in Fin-de-Siècle Europe* (Chicago: University of Chicago Press, 2008).

8. Chase, *Inciting Laughter*, 3.

9. Ibid., 43.

10. No attempt is made here to provide a comprehensive list of books on the general history and theory of humor, which is too extensive to be useful. For works on Hungarian Jewish humor, see Adam Biro, *Two Jews on a Train: Stories from the Old Country and the New* (Chicago: University of Chicago Press, 2001); Adam Biro, *Is It Good for the Jews: More Stories from the Old Country and the New* (Chicago: University of Chicago Press, 2009); László Erőss, *A pesti vicc* [The Budapest joke] (Budapest: Gondolat Kiadó, 1982); István Hajdú, *Osztropoli Herschel ostora: Viccek, adomák és bölcs mondások a zsidó folklorból* [The whip of Herschel Osztropoli: Jokes, anecdotes and wise sayings from Jewish folklore] (Budapest: Minerva, 1985); Imre Nagy, Ötezer vicc [Five thousand jokes] (Budapest: Ojság, 1932). For a selection of general works on Jewish humor, see Avner Ziv, ed., *Jewish Humor* (Tel Aviv: Papyrus, 1986); Avner Ziv and Anat Zajman, eds., *Semites and Stereotypes: Characteristics of Jewish Humor* (Westport, CT: Greenwood Press, 1983); Arthur Asa Berger, *The Genius of the Jewish Joke* (New Brunswick: Transaction Publishers, 2006); Sarah Blacher Cohen, *Jewish Wry: Essays on Jewish Humor* (Detroit: Wayne State University Press, 1991); Sig Altman, *Comic Image of the Jew: Explorations of a Pop Culture Phenomenon* (Madison, NJ: Fairleigh Dickinson University Press, 1971).

11. Mary Douglas, *Implicit Meanings: Essays in Anthropology* (London: Routledge & Kegan Paul, 1975).

12. Ibid., 98.

13. See Henri Bergson, *Laughter: An Essay on the Meaning of the Comic* (London: Macmillan, 1911); and Sigmund Freud, *Wit and Its Relation to the Unconscious* (New York: Dover, 1993).

14. Douglas, *Implicit Meanings*, 95.

15. Ibid., 98.

16. For a discussion of the political links between anti-Semitism and the crisis of modernity, see Shulamit Volkov, *Germans, Jews, and Antisemites: Trials in Emancipation* (Cambridge: Cambridge University Press, 2006).

17. See Sander L. Gilman, *Jewish Self-Hatred: Anti-Semitism and the Hidden Language of the Jews* (Baltimore: Johns Hopkins University Press, 1986); and Paul Reitter, *On the Origins of Jewish Self-Hatred* (Princeton: Princeton University Press, 2012). For an analysis of *Borsszem Jankó* from this perspective, see Kati Vörös, "Judapesti buleváron: A 'zsidó' fogalmi konstrukciója és vizuális reprezentációja a magyar élclapokban a 19. század második felében" [On the boulevard of Judapest: The theoretical construction and visual representation of the "Jew" in Hungarian humor magazines in the second half of the nineteenth century], *Media Kutató* (Spring 2003), http://www.mediakutato.hu/cikk/2003_01_tavasz/02_judapesti_bulevaron.

18. Csicseri Bors, "A 'Borsszem Jankó' története," 6.

19. "Ágai Adolf," *Füstölő* [Smoke-house] (November 1, 1881): 5.

20. Adolf Ágai to Béla Tóth (July 25, 1903), in Magyar Nemzeti Múzeum Könyvtára [Library of the Hungarian National Museum] Fond 1949, no. 100.

21. Csicseri Bors, "A 'Borsszem Jankó' története," 11.

22. Ibid., 2.

23. Mór Ludassy (1825–1885) was a Hungarian journalist, writer, and editor, who in the early 1860s moved to Vienna, where he became a contributor to the journal *Debatte*. He was known as a passionate advocate of the Compromise Agreement between Austria and Hungary and gained influence with Gyula Andrassy as a spokesman for this cause. The Deák Party was a political group that came into existence in 1865. Under the leadership of Ferenc Deák, the titular head of the group, it negotiated the Compromise Agreement that gave rise to the Austro-Hungarian monarchy.

24. Csicseri Bors, "A 'Borsszem Jankó' története," 2.

25. Ibid., 2.

26. Csicseri Bors, "Andrássy Gyula gr.—és a 'Borsszem Jankó'" [Count Gyula Andrássy and the "*Borsszem Jankó*"], *Borsszem Jankó* (February 23, 1890): 6.

27. Ibid., 5.

28. The actual remark was made in the context of recruiting Jews for political office in the newly elected parliament of 1867. "I consider it desirable," he claimed, "that the emancipation of the Jews be translated into deeds as well and since there exist so much outstanding talent among them, these intelligent individuals should take their place in the realm of the legislature for the good of the nation." Quoted in Tibor Frank, "Magyar és zsidó: A Wahrmann-életrajz kérdései" [Hungarian and Jewish: The problematic of the Wahrmann biography], in Frank, *Honszeretet és felekezeti hűség*, 59.

29. Lenke Steiner, *Ágai Adolf, 1836–1916* (Budapest: n.p., 1933).

30. For the convergence between Jews and Hungarian liberal nationalism, see Jakab Katz, "The Uniqueness of Hungarian Jewry," *Forum*, no. 2 (1977): 45–53.

31. Porzó (Adolf Ágai), *Por és hamu: Barátaim és jó embereim emlékezete* [Dust and ashes: Memories of friends and collaborators] (Budapest: Az Athanaeum R. Társulat Kiadása, 1892), 218.

32. Porzó (Adolf Ágai), *Új hantok* [New graves] (Budapest: Athanaeum Könyvkiadó, 1906), 1.

33. Ibid., 2.

34. Ibid., 19. The original of the sentence is: "Dulce et decorum est pro patria mori."

35. Quoted in Steiner, Ágai Adolf, 19.

36. Ferencz Székely, "A Kagál," *Borsszem Jankó* (October 1, 1916): 8.

37. Csicseri Bors (Adolf Ágai), "1–2000: Melléklet a 'Borsszem Jankó' 2,000 számához" [1–2000: Special edition to the two thousandth number of the *Borsszem Jankó*], *Borsszem Jankó* (April 8, 1906): 5.

38. Adolf Ágai to Ferencz Márton (February 18, 1884), Magyar Nemzeti Múzeum Könyvtára, Abonyi hagyaték, Fond 1/11.

39. For a recent study of the social and cultural strategies associated with Hungarian Jewish assimilation, see Miklós Konrád, *Zsidóságon innen és túl: Zsidók vallásváltása Magyarországon a reformkortól az első világháborúig* [Beyond and within Jewish identification: Religious conversion of Jews in Hungary from the age of reform to the First World War] (Budapest: MTA Bölcsészettudományi Kutatóközpont Történettudományi Intézet, 2014).

40. The archbishopric of Esztergom was a historic diocese in the territory of Upper Hungary. Though the source does not identify Ágai's interlocutor, it was almost certainly János Simor, who was archbishop between 1867 and 1891.

41. Dr. Miksa Schächter, "Ágai Adolf dr. és a zsidóság" [Dr. Adolf Ágai and his Jewish identity], *Múlt és Jövő* [Past and Future] 6 (November 1916): 440.

42. See András Gerő, "Zsidó utak—magyar keretek a XIX. században: *Liberálisok, anitszemiták és a zsidók a modern Magyarország születésekor* [Jewish paths and Hungarian frames: Liberals, anti-Semites and Jews at the origins of modern Hungary], in *Zsidóság a dualizmus kori Magyarországon: Siker és válság* [Jewry in Dualistic Hungary: Success and crisis] (Budapest: Pannonica Kiadó, Habburg Történeti Intézet, 2005), 58–72; and András Kovács, "A magyar zsidók és a politika" [Hungarian Jews and politics], *Világosság* 39, no. 2 (January 1998): 78.

43. Csicseri Bors, "Andrássy Gyula gr.," 6.

44. "A 'Borsszem Jankó' látogatói'" [The visitors of *Borsszem Jankó*], *Bosszem Jankó* (March 15, 1868): n.p.

45. Lipót Arany, "Ágai Adolf a magánéletben" [Adolf Ágai in private life], and "Ágai Adolf emléke: Születésének századik évfordulója alkalmából" [Memories of Adolf Ágai: Commemorating the hundredth anniversary of his birth], *Újság* (March 29, 1936): 31.

46. David Kunzle, *The History of the Comic Strip: The Nineteenth Century* (Berkeley: University of California Press, 1990), 6.

47. Csicseri Bors, "A *Borsszem Jankó* története," 7.

48. Adolf Ágai to Ferencz Márton (March 1, 1898), Magyar Nemzeti Múzeum Könyvtára, Abonyi hagyaték, Fond I/11.

49. "Borsszem Jankó estélye" [The soirée of Borsszem Jankó], *Borsszem Jankó* (December 26, 1875): frontispiece.

50. "Ujabb tanács" [More advice], quoted in *Egyenlőség* [Equality] 8, no. 6 (February 10, 1889): 8.

51. *Bolond Miska* [Mike the fool] (November 5, 1865), in *Mokány Berczi és Spitzig Itzig, Göre Gábor mög a többiek* . . . *A Magyar társadalom figurái az élclapokban 1860 és 1918 között* [Mokány Berczi and Spitzig Itzig, Göre Gábor and the others . . . The figures of Hungarian society in the humor magazines between 1860 and 1918] (Budapest: Magvető Könyvkiadó, 1988), 518.

52. "Királyutczai levél: Az új nemesekrűl és a régi goleszrul" [Letter from the Király Street: About the new nobility and the old god], *Borsszem Jankó* 3 (May 1, 1870): 187.

53. "Királyutcai levelek" [Letters from the Király Street], *Borsszem Jankó* (January 12, 1868): 18.

54. "Spitzig Itzig, Nyilt levél az aszódi zsidókhoz" [Itzig Spitzig's open letter to the Jews of Aszód], *Borsszem Jankó* (May 16, 1875): 9.

55. For diverging interpretations of *Mauschel*, see Gilman, *Jewish Self-Hatred*; Scott Spector, *Prague Territories: National Conflict and Cultural Innovation in Franz Kafka's Fin de Siècle* (Berkeley: University of California Press, 2000); Paul Reitter, *The Anti-Journalist: Karl Kraus and Jewish Self-Fashioning in Fin-de-Siècle Europe* (Chicago: University of Chicago Press, 2008).

56. Adolf Ágai, "Édes atyám" [My father], in *Az örök zsidó: Régi naplók, életképek, 1862–1906* [The eternal Jew: Diaries and accounts of everyday life, 1862–1906], ed. János Kőbányai (Budapest: Múlt és Jövő Kiadó, 2010), 12.

57. Steiner, *Ágai Adolf*, 2.

58. Aladár Komlós, *Magyar-Zsidó szellemtörténet a reformkortól a holocaustig* [Hungarian-Jewish intellectual history from the Age of Reform to the Holocaust] (Budapest: Múlt és Jövő Kiadó, 1997), 2:54.

59. Theodor Herzl, *Zionist Writings: Essays and Addresses*, trans. Harry Zohn (New York: Herzl Press, 1973), 1:164.

60. Aladár Komlós, "Ágai Adolf zsidósága" [The Jewish identity of Adolf Ágai], in Kőbányai, *Az örök zsidó*, 226.

61. For a discussion of this concept, see Chase, *Inciting Laughter*, 1–19. See also Susan Purdie, *Comedy: The Master of Discourse* (New York: Harvester Wheatsheaf, 1993).

62. Homi K. Bhabha, "Foreword: Joking Aside: The Ideal of a Self-Critical Community," in *Modernity, Culture and "the Jew*," ed. Bryen Cheyette and Laura Marcus (Cambridge: Polity Press, 1998), xvii, xix.

63. Chase, *Inciting Laughter*, 3, 10–11.

64. *Bolond Miska* (November 5, 1868), in *Mokány Berczi és Spitzig Itzig, Göre Gábor mög a többiek*, 518.

65. Douglas, *Implicit Meanings*, 107.

66. "Hajdan, Most" [Then and now], *Borsszem Jankó* (August 8, 1869): 316–317.

67. Arendt, "The Jew as Pariah," 280.

68. "Tönődések Seiffensteiner Salamontól" [Salamon Seiffensteiner's reflections], *Borsszem Jankó* (March 25, 1883): 2.

69. "Tönődések Seiffensteiner Salamontól" [Salamon Seiffensteiner's reflections], *Borsszem Jankó* (February 21, 1884): 4.

70. "Tönődések Seiffensteiner Salamontól" [Salamon Seiffensteiner's reflections], *Borsszem Jankó* (February 25, 1882): 4. The book he was referring to was Samuel Kohn's *Zsidók története Magyarországon* [The history of the Jews in Hungary] (Budapest: Athenaeum, 1884).

71. "Tönődések Seiffensteiner Salamontól" [Salamon Seiffensteiner's reflections], *Borsszem Jankó* (August 5, 1883): 8.

72. Adolf Ágai to Mari Jászai (January 25, 1902), Országos Széchényi Könyvtár, Szinháztörténeti Osztálya 1950, no. 4347.

73. Arthur Koestler, *The Act of Creation* (New York: Macmillan, 1964), 35.

74. For an account of the story, see György Kövér, "Seiffensteiner Salamon lidérces álmai" [Salamon Seiffensteiner's nightmares], *Irodalmi és társadalmi havi lap* [Literary and social monthly], nos. 7–8 (2006): 54–61.

75. Salamon Seiffensteiner, "Jeruzsálemben: Seiffensteiner Salamon elbeszélése nyomán" [Report from Jerusalem: Based on the account of Salamon Seiffensteiner], in *Czu Tumm! Hexti Atiszemida Nopdár 1883-ra* [Czu Tumm! Hexti's anti-Semitic calendar for 1883], Szeageszdete a Kraxelbuber Tobias [Edited by Tobias Kraxlebuber] (Pudibest: Az Athenaeum R. Társulat Kiadása, 1883), 77.

76. This was probably a distortion of the name Károly Eötvös, the defense attorney of the Tiszaeszlár Jews.

77. Seiffensteiner, "Jeruzsálemben," 83.

78. Ibid., 85.

79. See *Vasárnapi Újság* [Sunday paper] 30, nos. 26 and 29 (1883).

Chapter 5. The Scandal of the Budapest Orpheum

1. See Theophile Gautier, *Mademoiselle de Maupin* (New York: Boni and Liveright, 1918). For an interpretation of Gautier's work, see Mary Gluck, *Popular Bohemia: Modernism and Urban Culture in Nineteenth-Century Paris* (Cambridge, MA: Harvard University Press, 2005).

2. For a different perspective on the cultural status of the two cities, see András Gerő, "Zwei Städte, zwei Sätze: Wien und Budapest zur Jahrhundertwende," in *Zeit des Aufbruchs: Budapest und Wien zwischen Historismus und Avantgarde*, ed. Katalin Földi-Dózsa and Marianne Hergovich (Vienna: Kunsthistorisches Museum, Skira, 2003). See also Péter Hanák, *The Garden and the Workshop: Essays in the Cultural History of Vienna and Budapest* (Princeton: Princeton University Press, 1998).

3. Salamon Ödön, "Budapest a nyugat városa" [Budapest, a western city], in *A mulató Budapest* [Budapest, the city of entertainment], ed. Henrik Lenkei (Budapest: Singer és Wolfner, 1896), 17.

4. Porzó, *Utazás Pestről–Budapestre*, 404.

5. Dezső Gyárfás, *Orfeum: Egy szinész élete* [Orpheum: The life of an actor] (Budapest: A Kultúra Könyvkiadó Nyomda, 1920), 41.

6. See Péter Gál Molnár, *A pesti mulatók: Előszó egy szinháztörténetéhez* [Budapest nightlife: A foreword to the history of the theater] (Budapest: Helikon Kiadó,

2001). See also Miklós Konrád, "Orfeum és zsidó identitás Budapesten a század-fordulón" [Orpheums and Jewish identity in Budapest at the turn of the century], *Budapesti Negyed* [Budapest and its neighborhoods] 16, no. 2 (2008): 351–368.

7. A notable exception to this generalization were the publications of the *Budapesti Negyed*, a series of outstanding studies about Budapest popular culture that was active between 1993 and 2010.

8. See Moritz Csáky, *Between Escapism and Reality: The Ideology of the Viennese Operetta* (London: Austrian Cultural Institute, 1997); Péter Hanák, "A bécsi és a budapesti operett kultúrtörténeti helye" [The cultural historical role of the Viennese and Budapest operetta], *Budapesti Negyed* 5, nos. 16–17 (1997): 9–30; Ivan Sanders, "Eternal Operetta," *The Hungarian Quarterly* 189 (2008): 145–150.

9. Sándor Galamb, *A magyar operett első évtizede* [The first decade of the Hungarian operetta] (Budapest: Franklin Nyomda, 1926), 366.

10. Képviselő Házi Napló, 1887–1892 [Parliamentary Records 1887–1892], vol. 24 (Budapest, 1891), 373, in Miklós Konrád, "Orfeum és zsidó identitás Budapesten a század fordulón," 4.

11. "Die Spectakelsteuer in Budapest," *Internationale Artisten-Revue* 1, no. 1 (November 8, 1891): n.p.

12. "Beköszöntő" [Introduction], *Mulató Budapest: A budapesti szinházak és multók napilapja* [Budapest entertainment: The daily paper of the theaters and music halls of Budapest] 1, no. 1 (October 30, 1901): n.p. *Mulató Budapest* was one of several ephemeral guides to Budapest commercial entertainment to emerge between 1890 and 1906 that bore slight variations of the same name.

13. Endre Nagy, *A kabaré regénye* [The novel of the cabaret] (Budapest: Magvető Könyvkiadó, 1958), 217, 292.

14. For the connections between commercial entertainment and lower-middle-class Jewish identity, see Konrád, "Orfeum és zsidó identitás Budapesten a század fordulón."

15. "Pesti éjjel" [Nightlife in Budapest], *A mulató Budapest* [Entertainment in Budapest] 1, no. 5 (November 17, 1906): n.p.

16. *Journal de Budapest* (December 22, 1901): n.p.

17. *A Szinház* [The theater] (1904), 12, quoted in Molnár, *A pesti mulatók*, 193. Révay Street was the location of the Folies Caprices.

18. Nagy, *A kabaré regénye*, 147.

19. Samu Haber, "A gajdosok" [Ribald voices], *Egyenlőség* (February 7, 1897): 6.

20. "Bemutató, [Introduction], *Mulatók Lapja* (January 26, 1890): n.p.

21. Károly Somossy, "Somossy Orfeuma, Nagy mező-utca 17," Plakát-és aprónyomtatványtár [Collection of posters and leaflets], Országos Széchéynyi Könyvtár, Budapest.

22. Gyárfás, *Orfeum*, 35.

23. Elemér Boross, *Velük voltam* [I was with them] (Budapest: Szépirodalmi Könyvkiadó, 1969), 83.

24. Jenő Heltai, *Szines kövek: Elbeszélések, emlékezések* [Colored pebbles: Anecdotes and memories] (Budapest: Szépirodalmi Könyvkiadó, 1957), 497.

25. István Bródy, *Régi pesti dáridók: Egy letünt világ regénye* [Old night spots of Pest: The novel of a lost world] (Budapest: n.p., 1940), 14.

26. Quoted in T. J. Clark, *The Painting of Modern Life: Paris in the Art of Manet and His Followers* (Princeton: Princeton University Press, 1984), 34.

27. Gyárfás, *Orfeum*, 35.

28. Vilmos Tarján, *Pesti éjszaka* [Budapest nights] (Budapest: Általános Nyomda, Könyv-és Lapkiadó Rt., 1940), 23. Dob Street was one of the more impoverished streets in the neighborhood.

29. See Molnár, *A pesti mulatók*, 5.

30. Playbill of the Friedman Orpheum, in Plakát és aprónyomtatványtár, OSZK.

31. Nagy, *A kabaré regénye*, 292.

32. Gyárfás, *Orfeum*, 15.

33. Emil Dacsó, "Orfeumok, chantanteok" [Orpheums and chantants], in Lenkei, *A mulató Budapest*, 304.

34. Porzó (Adolf Ágai), "Budapest chez nuit" [Budapest by night], *A Hét* [The week] 1, no. 14 (April 6, 1890): 224.

35. Pepi Littman (1877–1930) was a member of the itinerant Broder Singers and became famous for performing in drag as a young Hasidic man, clothed in satin coat and white knee socks and breeches. She performed in Galicia, Romania, and Hungary, where she was especially popular for her Yiddish, often sexually explicit, songs and ditties. For Hungarian intellectuals' complicated attitude to Yiddish, see Ignotus, "Zsargon" [Jargon], *Nyugat* [West] 1, no. 20 (October 16, 1908): 247–256.

36. Tarján, *Pesti éjszaka*, 23.

37. Boross, *Velük voltam*, 85.

38. Ibid., 82.

39. Judith R. Walkowitz, *Nights Out: Life in Cosmopolitan London* (New Haven: Yale University Press, 2012), 64.

40. *Krúdy Gyula Budapestje: Megjelent az iró születésének 100. évfordulójára* [The Budapest of Gyula Krúdy: Published in honor of the 100th anniversary of the author's birth] (Budapest: Fővárosi Szabó Ervin Könyvtár, 1978), 106.

41. Yvette Guilbert (1865–1944) was a French cabaret singer and actress, associated with a modernist performance style. Jean-Paul Habens (1845–1908), also known as Paulus, was a celebrated French café-concert singer, renowned for the patriotic military songs he performed at the Eldorado. Caroline "La Belle" Otero (1868–1965) was a Spanish-born actress, singer, and dancer who became a star at the Folies Bergère in Paris and was one of the most flamboyant figures of Parisian music hall. Armand Ary was a celebrated singer and actress at the Folies Bergère; she is best known today for lithographs advertising her performances. The Barrison Sisters were a risqué vaudeville troupe who performed in the United States and throughout Europe between 1891 and 1900. Their style spawned countless imitators as well as fashion trends. Carola Cecilia was the star of the Somossy Orpheum, notorious for the extravagance of her personal life and performance style. She was particularly famous for her cross-dressing roles in tight male attire or Hussar costumes.

42. Emil Dacsó, "Orfeumok, chantanteok," in Lenkei, *A mulató Budapest*, 300.

43. Molnár, *A pesti mulatók*, 69.

44. Gyula Krúdy, *Világ* (May 17, 1925), in Molnár, *A pesti mulatók*, 48.

45. Jenő Zichy (1837–1906), who belonged to one of the oldest aristocratic families, was a member of parliament as well as an ethnographer known for his expeditions to Russia and Central Asia, where he hoped to discover the ethnic roots of the Hungarian people.

46. "Hogy mulatott Somossy?" [How did Somossy carouse?], *Pesti Napló* (March 5, 1903), in Molnár, *A pesti mulatók*, 51.

47. "A mulatás művészete" [The art of revelry], *Mulatók Lapja* (February 16, 1890): n.p.

48. "A földtől az Olympuszig" [From the earth to Olympus], *Mulatók Lapja* (January 26, 1890): n.p.

49. Lászlo V. Urbán, ed., *Heltai Jenő Századelő—Tudósitás a Duna-Parti Párizsból* [Jenő Heltai early twentieth century—Reports from the Paris on the Danube] (Budapest: Officina Nova, n.d.), 6.

50. Shane Vogel, *The Scenes of Harlem Cabaret: Race, Sexuality, Performance* (Chicago: University of Chicago Press, 2009), 29.

51. Peter Bailey, *Popular Culture and Performance in the Victorian City* (Cambridge: Cambridge University Press, 1998), 126.

52. Ibid., 137.

53. Géza Boros, *Folik vagy nem folik? Egy kupléénekes emlékei* [Follies or not follies? The memories of a music hall singer] (Budapest: Klein Jenő Nyomda, 1942), 79.

54. The lyrics of music hall songs were published in cheap editions that were associated with both the author of the songs and the music hall where they were performed. See *Szőke Szakáll legójabb kupléi: A Steinhardt mulató és a Folies Caprice műsorából* [The newest songs of Szőke Szakáll: From the program of the Steinhardt music hall and the Folies Caprice] (Budapest: Ehrenfeld Testvérek, n.d.); *Vasvári Mulató műsorából: Egy délután a Weingrúbernél; Szöveget es zenéjét irta: Sas Náczi* [From the Vasvári music hall: An afternoon at Weingrúber's; Lyrics and music written by Náczi Sas] (Budapest: Zeizler Nyomda, 1911); *A Steinhardt mulató műsorából: Hunyadi Emil kupléi* [From the program of the Steinhardt music hall: The songs of Emil Hunyadi] (Budapest: Grűnwald, 1913).

55. Géza Steinhardt, *Steinhardt Mesél: Tréfák, adomák, elbeszélések* [The stories of Steinhardt: Jokes, anecdotes, and recollections] (Budapest: A Szerző Kiadása, 1935), 3.

56. Szőke Szakáll was the stage name for Jenő Gerő, who went on to have a successful movie career in Germany and Hungary in the 1920s and 1930s. Forced to emigrate in 1940 after the Nazi invasion of Hungary, he moved to Hollywood, where he performed under the name of S. Z. Sakall. Known for his good-natured fatherly roles, S. Z. Sakall's most memorable Hollywood creation was the headwaiter Karl in the film *Casablanca*.

57. "Ruha nélkül egyenlők az emberek" [Without clothes all people are equal], in *Szőke Szakáll legújabb kupléi*, n.p.

58. Endre Nagy, "Conférenceok a közönségről: Miből lesz a közönség?" [Conference about the audience: How is the audience constituted?], *Új Idők: Szépirodalmi, Művészeti és Társadalmi Képes Hetilap* [New Times: Illustrated literary, artistic and social weekly] 19, no. 24 (June 8, 1913): 605.

59. Lauren Berlant, "Intimacy: A Special Issue," *Critical Inquiry* 24, no. 2 (Winter 1998): 281–288. In the same issue, see also Lauren Berlant and Michael Warner, "Sex in Public," 547–566.

60. Clark, *The Painting of Modern Life*, 237–238.

61. Bailey, *Popular Culture and Performance in the Victorian City*, 130.

62. Barry J. Faulk, *Music Hall and Modernity: The Late-Victorian Discovery of Popular Culture* (Athens: Ohio University Press, 2004), 12.

63. Charles Rearick, *Pleasures of the Belle Époque: Entertainment and Festivity in Turn-of-the-Century France* (New Haven: Yale University Press, 1985), 62.

64. Bailey, *Popular Culture and Performance in the Victorian City*, 126, 148.

65. Vogel, *The Scene of Harlem Cabaret*, 22, 36.

66. Marline Otte, *Jewish Identities in German Popular Entertainment, 1890–1933* (Cambridge: Cambridge University Press, 2006).

67. Kalabriasz is a card game for two, three, or possibly four players that resembles Piquet and is played with the same thirty-two-card deck. The game probably originated in Hungary, but it was known throughout Europe by a variety of names such as Klabiash, Klabberjass, Clobby, or Clobber. For convenience, I have consistently used the German title, "Eine Klabriaspartie," to refer to the skit, though it was also referred to in Hungarian as the "Kalábriász-parti."

68. "Eine Klabriaspartie" seems to have resonances to this day. I received a letter recently from an American reader of one of my articles who inquired about the physical location of the Café Abeles. From the letter, it emerges that the epithet "Café Abeles" had entered into family legend as synonymous with someone who cheated at cards. In such circumstances, the father would invariably reprimand the offending member with the question: "Wo spielen wir, im Café Abeles?" (Where are we playing, in the Café Abeles?). The family had immigrated to the United States from Vienna and Budapest, and the son logically assumed that the Café Abeles must have been a real place in either of these cities. He was surprised to learn that it was a symbolic place that had entered common usage from the fame of "Eine Klabriaspartie."

69. See Georg Wacks, *Die Budapester Orpheumgesellschaft: Ein Vairete in Wien, 1889–1919* (Vienna: Holzhausen, 2002).

70. See Otte, *Jewish Identities in German Popular Entertainment*, 125–197.

71. A graphic account of the improvisations of Rott is provided in Molnár, *A pesti mulatók*, 204.

72. See Adolf Bergmann, Eine *Klabriaspartie* (Vienna: National Verlag, n.d.), in Österreichische Nationalbibliothek, Theat.-S. 844287; *Eine Klabriasparthie* (Original-posse von Caprice [Anton Oroszy]), in *Caprice: Humoristisch-Satyrisches Wochenblatt* [Caprice: Humorous and satirical weekly] 1, nos. 20–39 (1902): 14–21.

73. Gershom Scholem, *From Berlin to Jerusalem: Memories of My Youth*, trans. Harry Zohn, foreword by Moshe Idel (Philadelphia: Paul Dry Books, 2012), 15–16.

74. See George L. Mosse, *German Jews beyond Judaism* (Bloomington: Indiana University Press, 1985); and David Sorkin, *The Transformation of German Jewry, 1780–1840* (New York: Oxford University Press, 1987).

75. Molnár, *A pesti mulatók*, 205.

76. Szinházi krónika [Theater chronicle], "A klasszikus orfeum" [The classical Orpheum], *A Hét* [The week] 6, no. 18/279 (May 5, 1895): 289–290.

77. Heltai, *Szines kövek*, 498.

78. Jenő Heltai, *Tollforgatók: Hét sovány esztendő; Az utolsó bohém, Jaguár* [Scribblers: Seven lean years; The last bohemian, Jaguar] (Budapest: Szépirodlami Könyvkiadó, 1968).

79. "Filozófia" [Philosophy], *Fidibusz* 1, no. 3 (December 15, 1905): n.p.

80. Urbán, *Heltai Jenő Századelő*, 5.

81. Quoted in Andor Zsoldos, *Theodor Herzl: Emlékezések* [Theodor Herzl: Reminiscences] (New York: World Federation of Hungarian Jewry, 1981), 19–20.

Chapter 6. Critical Cross-Dressing and Jewish Bourgeois Identity

1. See Yehudah Don and Victor Karády, eds., *A Social and Economic History of Central European Jewry* (New Brunswick: Transaction, 1990).

2. See Rolf Muller, ed., *Beksics Gusztáv* (Budapest: Uj Mandátum Könyvkiadó, 2005).

3. Gusztáv Beksics, "Polgári elem a magyar társadalomban" [The bourgeois element in Hungarian society], *Magyar Salon* [Hungarian salon] (April 1885): 44–45.

4. Marion Kaplan, *The Making of the Jewish Middle Class: Women, Family, and Identity in Imperial Germany* (New York: Oxford University Press, 1991), 7.

5. Beksics, "Polgári elem a magyar társadalomban," 55.

6. For a discussion of the Wohl sisters, see Fanni Borbiró, "'Csevegés, zene és egy csésze tea': A Wohl-nővérek a pesti társaséletben" ["Gossip, music and a cup of tea": The Wohl sisters in the social life of Budapest], *Budapesti Negyed*, no. 46 (2004): 350–376.

7. Egy Nagyvilági Hölgy (Janka and Stephanie Wohl), *Illem: A jó tarsaság szabályai—Útmutató a művelt társaséletben* [Politeness: The rules of good society—Guide to cultivated social life] (Budapest: Az Athenaeum R. Társulat Kiadása, 1891), 5.

8. Ibid., 98, 99, 102–103.

9. Ibid., 17.

10. Ibid., 156, 57, 222.

11. Ibid., 7.

12. Porzó (Adolf Ágai), Bevezetés [Introduction], in *Nem illik: Útmutató a tarsadalmi érintkezésben töobbé kevésbé elterjedt visszaságok, nyelvi hibák s egyéb botlások elkerülésére* [It is not polite: Guide to the avoidance of obstacles to social interaction associated with more or less frequently committed faults, linguistic mistakes and other missteps] (Budapest: Singer és Wolfner Kiadása, 1886), xxvi.

13. József Kiss, "Egy levél egy évfordulóról és egy szerkesztőről" [A letter about an anniversary and an editor], in *Kiss József kerekasztala: A költő prózai irásai és kortársainak visszaemlékezései* [The round table of Jozsef Kiss: The prose writings of the poet and the remembrances of his contemporaries] (Budapest: Kiss József prózai munkáinak kiadóvállalata, 1934), 21–22.

14. József Kiss, "Előfizetési felhivás és gyüjtőiv" [Call for subscribers and list of subscriptions], *A Hét* 1, no. 1 (1890): 20.

15. Ibid., 19.

16. Kiss's unpublished correspondence is full of letters responding to his urgent pleas for recruiting subscribers. "My intention was and continues to be," wrote a typical correspondent, a certain Dr. Herzl, "to recommend your journal—which I consider among the best edited Hungarian weeklies—to all the families I am acquainted with. I did this faithfully, mentioning and recommending your journal whenever the opportunity presented itself, without exercising undue pressure on anyone. From several sources, I received a negative answer, several promised to subscribe, the majority said that they were already receiving *A Hét*. I could not ascertain the truth of this fact, since I have not seen the subscription list." Dr. Izidor Herzl to József Kiss (April 16, 1902), Petőfi Literary Museum, Budapest (V5239/160).

17. Paula Frőhlichné Moricz to József Kiss (November 11, 1897), Petőfi Literary Museum, Budapest (V5239/129/1–3).

18. József Kiss, "Egy levél egy évfordulóról és egy szerkesztőről," in *Kiss József kerekasztala*, 22.

19. Tamás Kóbor, quoted in *Kiss József kerekasztala*, 5.

20. See Carl Schorke, *Fin-de-Siècle Vienna: Politics and Culture* (New York: Knopf, 1980).

21. For a somewhat different comparison between Viennese and Budapest modernity, see Peter Hanák, *The Garden and the Workshop: Essays on the Cultural History of Vienna and Budapest* (Princeton: Princeton University Press, 1998).

22. See *Emma asszony: A Hét szakácskönyve* [Mrs. Emma: The cookbook of *A Hét*] (Budapest: Vince Kiadó, 2009).

23. See Elaine Showalter, "Critical Cross-Dressing: Male Feminists and the Woman of the Year," in *Men in Feminism*, ed. Alice Jardine and Paul Smith (New York: Methuen, 1987), 116–132. See also Marjorie Garber, *From Vested Interests: Cross-Dressing and Cultural Anxiety* (New York: Routledge, 1992).

24. See Sander L. Gilman, *The Jew's Body* (New York: Routledge, 1991).

25. See Otto Weininger, *Sex and Character: An Investigation of Fundamental Principles* (Bloomington: Indiana University Press, 2005). For a historical account of the phenomenon, see András Gerő, *Neither Woman nor Jew: The Confluence of Prejudices in the Austro-Hungarian Monarchy at the Turn of the Century* (Boulder: Social Science Monographs, 2010).

26. Ignotus, *Emma asszony levelei: Egy nőimitátor a nőemancipációért* [The letters of Mrs. Emma: A female impersonator's fight for female emancipation] (Budapest: Magvető Könyvkiadó, 1985), 60–61.

27. For a discussion of the gender conflicts inherent in Jewish assimilation, see Paula E. Hyman, *Gender and Assimilation in Modern Jewish History: The Roles and Representations of Women* (Seattle: University of Washington Press, 1995).

28. Nagy, *A kabaré regénye*, 250.

29. Ignotus, *Emma asszony levelei*, 44, 57, 212.

30. Ibid., 73.

31. Ibid., 69, 48, 50.

32. Ibid., 33, 34.

33. Ibid., 49.

34. Ibid., 195, 200.

35. Ibid., 102.

36. Hermann Nothnagel (1841–1905) was a distinguished representative of the Vienna School of Medicine.

37. Ignotus, *Emma asszony levelei*, 131.

38. Ibid., 74.

39. Ibid., 220, 266.

40. Ibid., 303.

41. Ibid., 309.

Epilogue

1. See Ilse Josepha Lazaroms, "Marked by Violence: Hungarian Jewish Histories in the Wake of the White Terror, 1919–1922," *Zukot* 11 (2014): 1–10.

2. See Victor Karády and Péter Tibor Nagy, *The Numerus Clausus in Hungary: Studies on the First Anti-Jewish Law and Academic Anti-Semitism in Modern Central Europe*, Research Reports on Central European History (Budapest: Pasts Inc. Center for Historical Research, 2012); and Mária M. Kovács, *Törvénytől sújtva: A numerus clausus Magyarországon, 1920–1945* [Persecuted by the law: Numerus clausus in Hungary, 1920–1945] (Budapest: Napvilág Kiadó, 2012).

3. Raphael Patai, *The Jews of Hungary: History, Culture, Psychology* (Detroit: Wayne State University Press, 1996), 474.

4. Ernst Falzeder and Eva Brabant, eds., *The Correspondence of Sigmund Freud and Sándor Ferenczi*, vol. 2, *1914–1919* (Cambridge: Belknap Press of Harvard University Press, 1996), 297.

5. Ibid., 302.

6. Ibid., 365–366.

7. Tibor Frank, *Double Exile: Migrations of Jewish-Hungarian Professionals through Germany to the United States, 1919–1945* (Oxford: Peter Lang, 2009).

8. Molnár, *A pesti mulatók*.

9. A similar attempt was undertaken a little later by Aladár Komlós in *Zsidók a válaszuton* [Jews at the crossroads] (Presov: Minerva, 1921).

10. Hugo Bettauer, *De Stadt ohne Juden: Eine Roman von ubermorgen* (1922; repr., Hamburg: Achilla Presse, 1996).

11. Tamás Kóbor, *Mi az igazság? A zsidókérdésről* [What is the truth? The Jewish question] (Budapest: Garai Nyomda, 1920), 15.

12. Ibid., 11.

13. Ibid., 10.

14. Jozsef Kiss, "Függelékek végrendeletemhez" [Appendix to my final will and testament], Petőfi Literary Museum, Budapest (V5239/442).

15. Béla Borsody Bevilaqua and Béla Mozsáry, *Pest-budai kávéházak: Kávé és kávémesterség, 1535–1935* [The coffee houses of Pest-Buda: Coffee and the coffee professionals], 2 vols. (Budapest: Athanaeum, 1935), 1:102.

INDEX

Page numbers in italics refer to figures.

George L. Mosse Series in Modern European Cultural and Intellectual History

STEVEN E. ASCHHEIM, STANLEY G. PAYNE,
MARY LOUISE ROBERTS, AND DAVID J. SORKIN

Series Editors

Of God and Gods: Egypt, Israel, and the Rise of Monotheism
JAN ASSMANN

The Enemy of the New Man: Homosexuality in Fascist Italy
LORENZO BENADUSI; translated by SUZANNE DINGEE and
JENNIFER PUDNEY

*The Holocaust and the West German Historians:
Historical Interpretation and Autobiographical Memory*
NICOLAS BERG; translated and edited by JOEL GOLB

Collected Memories: Holocaust History and Postwar Testimony
CHRISTOPHER R. BROWNING

Cataclysms: A History of the Twentieth Century from Europe's Edge
DAN DINER; translated by WILLIAM TEMPLER with JOEL GOLB

La Grande Italia: The Myth of the Nation in the Twentieth Century
EMILIO GENTILE; translated by SUZANNE DINGEE
and JENNIFER PUDNEY

The Invisible Jewish Budapest: Metropolitan Culture at the Fin de Siècle
MARY GLUCK

*Carl Schmitt and the Jews: The "Jewish Question," the Holocaust,
and German Legal Theory*
RAPHAEL GROSS; translated by JOEL GOLB

Reason after Its Eclipse: On Late Critical Theory
MARTIN JAY

Some Measure of Justice:
The Holocaust Era Restitution Campaign of the 1990s
MICHAEL R. MARRUS

Confronting History: A Memoir
GEORGE L. MOSSE

Nazi Culture: Intellectual, Cultural, and Social Life in the Third Reich
GEORGE L. MOSSE

What History Tells: George L. Mosse and the Culture of Modern Europe
Edited by STANLEY G. PAYNE, DAVID J. SORKIN,
and JOHN S. TORTORICE

The Perils of Normalcy:
George L. Mosse and the Remaking of Cultural History
KAREL PLESSINI

Shaping the New Man: Youth Training Regimes in
Fascist Italy and Nazi Germany
ALESSIO PONZIO

The Jews in Mussolini's Italy: From Equality to Persecution
MICHELE SARFATTI;
translated by JOHN and ANNE C. TEDESCHI

Jews and Other Germans:
Civil Society, Religious Diversity, and Urban Politics in Breslau, 1860–1925
TILL VAN RAHDEN; translated by MARCUS BRAINARD

An Uncompromising Generation:
The Nazi Leadership of the Reich Security Main Office
MICHAEL WILDT; translated by TOM LAMPERT